# THE OLD

## Ipswich Town v N

A History
(Second Edition)

SPORTS HISTORIES BY ROB HADGRAFT
PUBLISHED BY DESERT ISLAND BOOKS

FOOTBALL
*Ipswich Town: The Modern Era - A Complete Record* (2001, updated 2006)
*Ipswich Town: Champions of England 1961-62* (2002)
*Norwich City: The Modern Era - A Complete Record* (2003, updated 2010)
*The Old Farm: Ipswich Town v Norwich City - A History* (2005, updated 2010)
*Colchester United: From Conference to Championship* (2007)
*Chelsea: Champions of England 1954-55* (2004)
*Kilmarnock: Champions of Scotland 1964-65* (2005)
*Luton Town: Staring into the Abyss* (2008)
*Luton Town: Through the Trapdoor 2004-09* (2009)

ATHLETICS
*The Little Wonder: The Untold Story of World Champion Runner Alf Shrubb* (2004)
*Beer and Brine: The Making of Walter George, Athletics' First Superstar* (2006)
*Deerfoot: Athletics' Noble Savage* (2007)
*Tea With Mr Newton: 100,000 miles - The Longest Protest March in History* (2009)

# THE OLD FARM

## Ipswich Town v Norwich City

### A HISTORY
### (Second Edition)

Series Editor: Clive Leatherdale

Rob Hadgraft

DESERT ISLAND BOOKS

Second edition published in 2010
First edition published in 2005
by
DESERT ISLAND BOOKS LIMITED
7 Clarence Road, Southend on Sea, Essex SS1 1AN
United Kingdom
www.desertislandbooks.com


© 2005, 2010 Rob Hadgraft


The right of Rob Hadgraft to be identified as author of this work has been
asserted under The Copyright Designs and Patents Act 1988


British Library Cataloguing-in-Publication Data
A catalogue record for this book is available from the British Library


ISBN 978-1-905328-79-6

Printed in Great Britain

# Contents

# AUTHOR'S NOTE

The first Ipswich-Norwich derby game I witnessed was in 1974, just a few weeks after moving into the area to begin a career as a newspaper reporter. It was the 73rd meeting of the old rivals, a figure that had nearly doubled by the time this book was first published in 2005. That's a high number of games – an average of well over once a year since the first clash in 1902. They say familiarity breeds contempt.

No book about a fierce rivalry can be truly balanced if the author hails from one of the camps involved. I have a clear conscience. I watched that 1974 game, and subsequent derbies, with an unbiased eye, and I hope this neutrality means I have been even-handed in this book. I am also the author of histories of both clubs – *Ipswich Town: The Modern Era* (2001, 2006) and *Norwich City: The Modern Era* (2003, 2010).

In this book, when mentioning Ipswich and Norwich together, I place the Suffolk club first purely for alphabetical reasons. Likewise, City comes before Town when those terms are used together.

For consistency, I refer to Ipswich's Saturday night football paper by the colloquialism the *Green 'Un* and Norwich's version as the *Pink 'Un*, although officially they are known as *The Football Star* and *Eastern Football News*. The acronym *EADT* refers to the *East Anglian Daily Times*, *EDP* to the *Eastern Daily Press*, and *EEN* to the *Eastern Evening News*.

The above newspapers were valuable research sources, along with various matchday programmes, yearbooks and the following publications: *The Men Who Made The Town* (Almeida, 1985), *Canary Citizens* (Jarrold, 2001), *Pride of Anglia* (Nostalgia, 1993), *Ipswich Town: The Modern Era* (Desert Island Books, 2001), *Norwich City : The Modern Era* (Desert Island Books, 2003), *All I Want for Christmas* (Vision, 2004), *Norfolk'n'Good* (Yellow Bird, 1993), *The Second Coming* (Yellow Bird, 1997), *100 Great Football Memories* (Jarrold, 2002), *The Essential History of Ipswich Town* (Headline, 2001), *100 ITFC Greats* (Tempus, 2002), *The Canary Companion* (RJS, 2004); *Football Gentry: The Cobbold Brothers* (Tempus, 2006); *Where It Hurts* – Bryan Gunn (Vision Sports, 2007), *Full English* (Fabian Wilnis, 2009), plus websites such as Pride of Anglia, Those Were The Days, and Norwich City Mad.

ROB HADGRAFT
2010

# DEDICATION

This book is dedicated to those football-lovers who find local derbies a source of poetic inspiration, rather than merely an opportunity to kick lumps out of the other lot. In the interests of balance, here are some lines from either side of the Norfolk/Suffolk border:

ONE OF THE OTHER TIMES WE WON (April 1996)
    'The shortest moment of silence
        when Gunn kicked air
    and the ball fell from pitch to net'
        (Copyright: Mark Jarman)

IPSWICH NIL NORWICH WON (September 2005)
    'The onion bag bulged
        and the lump in my throat
    disappeared
        washed down with three points of victory
    "winning isn't everything
        it's the only thing".'
        (Copyright: S B Ingle, www.footballpoets.org)

# THE BATTLE OF THE FARMLANDS

At a tranquil spot, deep in rural England, the sources of the rivers Little Ouse and Waveney can be found just a few yards from each other. They trickle seawards in opposite directions to form the border between Norfolk and Suffolk. But don't be fooled by the area's quietude. Under huge, forbidding East Anglian skies, these soggy riverbanks represent a sort of 'no-man's-land' between communities, some of whom have for centuries harboured an intense mutual dislike.

Skirmishes between the 6th century Wuffinga dynasty, based in what is now the Ipswich area, and their more northerly neighbours, the Icelingas, first created what is now the county border. And although the Wuffingas probably didn't wear blue and white, and nor did their counterparts sport yellow and green, the local rivalry between them set the tone for the East Anglian football derbies of today.

The history books make clear that the hurling of abuse from Suffolk (the 'south folk') towards Norfolk (the 'north folk') and *vice versa* – occasionally spilling over into violence – is not exclusively a modern phenomenon. It began during a time long before the Victorians dreamed up organised football.

The Icelingas arrived on these shores via the Norfolk beaches in 499AD and quickly established themselves as the first Kings of East Anglia. More than 1,400 years later, Norwich City FC would emulate this pioneering spirit by becoming the region's first professional football club. The supremacy of the Icelinga settlers would subsequently be successfully challenged by the boys from the Wuffinga camp further south. Top-dog down there was the noble King Redwald, who cut a sort of pragmatic Bobby Robson figure. Redwald had set up shop in the Gipping Valley and transformed a minor trading post into a real European force – exactly what Robson would do centuries later.

The area between Ipswich and Norwich had, in fact, been a battlefield even before Redwald was in his pomp. An aggressive Celtic tribe called the Iceni were allowed to settle here by the Romans, but repaid the favour by attacking their hosts. Now that we've reached the 21st century, folk from Norfolk and Suffolk have generally learned to rub along together reasonably well. But on derby day – when Ipswich Town FC play Norwich City FC – tolerance and social niceties go out of the window. Old habits clearly die hard.

Ever since Roman times, as the *Daily Telegraph* recently noted, this sizeable wedge of England has lived in a world of its own. The world at large has come to view East Anglia as a somewhat eccentric outpost, where locals walk their geese to market, cultivate root vegetables, and support the Canaries or the Tractor Boys.

That last-mentioned pursuit is indeed a major feature of modern life in eastern England. The fan-bases of both clubs extend well outside the respective conurbations. Norwich fans come in their droves from places like King's Lynn, Cromer, Great Yarmouth and Swaffham. And many of the Ipswich faithful are based in Lowestoft, Sudbury, Stowmarket and Felixstowe. The influx of home fans to Carrow or Portman Roads on a matchday is, as a result, reminiscent of the rural hordes heading into town for market day.

Although the two football clubs sit in separate counties, some forty miles apart, they snarl at each other with an uncompromising passion. The A140 trunk road links the two places but, by modern motorway standards, involves a frustratingly slow and arduous trek. Even the swiftest of vehicles will usually need a full hour to get from one to t'other. The only other local rivalry in English football where the combatants are based as far as forty miles apart is a little domestic issue in Devon involving Plymouth Argyle and Exeter City.

Of course, if you cast your eyes outside this crowded little island of ours, the 'local derby' can be a very different animal. In Norway the media calls the game between Bodo-Glimt and Tromso 'the northern local derby of Norway' yet the two towns are 254 miles apart. In Russia, Baltika Kaliningrad's nearest opposition is Zenit St Petersburg, a distance of 600-plus miles – i.e. roughly the equivalent of Arsenal trying to inject a bit of local needle into a game with Austria Vienna. But, as you might expect, the Aussies can top even that: Perth Glory in the National Soccer League have as their nearest neighbour Adelaide City Force, roughly 1,700 miles distant. Compared to these, Ipswich and Norwich are like Siamese twins.

The battle lines between City and Town were originally drawn in the first half of the 20th century, but it wasn't until after the 1939-45 War that hostilities really began in earnest. Strangely, the very first Football League meeting between the two clubs took place on the very weekend war was declared. Because of this, the significance of the match became overshadowed by international events and many devoted fans had to miss the game due to other, more pressing considerations. Nevertheless, once the matter of the Second World War was out of the way, the battle for supremacy in East Anglian football got underway unhindered.

Just a few months after the War ended, a bumper crowd squeezed into Carrow Road for what was only the sixth visit by an Ipswich Town side for a first-team game. The previous five had all been non-league encounters, and only one of those generated any real excitement. But now, in December 1945, the locals were desperate for entertainment after the unrelenting misery of the war years. Euphoria greeted a 4-0 home win which the press would call Norwich City's most notable victory in 43 years as a professional club. Unlike City, Ipswich had closed down completely during the conflict and were clearly in need of more time to get going again. Their party slunk back into Suffolk on that chilly evening in disgrace. It had been their heaviest defeat in any competition in eight years and they vowed never to be humiliated in such fashion again. Just eleven weeks later they tasted sweet revenge when the 4-0 scoreline was reversed at Portman Road.

During the years of post-War austerity, football became firmly embedded in the fabric of a working man's life. The thrill of victory was all the more potent when a hated local rival was on the receiving end. Local derbies provided excitement and interest often missing with run-of-the-mill opponents from further afield. Derby games could provide a talking point for weeks in advance and for weeks afterwards.

It seems amazing that a few years earlier the celebrated sportsman and writer CB Fry publicly condemned the growing partisanship evident in football. Fry felt the game was being 'morally warped' by blinkered fans who supported one team come what may, and did not appreciate the skills of the opposition. The tribal loyalty associated with local derbies was anathema to him. Were he alive today, one wonders what on earth Fry would have made of the rabid relish with which East Anglian fans anticipated the return of their local derby after two seasons' absence from the fixture list.

The passion and depth of feeling surrounding an Ipswich-Norwich derby certainly shouldn't be underestimated in relation to the better-known big-city versions. One man who knows this from first-hand experience is Joe Royle, who has played and managed in the Merseyside, Manchester and Bristol derbies, as well as witnessing the East Anglian affair from both sides of the fence. Royle, a former Norwich player and later manager of Ipswich, reckons the East Anglian derby has a seriousness and lack of humour not evident in the big city clashes. He reflected:

'At Everton I used to dread our keeper Gordon West launching the ball into the air, with big Ron Yeats breathing down my neck and Tommy Smith shouting "snap his back, Ron". But I soon learned in those games to keep moving to avoid a rabbit punch. It was ninety minutes of madness. But the difference between the Liverpool and Manchester derby games and the ones here in East Anglia is the lack of humour here. There is forty miles between Ipswich and Norwich but the two Manchester clubs are separated by only two miles and the Mersey sides by one mile, but absence certainly doesn't make the heart fonder down here.'

By 'lack of humour', one assumes Royle was referring to the intense seriousness with which East Anglian fans take their derby. Blue scousers and red scousers will scream abuse at each other for ninety minutes, but are then known to share a beer and a laugh together afterwards. That doesn't happen in East Anglia.

Despite this, the meetings of the Canaries and Tractor Boys down the years have sparked the occasional bout of levity. From the cartoons of yesteryear by Harry Banger and Oliver Westlake in the local press, to the 'creative' terrace chants and witty barbs of today's websites, the rivalry has always had its funny side. Often it can be a dark and unsmiling humour: the sort of thing that strikes an outsider as comical, but is deadly serious to those involved. Here's an example: this author recently spoke to a committed Ipswich fan who proudly stated he never changes an electrical plug at home – because he would be forced to deal with a yellow and green coloured wire. He wasn't smiling when he said it.

In the twilight of his playing career, centre-forward Joe Royle would face Ipswich three times while wearing Norwich colours. Ipswich fans don't forget that sort of thing. When he became their manager in 2002, many years later, there was a storm of protest from supporters who objected to the appointment, simply on the grounds he'd once worn Norwich's yellow and green. The big man displayed restraint and dignity in the face of this and his patience eventually paid off. Viewed in the cold light of day, the reasoning behind the fans' antipathy is bizarre and illogical, especially considering Royle's impressive CV and background. But that's the local derby effect for you. It would need time and a high number of victories before the fans allowed Royle forgiveness for his 'tainted' past.

Having sampled footballing life on both sides of the border, Royle became well-placed to express the view that Ipswich Town and Norwich City are different from many English football clubs in that they are truly the 'heartbeat of their county' – and that it would be wrong to think of football in this rural area as a calmer and less intense affair than in the cities:

'What you do realise as you get older is how much a town's football team means to people. For many people it's their life, not just at the weekend, it's also a topic of conversation during the week. It's a passion, it's their social life, they meet people there. I think there was a time when football probably lost its way a little bit, with the people that supported it, but there are good signs now, with community programmes and so forth, that it's coming back. It is so important for the people here. I'm bound to upset somebody by saying that Ipswich isn't as big as Manchester, but it means just as much to them.'

Royle's less-than-enthusiastic reception at Ipswich mirrored the experiences of Keith Bertschin and Trevor Putney when they joined Norwich in 1981 and 1986, respectively. As a former Ipswich striker, Bertschin's arrival was greeted by tutting and frowning by the Carrow Road faithful. Had manager Ken Brown really spent £200,000 on a player who hadn't quite made the grade at Ipswich? That was the question many asked, even though Bertschin had scored goals galore in the interim for Birmingham City. From the start of his Norwich stint, Bertschin was heartily barracked. There was no question of him being allowed to forget his past association with the old enemy. It would take many months before Bertschin's phenomenal work-rate and goalscoring habit convinced the fans he was made of the right stuff. When he banged in the winning goal in a 1983 FA Cup-tie against Ipswich, the last of the critics finally got off his back. Bertschin must have despaired in those early days at Norwich, but years later he reckoned he'd never had a moment's hesitation in joining them:

'It was just one of those things that happen in football. There was a very attractive offer on the table from Norwich and I decided it would be good for me. I knew the area – it was a nice place to play your football – so that held no worries for me. It wasn't a case of stepping into the unknown. And as it turned out, it was exactly the right decision.'

If anything, Putney's treatment was even worse than that of Bertschin. This was probably due to the fact that Putney moved to Norwich directly from Ipswich, whereas Bertschin had been elsewhere in the interim. It took Putney months to shake off the jeering, and his misery was prolonged by the fact that he was injured in his first match and needed time to establish himself as a regular. Putney recalled how his name would prompt booing when the teams were announced, and how it used to upset his wife and daughters sitting in the stands.

One man who has only happy memories of Carrow Road, however, is current Premiership manager Steve Bruce. The Birmingham City boss has a long personal history of appearing in derby games, most notably the fiercely-contested Manchester version. However, he casts his mind back to his time in East Anglia when asked about his favourite derby memory of all. The burly defender explained:

'My best experience of a local derby was between Norwich and Ipswich in the 1985 Milk Cup semi-final when I scored the goal in the last twenty seconds which took us to Wembley. People might not realise that this is a big derby, as they both have a lot of pride in their clubs, and even though they are not from the same city there is still a big rivalry. If you add to that the fact we were 0-1 down from the first leg and came back to win 2-1 on aggregate in the semi-final of a cup then it makes it an even better atmosphere. On a personal level, I have always done quite well in local derbies.'

Bruce acknowledged that a local derby often means much more to the supporters than it does to the players. But he claimed that he was not indifferent to the special atmosphere that is created when local rivals meet:

'I associate with football fans in general because of my upbringing. I know what it's like to support a football team and I know what it means to the people because when I was a kid I knew what it meant to me. As a boy growing up I was very aware that the local rivalry between Newcastle and Sunderland was massive. Malcolm MacDonald, Tony Green and Jim Smith were all idols of mine and as a kid in the early 1970s I never used to miss a game and crawled under the turnstiles like everyone else.'

Bruce's point about a local derby meaning more to fans than players was endorsed on more than one occasion by John Bond, who had a colourful seven-year stint managing Norwich in the 1970s. Seemingly weary of the extra pressure to get a result in clashes with Ipswich, Bond sighed:

'Local derbies are tremendous for the fans and of course we welcome the large crowd, but quite frankly I wish it was all over. Far too much importance is attached to a single game and a single result when – at the end of the day – it will be no more important than any other First Division match we will play in over the season.' Few committed fans would agree, but you can understand this point of view.

Midlander John Deehan is one of a select band of players who have performed with some measure of success on both sides of the East Anglian border. He had a total of seven years at City as player, coach and manager, and two seasons with Town. He found that the local derby atmosphere was always highly potent in Eastern England:

'For the players there's an edge to that game. There's intense pressure and expectation. It means so much to both sets of supporters. Any one of the players could be a hero, but a horrible thing is that one of those players might be held responsible for defeat. If you're a local boy and you score the winning goal, you've got three seasons' grace. Alternatively, if you make a mistake in a game like this one, it can turn your career. I've seen it happen. I saw [Norwich's] Rob Ullathorne score an own-goal against Ipswich – he was very unfortunate. But after that he found it very difficult to win over the fans again.'

The personnel who wear the shirts come and go at a football club, but generally the fans don't switch allegiance. And their hatred of the local enemy won't fade away either. A survey during the 2003-04 season by 'The Football Fans Census' concluded that 83 per cent of supporters feel 'intensely' or 'very intensely' about their main rivals. Furthermore, around 70 per cent said they would be 'angry' if a player or manager from their team moved to their local rivals. Only 15 per cent would be angry if the move was in the other direction, however.

The survey showed that Ipswich and Norwich were on the list of only 44 out of the 92 League clubs who had a two-way rivalry with another club (i.e. both sides agree about being each other's main rival). Of this list, only one other pairing (Colchester and Wycombe, who have a history of non-league rivalry) were further apart geographically than City and Town. The survey concluded that the Celtic-Rangers clash is widely regarded as the fiercest of all UK derbies, while the Merseyside version is the most amicable. The East Anglian derby falls somewhere in between. Celtic and Rangers might be 'The Old Firm', but Ipswich and Norwich are entitled to the play on words that gives 'The Old Farm'.

At the end of the 2004-05 season, Norwich's relegation on the final day, plus Ipswich's play-off failure a short while later, meant the two clubs found themselves back in the same division of the League once again. The game at Portman Road in September 2005 was the 140th meeting between the clubs, around a quarter of which (36) had been friendlies, testimonials or charity games. It is interesting to note that Ipswich have not met any other club as often as they have Norwich in League games. The same is not true *vice versa*, however, for Norwich have a longer League history than their rivals.

As the two teams prepared for their first encounter of 2010-11 season, the statistics showed that in their 147 previous meetings, Ipswich won 61 games, Norwich 59 and 27 were drawn. Ipswich had scored more goals – 216 to 201 – but overall it could hardly be much closer. If you disregard the 36 'non-competitive' games on the list, things are even tighter: Ipswich have won 46 of the league and cup encounters and Norwich 45, with 20 drawn. It should be noted that my statistics include the eight games between 1905 and 1938 in which Ipswich fielded their first team, and Norwich their second eleven (these were Southern

League, Southern League Cup and friendly games, played at a time when Norwich's first-choice side was occupied by Football League action).

Although Norwich City turned professional 34 years earlier than Ipswich Town, the Suffolk club quickly worked their way up through the leagues to catch their rivals. Ipswich made up for lost time by winning the League championship once (1961-62) and becoming runners-up twice (1980-81 and 1981-82), while Norwich's best League showings in the top flight were third (1992-93), fourth (1988-89) and fifth (1986-87). Ipswich have won the FA Cup once, (1977-78) with Norwich never making the final, while in the League Cup Norwich have triumphed twice (1961-62 and 1984-85) and been runners-up twice, with Ipswich not reaching any finals.

Ipswich have the edge in Europe, having won the UEFA Cup in 1980-81 and been involved in some 62 ties, while Norwich, curtailed by the ban on English clubs, can only point to a wonderful win at Bayern Munich as a highlight. Outside of the top flight, Ipswich have won five divisional titles to Norwich's four. So in terms of honours won, Ipswich are ahead but, of course, Norwich fans will counter with a few claims of their own – e.g. the Canaries have reached Wembley cup finals more often, have generally attracted bigger crowds to home fixtures over the years, and (at the time of writing) they've won 43 competitive derbies against Ipswich's 42.

The clubs have been squaring up to each other since well before the First World War and there's certainly no sign of the mutual dislike easing. These days more is made of their local rivalry than ever before, partly thanks to the intensive and detailed coverage that the regional media give their local clubs. Ipswich's affairs are covered in great depth by the *East Anglian Daily Times*, *Evening Star*, the *Green 'Un*, BBC Radio Suffolk and SGR, while Norwich go under the microscope in the *Eastern Daily Press*, *Eastern Evening News*, the *Pink 'Un*, BBC Radio Norfolk and Radio Broadland. In addition, BBC East TV and Anglia TV do their best to cover both clubs from a 'neutral' viewpoint.

This book traces the history of a local derby that is more than 100 years old, but is these days in better health and more robust than ever before. Call them what you will – Binmen or Tractor Boys, Canaries or Budgies – they've both come a long way since that first confrontation in 1902, which was a relatively polite and rather restrained affair.

In 2010 the modern-day Wuffingas hate their Icelinga counterparts with a vengeance and the feeling is entirely mutual. Peace and goodwill in these more civilised times? You must be joking.

# 'I'D RATHER FACE A PACK OF WOLVES THAN PLAY NORWICH'

### (1902-27)

It is hard to believe now, but there was a time when Ipswich Town and Norwich City were not the top dogs on the East Anglian football scene: At the start of the 20th century, Lowestoft Town and the Church of England Young Men's Society (CEYMS) were the sides everyone wanted to beat.

The point at which this state of affairs slowly began to change can be traced back to Saturday, 19 April 1902. The winds of change were blowing that day at England's most easterly football ground – Crown Meadow in Lowestoft – on the final day of the 1901-02 football season. The locals were in fine voice and generating an atmosphere of rare excitement for the visit of Ipswich Town. On a brisk afternoon, with a freshening breeze off the North Sea, Lowestoft swept Ipswich aside by 9-0, a sensational result which saw the home side make virtually certain of their fourth Norfolk and Suffolk League title in five years.

The remarkable nine-goal flourish not only sparked great celebrations at homely Crown Meadow, it caused deep gloom in both Ipswich and Norwich. In winning the title again, Lowestoft had narrowly pipped the best football teams that these two bigger towns could muster. Ipswich had gone into the game on a do-or-die mission, knowing that victory would probably clinch their very first league title, but anything less would let in Lowestoft. To the horror of the travelling band of Town supporters, their highly respected captain and goalkeeper Phillip Cornell had a nightmare afternoon, five goals flying past him even before half-time. This demoralising day would lead to the moustachioed Cornell handing over the captaincy, but it would generate a hardening of resolve in the Ipswich camp. The following campaign they could, and would, do much better.

When news filtered through to Norwich of events at Crown Meadow, the realisation that feisty Lowestoft and their raucous supporters were celebrating yet again proved to be the last straw for two senior figures at second-placed CEYMS, who were inactive that afternoon. Robert Webster and Joseph Nutchey, captain and vice-captain respectively, walked out on their teammates and decided to form a brand new club in

Norwich. They were sick and tired of playing second fiddle to teams like Lowestoft and wanted to create an outfit that had more ambition than CEYMS; one that would transport them to regional glory. They convened a meeting at a city-centre restaurant and announced that their new club would be called Norwich City.

Webster and Nutchey were schoolmasters and their determination and influence meant the new club had no problem getting quickly elected to the Norfolk and Suffolk League for the 1902-03 season. The league had been formed in 1897 and was the first of real stature in the eastern counties. Nutchey and Webster persuaded the Norfolk FA to allow them to use a site on Newmarket Road as their home ground. Blue and white kit was purchased and Norwich City declared its nickname would be 'The Citizens'. Having recruited CEYMS star player Bob Collinson as captain, the two schoolmasters were optimistic that their new outfit was ready to teach the region's other teams a footballing lesson.

Optimism undimmed by early exits at the hands of Lowestoft in both the FA and Amateur Cups, Norwich City got their inaugural league campaign off to a winning start in September 1902 over the border in Suffolk with a 4-2 beating of Beccles Caxton. Their first home league game would be several weeks later when the visitors were the men from Ipswich Town.

By now the Ipswich club had been operating for some 24 years, originally as Ipswich AFC and playing at Broom Hill, beside Norwich Road. The players changed in a shed behind the Inkerman pub and most were ex-Ipswich School pupils, as was the President of the club, the Tory MP Thomas Cobbold. Ipswich Town FC was created in 1888 when IAFC amalgamated with the town's rugby club and, when the latter folded, the round-ball lovers were left to enjoy exclusive use of the Portman Road ground. Town were very much an amateur outfit – eschewing the chance to join the Southern League in order to maintain their strong 'play for fun' ideals. Skipper Philip Cornell and his teammates enjoyed their football but remained determined to topple the less urbane 'oiks' from Lowestoft who were established as Suffolk's top side.

Some observers felt the well-connected Ipswich players and officials were falling behind as standards in East Anglian football began to improve fast. The football correspondent of the *East Anglian Daily Times* called for the club to turn professional in order to make Ipswich a force in the game:

'. . . while everywhere there had been a welcome improvement in the style of playing of local clubs, together with an encouraging increase in the number of followers of the game, Ipswich is the excepted place.

Ipswich Town has so degenerated that there are still slight hopes of having a good club in the town for some seasons to come, and it seems to me that the best policy would be forthwith to start a professional club in the town.' His words would fall on deaf ears and professionalism remained a long way off in Ipswich.

At Norwich City, however, there existed a stronger sense of purpose and ambition. Major interest was generated in November 1902 as the club's first home league match, against Ipswich, loomed. City's fine away win at Beccles had put them in good heart, but nobody quite knew which Ipswich team would be turning up at Newmarket Road on Saturday, 15 November. Would it be the slick, confident outfit who'd hammered champions Lowestoft 5-0 on 25 October, or the dispirited group of players that had gone down by the same score to the same opposition just a fortnight earlier?

Ipswich were at the time fielding an inexperienced and youthful forward line and the Norwich-based *Eastern Evening News* shared the widespread surprise at their hammering of Lowestoft: 'It was never imagined they could put so much vim into their play.' The paper also pointed out how some of the Lowestoft players had been rattled by the constant 'chipping' they received from the Ipswich crowd that day. This abuse was mentioned in other reports too, and underlines how Town fans regarded Lowestoft – not Norwich – as their most hated rivals of this era.

Town warmed up for their first meeting against Norwich City with a friendly at home to Guy's Hospital on 8 November, beating a weakened opposition 4-1. The visitors were missing several regulars and had to start minus key player Frankenburg, who missed his train. Ipswich generously tried to even things up by offering their own semi-fit player William Murdoch to plug the gap, but in fierce winds Town were always much the stronger side.

The fixture at Norwich generated plenty of interest in Ipswich and supporters were told a 'special' train would be leaving at noon for the game. Kick-off would be 2.30. Such travel arrangements must have drawn envious glances from fellow N&S league side Beccles Caxton, who that week had to withdraw from a big Amateur Cup-tie at Harwich and Parkeston due to a lack of funds and logistical problems. They simply didn't have the money or resources to get home the same night after the game, so scratched from the competition.

Despite dark skies and chilly conditions, a crowd of 1,700 – said to have 'greatly exceeded all expectations' – gathered at Newmarket Road for the game with Ipswich. The record books have it down as the first of the East Anglian derbies, but, of course, it was not referred to in such terms at the time. Norwich secretary Arthur Turner and treasurer Nutchey were delighted to report that takings at the gate had reached £20. It proved an eventful game, with Charlie Woodward striking a post in the first half for the visitors from Suffolk, the same player missing an open goal just before the interval. According to one report, Town's new centre-forward Woodward was not altogether a success in his new role: 'But [he] might improve if he eliminates the kick and rush style he resorts to at most inconvenient times.' Woodward's colleague, Ward, won high praise, however, for his tricky play out on the right wing and for proving a more than able deputy for the stalwart Harry Steel, who was absent due to Cambridge University commitments.

On the hour, the first goal in an Ipswich-Norwich contest arrived. Norwich outside-left Tommy Newell sent over a centre which dropped at the feet of skipper and inside-left Bob Collinson. Everyone expected the talented Collinson to have a crack at goal, but he unselfishly turned the ball aside to outside-right Fred Witham, who converted the chance in style. There were vigorous claims of offside from Ipswich, but the referee, Mr MacQue from London, was well positioned and perfectly happy. The goal proved to be the winner and the Ipswich papers reckoned their side had been decidedly unlucky and deserved at least a draw.

Town created 'greater havoc' but passed up many golden opportunities, thanks partly to good goalkeeping by William 'Dillo' Sparkes, said the *EADT*. The paper condemned persistent fouling by Norwich's Yallop brothers (George and Jack, both half-backs) which they felt tended to spoil the game as a contest: 'A continuance of this practice is not likely to advance the reputation of Norwich City and a timely admonition by the captain of the club may have the desirable effect of the two players in question receiving less attention from the referee in future.' The football correspondent at Norwich's *EEN*, meanwhile, said it was not important that Ipswich had been the better side because: 'The two points are safely in City's locker and the result is the concrete thing. For a new club, the City is making real headway and it is within the range of possibility that Bob Collinson's pack will finish in front of the other Norfolk clubs.'

The win over Ipswich left Norwich top of the N&S League that evening and Collinson was highly encouraged by the start his new club had made. Born in Yorkshire 26 years earlier, he had been a brilliant scholar and all-round sportsman, who represented Yorkshire at rugby and cricket, played football for Switzerland while studying in Zurich and who starred in Norfolk athletics. Having scored thirty goals in 25 games in 1901-02 for CEYMS, he'd 'defected' to City along with several others.

He could also play in defence and would go on to become a director of the club, working as an analytical chemist in Norwich after hanging up his boots.

Ipswich's party had not been the only important visitors to Norfolk that day in November: Kaiser Wilhelm, the Emperor of Germany, was at Sandringham to see the King and Queen. Duck shooting and tree planting were on their schedule. Norfolk police were keeping a careful eye on the royal residence after dealing with two mysterious women who'd arrived in the area from London wanting to personally hand over a letter addressed to the King. They were spirited away and declared by a doctor to be a deranged Irishwoman and her imbecile daughter. The contents of the letter remain a mystery.

Despite losing key players and officials to Norwich City, the CEYMS side continued to feature prominently in local soccer and remained one of the stronger outfits. The events of 1902 led to some ill-feeling between the two Norwich-based clubs, and when they faced each other this was really the only true 'local league derby' at the time. Although Ipswich against Norwich had quickly grabbed the imagination, it would be some years before these two regarded the other as their main rivals. For their part, CEYMS were bloody but unbowed by the exodus of their best men and, indeed, some 100 years later the club was still going strong, albeit playing in Division Three of the Anglian Combination League, usually in front of two men and a dog.

Ipswich had an early chance to gain revenge over Norwich, for the return match was staged just four weeks after the first meeting. By this time City had suffered the permanent loss of popular goalkeeper Sparks, who'd dislocated his shoulder and quit football. Town went into the game in second place, just ahead of Norwich, who'd played fewer matches. London-based referee Mr MacQue was again in charge for the 2.15 kick-off, and a train containing City players and supporters left Norwich Thorpe Station shortly before noon on a bright, crisp day.

Once again City had less of the play territorially but would teach Town a lesson in taking chances. Ipswich's early superiority was rewarded when Woodward took a pass from Steel and beat keeper Jeffries. One effort then skimmed the bar before Tommy Newell set off on a fine run down the left and set up Bill Horton for Norwich's equaliser. More Ipswich pressure came to nothing and, against the run of play, Fred Witham cracked City into the lead with a scorching low drive. The excitement didn't abate at half-time, because the teams turned round for an immediate restart. Scott Murdoch of Town had a goal disallowed for a foul on the keeper before his opposite number Rowland Palmer had to depart for treatment after being accidentally kicked in the mouth. It was a nasty injury that left him scarred for life.

Collinson, playing at central defence, had a fine game as City repelled the home side's desperate attacks and held on for victory. With the game having started late, at 2.30, it finished in seriously failing light. Doing 'the double' over Town left City second in the table, two points behind leaders King's Lynn with two games in hand. Ipswich dropped to fifth. The Ipswich inquest saw the *EADT* blame 'rather bad blunders' for the City goals. The paper's football writer 'Whistler' grudgingly stated that City were improving but were still a long way from being a very good side: 'They have a formidable defence but lack style.' Meanwhile, the *EEN* reported that City had been distinctly lucky, for there was no other explanation for the charmed life their goal enjoyed: 'The ball seemed to have taken on the temper of a mule, and refused to hit the target.'

Being immensely proud of their amateur status, Ipswich didn't go in for much training at this time, and the idea of increasing fitness and sharpening skills was taken far more seriously north of the border in Norfolk. Like Norwich, Yarmouth Town were another club keen to break the stranglehold that Lowestoft had on the N&S League and it was announced that: 'A gentleman in the town, who has some experience in these matters, has consented to take the Yarmouthians in hand two evenings a week and a good muster of players gathered for the first series of exercises devised by him at the Recreation Ground.' Systematic training was not normally part of the life of an amateur footballer at the time, but things were clearly beginning to change. The forward-thinking people at Norwich City, unlike their opposite numbers at Ipswich, were very interested in developing their club and putting things on a more professional footing.

The following season, the City and Town wouldn't meet until March of 1904, with Ipswich by now coping with a more overcrowded fixture list, having also joined the South East Anglian League along with four teams from Essex. City, boasting an array of new recruits from around the region, were in the better form just now, but the Ipswich *Evening Star* predicted a big gate for their visit, as Town were confident of collaring points from the team who earlier in the season had simply smothered all opponents. Heavy downpours before kick-off left the Portman Road turf in a bad way and the poor weather meant only 700 turned up instead of the anticipated 1,500.

An early slip in the mud by Ipswich full-back Ernie Betts allowed Horace King through alone to open the scoring for City. Percy 'Putt' Gooch took advantage of poor defending to double the lead fifteen minutes later. The Scot Robert Doig then banged in Gerald Lewis's fine centre after a number of near misses to bring Ipswich back into it. But two minutes later City's Tommy Newell's long-range effort was fumbled into his own net for 1-3, and then Horace 'Moosh' King, looking suspiciously offside, converted a Newell pass for the fourth. After the interval Ipswich's misery was compounded when the off-colour Cornell only half-cleared from Gooch, and Palmer put City further ahead. Near the end Palmer centred from the right for King to fire in the sixth goal. The mud-spattered home defenders looked thoroughly demoralised and apparently made little effort to stop him.

Town restored some confidence a week later when a much-changed team beat CEYMS 3-2 just three days before they were to take on City in the return game at Norwich. This game didn't capture the public imagination for some reason and the attendance was poor, suggesting other attractions in the area on this Easter Monday afternoon. Referee Landraggin of Kent allowed the game to start despite the Ipswich players taking the field in what the *EADT* called 'a perfect medley of colours – chocolate red, pink, and blue of all shades'.

The reason for Ipswich looking like a scratch team was the presence of around half-a-dozen reserves in the side, most of whom were wearing the colours of their former club, the now-defunct St Clements Rangers. Ipswich always adhered to amateur rules and therefore had to be careful over purchasing kit for its players – and this bizarre spectacle was the result.

Not only were Ipswich multi-coloured, they were under-strength: A fortnight earlier they'd won the Suffolk Senior Cup but only two of the trophy-winning eleven played at Norwich, a decision that raised complaints from the home club. As it transpired, the makeshift side gave City a fine game, so there was no cause for grumbling, said the *Evening Star*. Norwich attacked strongly and Palmer headed them in front from a fine cross, with several Town defenders having stopped to appeal vainly for offside. The visitors drew level when a wind-assisted shot from Walter Cotton deceived the shaky-looking stand-in keeper Lloyd Mitchell. After the 1-6 disaster earlier, Town were delighted to hold on for a point and remain in mid-table just a point or two behind City.

Around Christmas 1904 came dramatic news that an FA Commission was to examine the books of three local clubs – Lowestoft, Kirkley and Norwich – after allegations that amateur rules had been contravened. Kirkley's affairs were generally found to be in good order, although one player was suspended for claiming too many expenses when turning out for the county side. Lowestoft, however, were censured, several officials being suspended over an episode when money was raised to help player Fred Timoney emigrate and make a fresh start in life. Lowestoft paid the FA a restitution of two guineas to keep their amateur status.

Norwich City's books were examined in London and serious irregularities found. The FA's panel came to Norwich for a six-hour hearing at the Bell Hotel and duly removed City from the Amateur Cup and declared them to be a professional club. Three officials – including founders Nutchey and Webster – were suspended until the end of the season. The punishments were imposed for the hiring of a gymnasium for training, paying for massage treatment and 'amusements' for the players, and the making of an £8 payment to player Bertie Playford who'd been crippled by injury and had to quit. Playford, the first Norwich player ever to score a hat-trick, had apparently been 'in dire need'.

The FA's verdict on Norwich didn't come as a great surprise in local circles and Lowestoft were particularly pleased the truth was now out in the open. Lowestoft had been furious with Norwich for 'poaching' four of their best players. This bad feeling had led to a number of unsavoury incidents at the Crown Meadow ground when Norwich visited, with City official Arthur Turner hit on the head by a rock. Locals blamed Turner for tempting their heroes away by giving them jobs in the city. It was Turner who was also held responsible for the payment of the gymnasium, kit fees and doctors' bills which had landed Norwich in trouble.

The scandal forced Turner to resign, although he would later return for a brief spell as manager. Norwich decided to accept their punishment and go one step further by seizing the moment and plunging fully into the world of professionalism. It was a high-risk strategy – the three suspended officials would have to be replaced and much other 'red tape' overcome – but it was the start of an exciting new era for the club.

As the decision to turn pro had been made in mid-season, the N&S League allowed Norwich to continue with their fixtures, and this meant the fifth meeting of Ipswich and Norwich would go ahead in January 1905. Ipswich were still seeking their first 'derby' win and could have done without the added pressure of a mix up at Ipswich Station before even starting the journey to Norwich. Club secretary George Wilding, the equivalent of a modern-day team manager, evidently got his calculations wrong during a head-count, allowing two of his men to go off and play for the reserves. Later, just as their train was entering Norwich, another head-count revealed only ten players in the party. The missing man was found to be wing-half CM Phillips, who, it emerged, was absent for conscientious reasons. He'd actually gone on strike, refusing to play against Norwich because they were turning their back on the amateur game.

'I would rather engage a pack of hungry wolves than come face to face with a professional,' he told a reporter.

With scandal-ridden City going well at the top of the table, the last thing Ipswich needed was to play them while a man short. City made numerical supremacy count and chalked up another win – their fourth in five meetings with Town – Bob Baker scoring after just two minutes following a free-kick. Winger Robert Ixer had to leave the field with a facial injury, meaning Town went down to nine men. The contest was as good as over when King scored from close range just before the break. Town did well to prevent further scoring and City won 2-0.

By the time of the return game at the end of April 1905 – the final match of the season – Norwich had not only clinched the N&S League championship, they had also turned fully professional. They had by now appointed a full-time manager in John Bowman, in readiness for joining the Southern League the following season, where they would be replacing Wellingborough. Their first-choice team had a friendly with Luton fixed up for the same day as the Ipswich game, so the eleven who took the field at Portman Road was something of a makeshift side. Ipswich took advantage and finally grabbed their first win in six attempts against Norwich. On a fine and dry afternoon, a bumper crowd of 2,000 urged Town forward and were ecstatic with ten minutes to go when right-winger Gerald Lewis ended a long run by calmly netting the only goal. In the frantic closing minutes Albert Bailey put a Town penalty wide and both sides hit the crossbar.

With Ipswich remaining steadfastly amateur, the April 1905 meeting of the clubs would be their last competitive meeting for 31 years. City's energy and ambition meant they were going onwards and upwards, but old-fashioned Town seemed content to plod on in their modest, somnolent way. Rather than improve playing standards, Town seemed more interested in creating the finest playing surface in the country. This was the stated ambition of club official Stephen Notcutt, who announced a plan to create a grandstand along the Portman Road side of the ground and a cinder track for athletics. Notcutt had the pitch levelled out and, carefully tended by the green-fingered W Baldry, it would soon win praise as the top playing surface anywhere in England, something it could still lay claim to 100 years later.

Despite a busy start to the 1905-06 season, their first Southern League campaign, Norwich fixed up half-a-dozen friendlies during the autumn, including a game at Portman Road on 1 November. As fully-fledged pros, City were now moving in exalted circles, competing with the likes of established clubs like Tottenham, West Ham, Luton and Southampton.

Games against Ipswich had become little more than training exercises. City's introduction to their new surroundings had been fraught with difficulties, however. *En route* by train for a game at Plymouth, they were met by a scene of carnage at Witham station in Essex, where the Cromer Express had derailed and mounted the platform. City players leaped from their train to assist in the rescue operation, but eleven people died and many more were badly injured.

In comparison, City's trip to Ipswich for the November friendly was a casual affair. They eased to a 5-0 win, fielding their full Southern League side. Second-best Ipswich were further hampered when wing-half Walter Cotton left the field after being kicked in the throat. The miserable Ipswich fans might have been quite pleased had they known that Town would not have to face the Norwich first team again for nearly 32 years.

Games against Norwich would not be especially badly missed in Ipswich, however, for Town had other bouts of 'local rivalry' to set the pulses racing and the cash-boxes rattling. There was Colchester Crown FC, for example. In October 1905 a Town player was allegedly deliberately kicked in the face by one of the Crown men, and the outraged Ipswich club later issued a statement that they would never play this opposition again. The scheduled return game was duly cancelled and Orwell Works stepped in for a friendly match instead. Town were fined for not fulfilling their proper fixtures as a result, but they felt justified in their actions.

Three days after the friendly that ended in a five-goal hammering for Ipswich, City sent a reserve side to Portman Road and almost repeated the trick, this time winning 4-0. The game was billed as a N&S League fixture, but when Norwich withdrew their reserves from this league soon afterwards, the game was expunged from the record books. The scoreline was hardly surprising as Town started with just nine men. Gerald Lewis took his place on the field long after kick-off, only to see Vigar and Brindley put City 2-0 ahead within minutes of his arrival. Ipswich then went back down to nine men when Vernon Lewis broke his nose in a collision with a teammate. A horse-drawn cab was summoned to take him to hospital. When Town officials decided their other missing player was definitely not coming, they asked the watching Albert Bailey to go home and get changed. While this was happening, Walter Cotton picked up a knee injury, hampering Town even further. Unsurprisingly, amid such chaos, Norwich added two further goals.

With Ipswich showing no signs of following City into professionalism at this point, it would now be many years before the clubs' paths would cross at any level. After playing each other four times in 1905, even the will to organise friendlies diminished and it would be nearly twenty years before further contests. This period would see enormous changes take place at both clubs, but mostly at Norwich. By the time City sent a reserve side to Portman Road for a friendly in April 1924, they were established as a Football League side, and enjoying their fourth season in Division Three (South). They'd also moved from their Newmarket Road ground, dismantling it lock, stock and barrel and transporting the pieces by horse and cart to The Nest, a disused chalk pit in Rosary Road. The club nickname had been changed from The Citizens to The Canaries in recognition of the local pastime of breeding exotic birds, and they'd also changed their colours from blue and white to yellow and green.

Back in Suffolk, Town had joined the Southern Amateur League and had closed down completely during the years of the First World War, largely because the authorities requisitioned the Portman Road site and didn't move out again until 1920. By the time hostilities were resumed with Norwich, Town had completed around a dozen seasons in the Southern Amateur League, along with teams like Westminster Bank, Aquarius and Old Parkonians. Ipswich won this league in 1922 and regularly pulled in four-figure crowds, but were still worlds away from Norwich's new level as a Football League club.

Absence apparently didn't make the supporters' hearts grow fonder and the 1924 friendly created little fuss despite the fifteen-year wait. It was a run-of-the-mill game played on a mild evening at Portman Road in April, both clubs fielding 'experimental' sides. City won 2-1 with goals from Silverthorne and Short, coming back from a goal down.

Three years later came the tenth meeting between the clubs and it was another Portman Road friendly, this time billed as a curtain-raiser for the 1927 Suffolk Senior Cup final between Brantham and Lowestoft taking place on the same pitch later on. When City and Town kicked off at 2pm around 4,000 were in the ground, but by the time the final whistle went it was nearer 8,000, with many of the cup finalists' followers having taken their positions. There were goals galore, City running out 6-3 winners, and, unusually for a friendly, there were moments of ill-feeling and derby-style peevishness: when City keeper Les Allman was penalised for carrying the ball, he petulantly booted it over the grandstand and into the cattle market next door. Recovery of the ball took a long time and Town officials complained afterwards that the incident had ruined the afternoon. They also registered their distaste over the visitors' negative tactic of repeatedly passing back to their goalkeeper from distance. Clear signs here then, possibly for the first time, that attitudes were beginning to harden and that a mutual dislike was developing between the two clubs.

2

# A Real 'Snorter' as
# War is Declared

(1936-39)

It took a dashing and well-connected former Scots Guards officer to shake Ipswich Town FC from its slumbers and usher in the world of professional football. Captain J M 'Ivan' Cobbold, an Old Etonian, made it his personal quest to build a club in Ipswich that would match the recent success and crowd-pulling ability of Norwich City.

Acting on advice from his close friend, the Arsenal chairman Sir Samuel Hill-Wood, the Captain was able to persuade the stubborn idealists running Ipswich Town that the time was right to bring professional football to Suffolk. The essence of his mission was to shift the club out of the comfort zone and make the most of the potential that was surely there. Pointing out that Ipswich was the largest town in England that was not represented at League level, he soon managed to get his plans rubber-stamped locally, thus ending years of pessimistic resistance to the idea.

The club was able to secure an immediate place in the Southern League and quickly appointed a new team-manager, the Brentford coach and former Irish international Mick O'Brien. Bankrolled by the aristocratic and wealthy board members, O'Brien was able to dangle enormous salary packages in front of potential signings, and the football world was amazed when Aston Villa's Scottish international Jimmy McLuckie succumbed and signed for this new non-league outfit from the Suffolk 'sticks'. With McLuckie on board, other experienced men were persuaded to follow. Town were on their way.

In the same week that the King scandalised the nation by setting off on a cruise with divorcee Wallis Simpson, Town kicked off their new era at home to Tunbridge Wells in front of a record crowd of over 14,000. This turnout proved East Suffolk could support professional football and Cobbold and his fellow directors were applauded for their foresight. Monitoring events with great interest were Norwich City, who seemed genuinely pleased at the arrival of a second professional set-up in the heart of East Anglia.

Since last meeting Ipswich on the football field, Norwich had experienced the highs and lows of life in the Football League. They'd successfully applied for re-election after finishing rock bottom of Division Three (South) in 1931. A rebuilding job was required on the team and things were going well until eighteen months later when manager James Kerr went down with bronchial pneumonia and died in hospital aged just 51. Former Southampton, Arsenal and England full-back Tommy Parker took over as manager and exceeded all expectations, leading City to the Third Division (South) title only twelve months later. Achieving Second Division status for the first time led to great celebrations in the city and the club realised it would need a new, larger ground to accommodate the upsurge in interest. Not that City had much choice, for The Nest was declared potentially unsafe by the FA anyway. With remarkably little ado, a brand new stadium was created at Carrow Road beside the Wensum River in just 82 hectic days. It was described as the largest building project the city had seen since the Castle went up nearly 900 years earlier.

These exciting developments at Norwich City during the mid-1930s clearly made an impression on Captain Ivan Cobbold, who'd become president of Town at around the same time as City moved into Carrow Road. Cobbold could see no good reason why Suffolk shouldn't also have a club and football ground that it could be proud of, and one that could compete on equal terms with the prospering Canaries.

Town's opposition in their new surroundings of the Southern League for the 1936-37 season was almost exclusively from the south and west of the country. Trips to Kent and Surrey would be among the shorter of the journeys they would have to undertake. However, there was one notable exception to this – as Norwich City reserves also played in the league.

It was significant that, for the first time, both Ipswich and Norwich would be facing an entire season with no other league fixtures against East Anglian opposition other than those against each other. In other words, City versus Town in the Southern League was the only 'local derby' each would encounter in league games. Hence, from the 1936-37 season onwards, this fixture suddenly took on a much greater importance. It quickly became the local derby of Norfolk and Suffolk, and not just another meeting between two local clubs. Ipswich would also develop a 'local' rivalry with up-and-coming Colchester United, based only eighteen miles away in Essex, but that little spat would only thrive for a limited period.

Meanwhile, in 1936, Town and the City second string side would confront each other three times in the final eight weeks of the calendar year. The first occasion was a Southern League Cup first-round tie at Portman Road when Town welcomed their neighbours into a newly improved stadium on a chilly Wednesday afternoon, confident of giving a good account of themselves after winning nine and drawing three of their first twelve games as a professional club. Town attacked with great enthusiasm, roared forward by a near-10,000 crowd (gate receipts £483), but found City keeper Fred Hall in inspired form. City survived a series of close shaves, including a disallowed goal, before Jack O'Reilly broke Ipswich hearts by seizing on George Edwards' through ball and thrashing home a late winner.

The Southern League fixture secretary had the foresight to pair Ipswich and Norwich reserves twice over the 1936 Christmas period. It meant players and fans faced minimal travelling problems over the holiday period, not to mention the excitement of two local derbies against fellow league title challengers in two days.

The first meeting was at Carrow Road on Christmas morning and saw 250 Town fans travel by train to help boost the crowd to 9,800, which was a Southern League record for Norwich. Town's balding skipper Jimmy McLuckie was in commanding form at left-half and his fierce free-kick was palmed away for a corner, which little Jackie Williams sent over for McLuckie to tuck home. Town repelled all Norwich efforts to equalise and clinched victory four minutes from time when home keeper Tom Knox fumbled a back-pass and Jock Carter slid the ball home.

On Boxing Day afternoon the sides faced each other again at Portman Road in front of a raucous crowd of 15,242, a ground league record. Unbeaten in the Southern League thus far, Town were shocked by an early strike by Bert Goffey, but Ambrose Mulraney pulled them level before the break. Moments earlier a rising shot by John Friar had nearly demolished the Ipswich crossbar before spinning along the bye-line, hitting a corner flag and going out for a throw. Friar was rewarded, however, late in the game when he put City ahead and then set up Goffey for the clincher.

The Christmas encounters were the first meetings between the clubs to generate substantial crowds and genuine local derby 'fever', so it was no surprise that two further games between the clubs were organised for the tail-end of the same season. The first was a contest for the Ipswich Hospital Cup on a Monday afternoon in late April, just a few days after Town had clinched the Southern League championship at the first attempt. Naturally there was an air of celebration even before the game began, and Norwich showed the new champions respect by sending their full-strength Second Division side for the occasion. Effectively then, this was the first time the two clubs' strongest possible sides had faced each other for a period of 32 years.

Just 48 hours before the Hospital Cup contest, Norwich had recorded a superb 5-1 win over star-studded Aston Villa in Division Two, but
this didn't worry Ipswich boss Mick O'Brien, who relished the chance to
test his men against a more senior team. He said Town were looking forward immensely to facing a Second Division side and he'd noted a serious outbreak of 'cup fever' in the town. Unsurprisingly the game proved
to be easily the most exciting of the nine annual Hospital Cup contests
so far staged at Ipswich, with five goals in a 38-minute passage of play
and incidents galore. John Friar opened the scoring for City with a shot
that went in off a post, but Jock Carter crashed home a George Dobson
cross in fine style to equalise. Town surged ahead before the break when
Dobson hit a volley into the roof of the net, giving keeper Harry Duke
no chance. Carter increased the lead and the thrills continued with Frank
Manders pulling one back for Norwich despite loud offside appeals.
Ipswich were gleeful at lifting the cup at the expense of their more celebrated neighbours and the *EADT* noted:

'There were scenes of great enthusiasm . . . the players being mobbed
as they made their way to the directors' box and afterwards carried shoul-
der-high to the pavilion, to the accompaniment of cheers and singing of
enthusiastic supporters.'

Inevitably the fifth and final meeting of these two sides that season,
just two days later at Carrow Road, proved something of an anticlimax
following the cup celebrations. The occasion was a testimonial for City
stalwarts Bernard Robinson and Jack Scott, with a bus strike helping keep
the crowd below 5,000. Few of the players could lift their game for such
a low-key event and the main feature of a rather lifeless affair was a first-
half hat-trick for Norwich's skipper Tom Halliday, playing in an unfamiliar attacking role. Robinson and Scott, who were being rewarded for six
years' service apiece, were assured of a good sum despite the poor gate
thanks to a pre-arranged agreement with Norwich officials.

After depositing the Hospital Cup into their trophy cabinet, Ipswich
officials could now turn their attentions to the matter of applying for a
place in the Football League. Captain Cobbold was convinced they had a
fair chance of success, despite having been a professional club for less
than twelve months and with only one – albeit highly successful –
Southern League season under their belts. Cobbold lobbied hard and was
rewarded with 24 votes when the full meeting of the League clubs took
place in early June. Sadly it was not enough and Aldershot and Exeter
were re-elected.

This temporary setback was followed by shocking news when manager O'Brien quit the club, shortly after signing an extension to his contract.

It emerged that he'd been having a relationship with the married landlady of one of Cobbold's pubs in Ipswich. His departure was described as 'due to personal problems'. The search for a replacement saw Captain Cobbold fail in an ambitious approach to Wolves' celebrated manager Major Frank Buckley, but he was successful when he turned his attentions to former Manchester United boss Adam Scott Duncan.

This flurry of excitement in 1937 meant all eyes were on Ipswich, and Norwich were in the unfamiliar position of playing second fiddle. Some Canaries fans naturally resented the publicity and success Ipswich were having, but the Norwich sporting press had no such qualms and spoke in favour of Town's ambition to join the Football League. Columnist 'Canary' wrote: 'Any suggestion that Norwich City are anything but favourably disposed towards the possibility of Ipswich being elected to the Third Division is entirely without foundation. Norwich City are the first club – and the only club so far – to raise the flag of the Football League in East Anglia, but they have no feeling of jealously or opposition to the Town. They wish to see them elected. Need I say more?'

The editor of *Eastern Football News* concurred with this view: 'Hearty congratulations to Ipswich – our nearest professional neighbours – upon winning the Southern League championship at the first attempt. The experiment of launching a professional club in an amateur stronghold has been completely justified and the attendances at Southern League matches this season has shown that in Ipswich and neighbourhood there is a large public interest . . . the success of Norwich has possibly helped to create some of that interest and when we recall the early struggling days of Norwich City and compare them with the enthusiasm displayed at Ipswich and the strong financial backing given to the new club, we realise the potentialities of a great future for pro football at Ipswich. The average attendance of 9,000 for Southern League football is really amazing – higher than most Third Division clubs. If ever a club and district had proved itself ready and deserving of a place in better company it was Ipswich Town. Their [recent] failure at the polls when seeking election to the Third Division was a bitter disappointment and we hope it will not discourage nor shake their determination to reach the desired goal.'

For the 1937-38 campaign then, it was back to Southern League action for Town and another Christmas double-header against Norwich reserves. Christmas Day morning saw Norfolk shrouded in fog, but it began to clear over Carrow Road just in time for the 11.15 kick-off. The weather kept the gate down to 7,100 but those who remained at their yuletide fireside missed a cracker. Les Maskell slotted Norwich ahead in the first minute, but it was not long before Jack Edwards, a failed

Norwich triallist, levelled with a brilliant solo effort. Winger Len Astill gave an eye-catching performance and put Town ahead from a cross by the returning Jackie Williams. Urged on by home fans who at times were considerably steamed up by Ipswich's robust tactics, City pulled level before the break through Maskell. On the hour Frank Manders dazzled three Town defenders with his ball skills before rifling home a marvellous winning goal.

Two days later action resumed at Portman Road on Boxing Day after-noon and City managed to quieten the home fans among the 13,643 crowd by completing a seasonal 'double'. Headed goals by George Edwards and Ben Burley within the first eleven minutes got City off to a sensational start and from then on it was generally a case of soaking up Town pressure and hanging on. Gilbert Alsop pulled a goal back, but Town then spent a fruitless hour chasing an equaliser. The holiday results kept the Southern League title race wide open and prevented Town from steaming clear at the top as they had the previous season. Both East Anglian sides remained in contention for most of that season, but ulti-mately it would be Guildford City finishing top of the pile. Town were five points behind in third and City Reserves fifth. New kids on the block that season were Ipswich's other 'neighbours', Colchester United, who had themselves recently turned professional and joined the Southern League too.

Despite not retaining their title, Cobbold and his well-paid manager Scott Duncan were keen to maintain their campaign to get Ipswich into the Football League. Their intense lobbying, featuring a slick printed brochure, saw them make good use of their contacts in boardrooms up and down the country. On the day of the annual meeting at the League's London headquarters, Cobbold and Duncan were to be found pacing up and down in the lobby, the former convinced they wouldn't get enough votes and the latter betting him a sovereign that they would be success-ful. Duncan won his bet when Town polled 36 votes, Walsall 34 and Gillingham 28, meaning Town would replace the Kent club in Division Three (South) for 1938-39. The good news was transmitted back to East Anglia and the Town directors were met that evening by hordes of cele-brating fans at the railway station and feted again later at the Town Hall.

Optimism was in the air north of the Suffolk-Norfolk border too, for City made a handsome profit during the season just finished, despite hav-ing recently erected the huge Barclay Stand to increase Carrow Road's capacity to 38,000. A record crowd of 33,346 had witnessed a recent thriller with Aston Villa and interest in Norwich City had reached new levels. The Canaries welcomed Ipswich's arrival on the League scene, but didn't anticipate having to play them for a while. What they didn't foresee was relegation for the Canaries at the end of the 1938-39 season, meaning both clubs would soon be lining up together in the Third Division (South).

Before then, and a week before Ipswich's Football League debut, City welcomed Town to Carrow Road for a friendly in August 1938 in aid of the Football League Jubilee Fund, which aimed to help ex-players who had fallen on hard times. Originally Southend United had been due to play City in this fixture, but the election to the League of Ipswich meant their presence would bring in a far bigger crowd and the arrangements were hastily amended. More than £1,000 was raised from a 17,829-turnout and both clubs benefited from a lively workout. There was general astonishment at the level of support Ipswich enjoyed that afternoon. The *EADT* noted:

'Packed excursion trains, dozens of buses and cars by the hundred brought into Norwich from Ipswich and other parts of Suffolk one of the biggest crowds of supporters for a visiting club that has ever invaded the Norfolk capital. Quite a number of enthusiasts made the 80 miles journey by bicycle. City fans were astounded at the Ipswich enthusiasm. It seemed they were outnumbered, so much blue and white was there displayed and around Carrow Road they were certainly outvoiced. It was Suffolk's first opportunity of uniting to express appreciation of election to the Football League . . .'

Town's new-look side, full of expensive signings, put up a spirited display and went ahead early on through Bryn Davies, but a City onslaught in response eventually saw George Law level matters and the game ended 1-1. Town would go on to enjoy a highly satisfactory debut season, finishing seventh, just eleven points behind champions Newport. Home crowds were generally 10-15,000, a healthy level and not far behind those at Carrow Road, where Norwich were having their worst season for many years. After losing their opening four games, City never really recovered and relegation was confirmed on the season's final day when they were unable to beat Nottingham Forest by the four-goal margin needed to stay up. As the local sporting press picked over the bones of an awful season, they could only find one ray of light: 'There will be keen interest in the dates of [next season's] derbies with Ipswich.'

The 1939-40 season commenced with a repetition of the Football League Jubilee Fund experiment of a year earlier, and the occasion drew nearly 12,000 to Portman Road. A fast, open game saw City take a lucky lead when Town's new signing Matt O'Mahoney attempted a clearance only to see the ball cannon into his own net off the leg of colleague Jack

Aquroff. Fred Jones equalised with a header and Fred Micheson slipped in a neat winner for Town after dribbling into the City box. The match meant little in comparison to the forthcoming first-ever Football League encounter between the clubs, but it raised another good sum for the Jubilee Fund and also gave Town fans bragging rights for few weeks.

From the day the 1939-40 League fixtures were published, fans of City and Town looked forward with relish to the first meeting of their clubs at this level. Little did they know how the big match would end up being completely overshadowed by major events completely out of the control of anyone involved in football. The forthcoming clash, scheduled for Portman Road on Saturday, 2 September took up countless column inches in the regional papers. Just seven days before the big game, the *Pink 'Un* postulated:

'What a game this will be! There are indications already that the record attendance for the ground of 28,194 who saw the Aston Villa cup replay last January will be exceeded. Local rivalry will always make for keen games and it is all to the good, but I hope there will be nothing that the clubs will regret next Saturday. It was keen enough in all consequence last week in what was virtually a friendly. City's first team, by the way, do not seem able to beat the Town, who won the Ipswich Hospital Cup at Portman Road in 1937, drew [at Norwich] a year ago in the jubilee match, and again beat City last Saturday in the jubilee match. City's one win was the benefit in 1937 which we won 3-1. I have no illusions about this game at Ipswich. It will be a snorter – all I hope is that the players will not pass the bounds of reasonable vigour and that we shall see nothing about which anybody can feel upset afterwards. Remember, the game's the thing.'

Thousands of East Anglians were keyed up as the game drew ever closer. But, by the Monday of the preceding week, conflict of a much more serious nature was beginning to occupy everybody's thoughts. International tension was increasing. It was clear by the end of August that war in Europe was a very real possibility. All of a sudden a football match, albeit a very special one such as this, seemed rather irrelevant in the great scheme of things.

The animated football chatter in factories and shops was replaced by long faces on Friday, 1 September when news came through that Hitler's troops had invaded Poland. There were serious doubts over whether football would go ahead the following day. Racing and cricket were among the sports that were affected by the Government's state of emergency. Many believed that entertainment such as the cinema and football provided an essential diversion 'at such a time of jitters', preventing unnecessary unrest and boosting public morale. Precautionary instructions were issued for 300,000 schoolchildren to leave London under special evacuation plans and London Zoo took the step of destroying all its poisonous animals.

The football programme was allowed to go ahead on 2 September, even though war looked inevitable on that morning. Buses which otherwise would have taken hundreds of City followers to Ipswich for the game were commandeered for the distribution of children to the county areas and it became clear that the attendance at Portman Road would be well below the ground record (28,194) that had been hoped for. The first League meeting of the great rivals would take place 'under circumstances which will be talked of by many generations of followers', observed the local press.

Shortly before Ipswich and Norwich kicked off in front of an inevitably reduced crowd of only 10,792, a crowded and expectant House of Commons heard Minister of Labour Ernest Brown move the first reading of the National Services (Armed Forces) Bill, making all fit British subjects between eighteen and forty liable for call up by the armed forces. The bill was passed by 340 votes to seven. Messages from the Prime Ministers of Canada, Australia and New Zealand arrived, declaring support for Britain now that Germany had been warned to withdraw from Poland. Portugal declared it would be remaining neutral along with Scandinavian nations.

Many City fans based in the Great Yarmouth area had to abandon plans to travel to Portman Road. The town was a hive of activity, with holidaymakers leaving the area in droves to return home. The town's hospital evacuated 80 per cent of its patients and the various civil defence sections declared themselves in a state of readiness. These were worrying times indeed: a doctor who remembered the misery of the First World War decided he couldn't face it all over again, and threw himself to his death off a cliff. News was received on the Saturday morning that Germany had systematically bombed military targets on the edge of Warsaw. Speculation was rife that the Cabinet would be enlarged for the war period by at least four ministers, with Winston Churchill and Anthony Eden expected to be among them.

It was a warm and humid afternoon when the local derby kicked off at Ipswich. Spectators and players alike seemed keen to forget what was happening in the world outside and the crowd made plenty of noise as the two teams tore into each other with gusto. The *EADT* described some of Norwich's tackling as 'deadly' and expressed distaste for the buffeting that City gave Town's diminutive winger Jackie Williams. Jackie

Little was spoken to by the referee for 'charging', and a City man given a lecture for a hostile lunge at Ambrose Mulraney. By now Charlie Fletcher was a passenger, having picked up an early injury, but Ipswich's ten fit men were able to match Norwich in this fast and furious contest.

The deadlock was not broken until the 65th minute, when Little beat John Milburn and Tom Smalley on the flank before centring for Fred Chadwick to head firmly home. City hit back immediately and the cool Milburn supplied John Church, whose cross was headed in by the on-rushing Bill Furness. Near the end Town almost grabbed a winner during an almighty goalmouth scramble that saw City keeper Harry Duke crawling around desperately trying to grab the ball. A draw was probably a fair result and the *Pink 'Un* reflected that it had been a 'great and tenacious battle, but as it ended the thought on most people's minds was when will they meet again?'

People rushed home from the game and tuned into their radios for news of the international crisis. They would hear later that evening that Prime Minister Chamberlain had entered the Commons debating chamber to loud cheering. He told a rapt audience that Britain was 'bound to take action unless German forces are withdrawn' and gave the news that the warning message delivered to German Foreign Minister Ribbentrop the previous evening had met with no response. The people of Britain took to their beds that night fearing the worst.

At breakfast time the following day, Britain sent an ultimatum to Germany that unless German troops were withdrawn immediately from Poland, Britain would go to war. No reply came before the ultimatum expired at 11am and fifteen minutes later Mr Chamberlain broke the news to the nation. Only a matter of minutes later the first air raid warning sounded across London. Although League football was suspended across the country, fans had reason to believe that some form of organised football would continue, albeit with makeshift teams and 'guest' players making up the numbers.

However, Ipswich fans were disappointed when, ten days after war was declared, their club issued a statement declaring that all football would cease. A fortnight or so later, a further statement was issued, saying that all operations at Portman Road would be closing down and – seemingly without any hint of apology – added that season-ticket holders would not be able to get a refund of their money. The only concession was that 'after the war they will have special consideration'.

Subsequently, Portman Road would be used for the occasional football match during the war years, but none involved Ipswich Town. Ironically, one of the teams using the lush Town's turf during this time was Norwich City, whose games there included a couple of comprehensive wins against Navy sides. Sadly Captain Cobbold, the man who'd taken the decision to close down ITFC during the war years, would never see the return of competitive action at Portman Road. Serving in the Welsh Guards, he was killed by a German bomb which destroyed a chapel in London during a religious service in June 1944.

Unlike Ipswich, Norwich continued playing and entered the regional competitions that were hastily arranged. The Town squad had looked strong in 1939 and Norwich were more than happy to have several of them travel up the A140 to appear as 'guests' for the Canaries. The list would include Mick Burns, Billy Dale, Ossie Parry, Jimmy McLuckie, Ambrose Mulraney, Jackie Little, and Fred Chadwick. Many of the Town's players continued living in the Ipswich area, many finding work at either Cobbold's breweries or at Churchman's tobacco factory.

How strange then, that just as serious hostilities had got underway between Ipswich and Norwich at Football League level, everything should be brought to a shuddering halt the very next day by the outbreak of another, more serious kind of war. East Anglian football fans, especially those who enjoyed the enthralling Portman Road game on 2 September, wondered how long they'd have to wait before they could next enjoy the cut and thrust of a local derby. The answer would prove to be six whole years.

# 3

# A SHIFT IN THE BALANCE OF POWER

## (1945-49)

Although life in general, and football in particular, would need time to return to normal after the end of the 1939-45 war, Ipswich Town and Norwich City were anxious to renew acquaintances as soon as possible. There had been no local derbies in East Anglia for six years, but the post-War 'transitional season' of 1945-46 saw the two clubs meet no fewer than half-a-dozen times over a six-month period.

They both became part of a makeshift regional competition, known rather confusingly as the Division Three (South) North League, which lasted just the one season. They met twice in this competition, twice more in the Division Three (South) North League Cup, and then twice more in a home and away contest for the Norfolk Jubilee Cup. With hindsight, the arrangement of six games between the same clubs in less than six months seems like overkill, but the soccer-starved fans lapped it up. The turnstiles clicked nearly 70,000 times in aggregate for these games, producing an average attendance of more than 11,000 at both grounds for the three matches they each hosted.

Although Norwich City had continued to function during wartime, unlike Ipswich, both clubs emerged from the conflict with severe financial problems. City were still suffering from debts incurred from the building of the Carrow Road ground and hadn't made much money from games played during hostilities. Spectators had usually been charged a shilling, and the players, many of them 'guesting' for the club, took home £1 10s per game. Although the directors were confident huge crowds would return to Carrow Road, there were still worries behind the scenes. Meanwhile, the mothballed Ipswich club had reported a financial crisis in 1943, when Captain Cobbold and his fellow directors had to somehow meet debts amounting to £14,000. After a German bomb killed Cobbold a year later, his widow Lady Blanche remained heavily involved at the football club and two of the couple's sons – John and Patrick – would later take turns as chairman.

Meanwhile, in 1945 Norwich scraped together the cash to re-turf the Carrow Road pitch and repaint the stands and dressing rooms in readiness for post-War football. They kicked off the 'transition' season with an 8-1 hammering of Watford but it would take a while before attendances crept into five figures again. The first re-match with Ipswich, on the first day of December 1945, proved a big draw, however, and 16,301 assembled inside Carrow Road to see the Canaries wallop their local rivals 4-0. The *Eastern Daily Press* reckoned City had never put up a better performance in the club's history than this humiliation of Scott Duncan's men. Guest players Sid Plunkett (Wolves) and Robin Newsome (West Brom) were playing with the permission of their 'first claim' clubs and scored the goals that left Town trailing at the interval. Making his third appearance in Town colours that afternoon was Tommy Parker, a North-Easterner stationed in Suffolk with the Navy. Following brilliant displays home and away against Watford, Parker worked relentlessly to get Town back into the game at Norwich, but the home side were too strong and Newsome and Jones completed the scoring.

Less than three weeks later came the chance of revenge for Town, but the Portman Road game lacked atmosphere because it had to take place on a Wednesday afternoon, having been rearranged due to cup commitments. Perhaps the 5,040 crowd was reasonable under the circumstances, but it was barely half Town's normal gate for that season. Parker gave another awesome display and City were put under heavy pressure for long spells, but their goal remained intact. Town had to be satisfied with a goalless draw, but the local press called it the best game of the season thus far – and that included at least three games featuring six goals or more. Although everyone knew that 'real' football would be returning in August 1946, there was no shortage of commitment in the series of games the club played in this transitional season.

The meeting of Ipswich and Norwich in the Division Three (South) North League Cup in February 1946 was another hard-fought humdinger, attracting 10,731 to Carrow Road. City caught Ipswich cold, netting after less than sixty seconds, when Vic Johnson nipped in front of goalkeeper Mick Burns to convert a deflected cross. Albert Day thought he had equalised but the referee changed his mind after giving the goal, indicating that Day's fellow guest player Harry Baird, making his Town debut, had handled. City hung on for a 1-0 victory.

Just seven days later came the return cup game at Portman Road, in which Norwich's normally resolute defence collapsed in the face of sustained late pressure by Ipswich. For 65 minutes the Canaries had kept Town at bay, their only real scares coming when George Perrett and Ian Gillespie hit the woodwork. But after Gillespie headed home a free-kick on 65 minutes, the floodgates opened and Town went on to win handsomely by 4-0. Ron Trenter slotted home the second, Day danced past three defenders for the third, and John Roy, a former Canary, crowned his impressive Town debut with the fourth.

The four games between the two rivals so far that season created enough interest and good football to vindicate the decision to arrange two more – a two-legged contest for the Norfolk Jubilee Cup at the end of the season. The first leg at Carrow Road in late April featured an heroic display by Town's Gillespie, newly signed from Crystal Palace after his earlier guest appearances. After an accidental kick in the head saw him carried off unconscious, Gillespie ignored medical advice and returned to play a key role in a 2-1 win. While Town were down to ten men, Plunkett converted Billy Furness's pass to put the Canaries in front. Undaunted, depleted Town threw men forward and were rewarded shortly before half-time when Geoff Fox converted the rebound from twenty yards after a Perrett effort was blocked. Strangely enough, City were less effective while Town were down to ten men and only stepped up their game when their opponents reintroduced the groggy Gillespie after the interval. Gillespie's heroics were hailed noisily by the Ipswich fans when he sent over a 50th-minute cross for Fred Chadwick to shoot home. The latter was playing his first game for years, according to the *EADT*, and was not fully fit after his 'privations in a Japanese PoW camp'.

Therefore, for probably the first time in a derby with Norwich, Ipswich were hot favourites going into the second leg. On the sunny first Saturday of May, roared forward by a crowd of 13,365, Town tore into their opponents in search of an early goal. City held out but some of the physical attention they paid to winger Roy incurred the wrath of the home fans. City's resolve was broken just before the interval when Parker shot Ipswich into a deserved lead. The aggregate lead was stretched to a three-goal margin when Matt O'Mahoney slammed home a free-kick. To their credit, City refused to fold and clawed it back to 2-2, with less than fifteen minutes left. Furness grabbed both goals, scrambling in the first and thundering the second in off the underside of the crossbar. On 79 minutes Town surged into a 5-3 aggregate lead and got one hand on the cup when Geoff Fox's free-kick was touched in by Jackie Little. Craggy skipper Dave Bell received the trophy from the Mayor, Mr F H Warner, and Town fans tossed their hats into the air in delight.

The last day of August 1946 dawned cool and showery as proper league football, as the English working-class man knew and loved it, was back again. The same fixture list prepared for the ill-fated 1939-40 season was reinstated and there was optimism galore as teams rebuilt in anticipation of a real boom season. In East Anglia, many folk worried and fretted over a potential failure of the harvest, but were glad to see football getting back to normal again. An indication that real football was back in business was the presence of the Ipswich *Green 'Un* and the Norwich

*Pink 'Un* on the news-stands on a Saturday night, after an absence of seven years. In common with many English towns and cities at the time, these local football papers (formally known as *The Football Star* and *The Eastern Football News*, respectively) were immensely popular and huge queues would build outside the newsagents and chip shops who sold them on a Saturday evening. Many an Englishman could now return to his enjoyable Saturday evening routine that involved picking up his footie paper, while walking the dog or popping into the pub for a pint.

Norwich now had a new team-manager in former Cardiff boss and Spurs and Wolves goalkeeper Cyril Spiers. Around eight City men who played before the War were still young and fit enough to make the first team squad in 1946-47 and Spiers brought in a number of additional new faces, including several from South Wales. Town, starting only their second full season as a Football League club, were still managed by Scott Duncan, and like City, believed they had assembled a squad good enough to challenge for promotion. Town were particularly pleased to capture the signatures of Tommy Parker and Irish international Harry Baird, both of whom had guested for the team while serving locally in the forces. The former would go on to create a club record number of appearances.

The Government, keen to help the masses' entertainment in these austere times, ruled that admission to senior football matches should be reduced from 1s 6d (7.5p) to 1s 3d. Although this helped gates soar even higher, it wasn't welcomed by most of the hard-up clubs, some of whom responded by refusing to provide change at the turnstiles. Buoyant Ipswich officials predicted around 25,000 would attend the visit of Norwich in the third match of the season, in early September. Perhaps they'd forgotten that many of their fans would be fully occupied in the fields with their harvesting duties at that time, for the gate totalled 20,120 – still a League record for the ground, however.

With their first League meeting declared null and void by the outbreak of war, this local derby was easily the most important clash between the two rivals to date. Both sides had made moderate starts to the campaign, but what went before had no bearing as the big crowd generated a marvellous atmosphere on a fine but breezy Suffolk afternoon. After a nervous opening, an incident in the fifteenth minute proved to be pivotal. Town winger Jack Connor collided with City keeper Fred Hall. The custodian received lengthy treatment and limped back into the action, but minutes later collapsed to the ground and was forced to retire. League debut-making winger Ralph Johnson was asked to take over the red jersey, perhaps a strange decision considering he'd banged in 123 goals in 107 wartime games for the club.

Hall's removal proved a mortal blow to City's hopes. Buoyed by their lucky break, Town pushed forward and within seconds Jack Connor had the ball in the net, but the effort was disallowed. Minutes later Albert Day flicked a shot past the bemused Johnson from a tight angle and Town were ahead. City officials pushed a heavily-strapped Hall back into the action and he spent the rest of the half hobbling around on the wing to little effect. After the break Hall returned to his goalmouth, but looked a forlorn figure. Three minutes later Parker's looping shot flew over his head and the hordes of Town fans in the Churchman's End were in raptures. John Roy, the ex-Norwich winger known as 'Wroxham' because of his Norfolk roots, centred for Parker to bullet a header past hapless Hall. Salt was rubbed into City wounds in the closing minutes when Day scored twice with little resistance from a disheartened defence to make it 5-0. Thirty-year-old Hall hobbled off sadly and would never see first-team action again.

The *Pink 'Un* reported that even Ipswich fans had acknowledged that the hammering was largely due to Hall's injury: 'It had been so obvious that it doesn't even merit discussion – however Norwich's problems do go a little deeper and lots of work needs to be done. It is hard to remember such a bad week for City in terms of injuries, illness and bad luck.'

That awful day triggered a long run of poor results for City, with 25 goals conceded in the next eight League games and an inexorable slide towards the foot of the Division Three (South) table. 'Seven years of war and don't-matter football had taken its toll,' wailed the *Pink 'Un*.

As the Canaries slipped and slithered their way through a severe winter, Town had a moderately good season, spending their time mostly in the top half of the table. A week before the return game with Norwich on the first Saturday of January 1947, the *Pink 'Un* columnist 'Wanderer' said this season was proving the most exasperating he'd known in thirty years of following the Canaries, particularly in respect of illness, injuries and consistency.

A week before welcoming Town to Carrow Road, City crashed 1-6 at Cardiff when a man from either side was sent off in front of 50,000. It left City third from bottom with just five wins and two draws from 22 games and the leakiest defence in the division. Town prepared for the derby game with an awful goalless draw at home to Leyton Orient. Both East Anglian clubs, particularly Norwich, were plagued by financial worries at this time, and the recent news that the Football League management committee was recommending wage increases for players to a maximum of £11 (£9 in the close season) and a minimum of £6 and £4, was hardly welcome.

A resolute defensive performance by Town won the day at Carrow Road, following an early breakthrough when Stan Parker prodded home Jackie Little's corner. City fielded a much-changed side and toiled in vain for an equaliser, much to the disappointment of the home element in a bumper 23,010 crowd. 'Ipswich are the luckiest team that's been here this season,' one Norwich fan was heard to say, a view that was disputed by a *Green 'Un* columnist, who accused Norwich of being punchless in attack and unable to make the most of territorial superiority. City's veteran wing-half Bernard Robinson, who seemed to save his best games for those against Ipswich, said he'd been with the club in both good times and bad, but he could fathom no concrete explanation for the club's current woes. He said it had grown into a huge job to get out of the current rut, and over-anxiousness had spread through the side like a virus.

At the end of this record-length season (on account of midweek games being banned), City would only escape finishing rock bottom of the League thanks to goal-average, but still had to undergo the indignity of applying for re-election. Town had a more satisfactory campaign, finishing sixth and with fewer financial worries than their rivals. Indeed, on the money front, Town were often grateful for the help of their vibrant and generous supporters' club. Around this time the fans paid for a new broadcasting system at the ground, a house in Christchurch Street to accommodate players, and they also footed the bill when gale-force winds lifted part of the East Stand roof clean off and into the cattle market next door.

Town's opportunity to complete a hat-trick of victories over City in 1946-47 presented itself towards the end of May, when the sides contested the Norfolk Jubilee Cup at a sun-drenched Carrow Road. The *Green 'Un* scribe reckoned the below-average gate of 11,361 was due to many local folk taking the opportunity of some early summer sun on the Great Yarmouth pleasure beach. The game was played for a piece of silverware given by Lord Fermoy to commemorate fifty years' work by the Norfolk FA. It had been more or less a 'white elephant' competition until these two senior clubs decided to compete for it.

After five successive defeats at the hands of Ipswich in league and cup games, Norwich were by now desperate to put one over Town and banish their own re-election blues in one fell swoop. In an evenly matched first half City took the lead on the half-hour when John Church cut in and set up Len Dutton for a fine goal. When Baird handled, Robinson stepped up to convert their second from the spot. Tommy Parker scored for Town after defensive hesitancy, but City hung on and deserved to lift the cup. It was a welcome boost as the club nervously waited for the

League's annual meeting and news of their ultimately successful re-election bid.

It is interesting to note that Ipswich were unable to give their formal backing to Norwich when the re-election procedure took place. This was not a snub, but simply down to the fact that they had yet to become 'full' FA members and therefore didn't qualify for a vote. A Town spokesman explained: 'When we gained admission to the league in 1937, Norwich, then a Division Two club, gave us their vote, but we cannot do the same for them in their application for re-admission as we are still voteless, but there is no question about their election, not only on the unanimous recommendation of the southern section, but by the spontaneous vote of the full members.' Ipswich's confidence about their rivals' fate would prove well-placed.

The 1947-48 season began with Ipswich, for the first time, able to realistically call themselves the top dogs in East Anglia. City boss Cyril Spiers knew it would need a major revival to get his club moving in the right direction again. In the Canaries' handbook he praised the loyalty and patience of City fans and promised more effort in 1947-48, admitting the previous disastrous season had seen them struggling along, with only one player capable of playing to the standard now required. Presumably he was referring to leading scorer Les Eyre, one of his handful of recruits from Cardiff after the War.

Extra effort or not, the new season failed to get off to a good start and City welcomed Ipswich to Carrow Road in September 1947 having only won one of their opening six games. Languishing at the foot of the table again, Spiers had already used around twenty players as he desperately sought a winning combination. He pleaded for more encouragement and support from the fans for his over-anxious players.

A good crowd of more than 23,000 turned up on a wet and gloomy afternoon at Carrow Road, with the City players under considerable pressure to produce a result against Ipswich to appease their unhappy fans. Umbrellas and raincoats were the order of the day as a huge contingent of around 5,000 away fans arrived drenched in Norwich throughout the morning, via a 'hitherto unseen gigantean procession of trains, buses and private cars', according to one report. City fans feared the worst when defensive stalwart Norman Low was declared unfit, but even they didn't expect the awful start when Ted Pole centred and Stan Parker put Ipswich ahead after thirty seconds. Things went from bad to worse and by half-time Town were 4-0 up – Stan Parker's headed goal followed by strikes from Bill Jennings and Tommy Parker. The home fans began barracking their own men well before the interval and it reached a crescendo less than two minutes after the restart when Day rocketed in a fine fifth goal for Town. Late in the game John Church pulled one back, but this did little to lessen the misery.

Even Ipswich fans seemed shocked by the level of abuse the City faithful directed at manager Spiers and his hapless team. A *Green 'Un* reporter noted: 'I don't want to gloat on the Norwich miseries and I am sure that the large contingent from Suffolk were on Saturday more sympathetic towards the Canaries than were their own so-called supporters. I am told that some of their forcibly-expressed comments disgusted even Ipswich fans. Although I urged that goals count, I was glad that the Town did not rub it in as they could easily have done. In fact our defence confessed that never had they earned a bonus so easily.'

A welcome, but minor comic diversion for the Norwich fans came when Ipswich winger Pole had a bizarre contretemps with the officials regarding a hole in the pitch that had appeared by the corner flag. Attempting to take a corner, Pole placed the ball on the outer edge of the quadrant so that it would not fall into it. The linesman wasn't having this, and rolled the ball back into the hole. Pole felt he couldn't take a corner from this position and moved it out again when the linesman wasn't looking. The home fans let out an indignant roar to alert the officials to what Pole had done, and a lengthy dispute ensued. Eventually Pole was forced to take the kick to avoid receiving a caution and did well to force the ball out of the dip and into the Norwich goalmouth. Like a golfer stuck in a bunker, he had to use his leg like a sand wedge.

In the subsequent weeks Ipswich crept up the table, while Norwich remained pinned to the bottom. Inevitably, Cyril Spiers' days were numbered and by Christmas he'd departed and returned to his former club Cardiff City. Doug Lochhead, the wing-half who had played for City for six seasons between the wars, was promoted to fill the vacancy. The crisis at Carrow Road meant it was a baptism of fire for the popular Scot, whose coaching and managerial career would later take him to Turkey and Holland during the early 1950s. Lochhead's first major action was to sign the Luton centre-forward Allenby Driver.

City went into the new year of 1948 with fewer points than any other League side in the country, and only one side had scored fewer goals. Driver made his debut in early January, scoring in a 2-2 draw with Watford, one of his former clubs. Suddenly City had more bite in attack and a degree of optimism returned to Carrow Road, for Driver's debut had been one of the best seen at the club in many a year. A last-minute equaliser at home to Brighton lifted City off the bottom of the table on the same day that Ipswich were having their outside hopes of promotion badly hit by a 0-4 thrashing at Bournemouth. This pair of results had the effect of geeing City up in advance of the forthcoming local derby with Town at Portman Road at the end of January.

Interest was massive in Suffolk, too, with Town boss Duncan reporting 'an extraordinary demand for tickets' from north of the county border. Duncan, whose job involved secretarial duties as well as team management, nearly lost sight of his desk as letters flooded in, around 1,000 arriving with the game more than a fortnight away. The *Pink 'Un* reported that a mass exodus of travelling fans from Norwich was on the cards – undaunted by nationwide petrol shortages and on a scale never before seen. Duncan confessed he was at his wits' end about how to deal with the postal applications:

'I am told that there are so many works and other trips booked up for the clash of the city and town that it is very difficult, even if it is possible, to book any sort of charabanc, bus or other means of getting to Ipswich by road that day.'

Duncan admitted the whole of Portman Road's seating allocation could have been filled by Norwich fans by mid-January twice over. This gives an idea of the scale of the problem that might well have ruffled even Duncan's well-known serenity and urbanity, commented the *Pink 'Un*. An Ipswich correspondent said he couldn't fail to be impressed by Norwich's interest in the game and pointed out that when a club on the bottom peg of the ladder can claim support like this, they need have no fear of not being re-elected.

The Norwich press responded by welcoming this last comment, saying it was good to hear 'our friends and rivals' saying this, but what Norwich supporters, all 30,000 of them, really wanted was to see the Canaries do something better than rely on the size of their support when it came to re-election. 'City must fight their way out of trouble and not rely on big crowds to get them re-elected – and what better way to start than at Portman Road?'

Meanwhile, Ipswich's recent poor form continued as the derby game loomed and they went down 1-4 at Brighton. City's revitalisation since Driver's arrival proved temporary, for they slipped to a home defeat by Bournemouth, sinking in consequence back to bottom of the League, after a back-pass by Bernard Robinson stuck in the mud and presented the visitors' South African centre-forward Dudley Milligan with an easy winning goal.

With just three wins, none of them away, from 24 League games, City were rank outsiders to win at Portman Road, but derby fever seemed to work its magic on their previously tentative and down-hearted squad. The presence of around 4,000 Norwich fans helped boost Town's average gate from 13,000 to just short of 20,000 and the visiting hordes certainly made their presence felt.

It was to be Norwich's day, from the moment before kick-off when a fan dressed as a canary paraded cheekily at pitch-side in front of the jeering Ipswich fans. City took a shock lead when Driver headed in George Morgan's cross after twenty minutes. Playing in his first East Anglian derby was City's new young keeper Ken Nethercott, a man who would go on to play more than 400 times for the club, and he kept the Canaries' lead intact as Ipswich battled for an equaliser. Twelve minutes from time he was finally beaten when Jackie Little swapped passes with Stan Parker and smashed a brilliant drive into the net.

But the biggest drama was yet to come. With just seconds remaining and a draw looking likely, the veteran Robinson shaped up to take a free-kick some forty yards out, close to the touchline. A shot from such a distance looked unfeasible, but 'Robbo' bludgeoned an immense drive towards Tom Brown's goal and the ball zipped past all and sundry to nestle in the net. There were just thirty seconds left and the Norwich fans could not contain their jubilation. They swarmed onto the pitch to celebrate a rare golden moment in a miserable era, and, moreover, an end to the run of defeats by the old enemy.

Their delight overshadowed the fact that City were still bottom of the League, but the fans clearly believed that this could be a turning point. Letters flooded into the local press, Mr J King of Norwich writing that he believed City had the most enthusiastic following in the country bar none, but warning that if this spirit was not to be curbed then the directors must sign fresh players. A *Pink 'Un* reporter said he was asked by Ipswich people how the City fans could take all their hammerings yet still turn up in big numbers. His answer was clear: 'Norwich can take their thrashings without too much whimpering, and here in Norfolk there is a deep affection for the Canaries which is not easily understood by other people.' Another City fan wrote: 'It was a silent and bewildered Ipswich crowd who filed out and I guarantee they must wonder and admire the loyalty and guts which we possess. Judging by what I saw of them, I never doubt for a minute that they would give short shrift to their own side if the positions in the table were reversed. I do not write that in any spirit of malice.'

Invigorated by this unexpected victory, City managed a late-season rally of sorts and came very close to avoiding the need for re-election. They won 3-1 at Bournemouth on the season's final day but their escape was foiled by the fact that Bristol Rovers and Leyton Orient also won elsewhere, while Brighton and Aldershot drew. It meant that City finished 21st of 22, the bottom three all on 34 points.

Ipswich, who were to finish an impressive fourth, actually played a key part in their local rivals' plight, for they collapsed 0-4 at home to Bristol Rovers that afternoon, thus allowing Rovers to creep ahead of City on goal-average. It must have crossed a few Norwich minds that City's plight might have contributed towards Town's poor display, but such a conspiracy theory surely holds little water. Anyway, for the second season running, City gained comfortably sufficient votes for re-election.

If any City players bore grudges over Town's capitulation against Bristol Rovers, they had the chance to exact revenge just four days later. The two East Anglian clubs renewed rivalry at Carrow Road for the Norfolk Jubilee Cup, and although the crowd was an understandably moderate 7,435, the game was keenly contested. Oscar Hold netted two opportunist efforts before half-time for City, and Town's only response was a second-half drive by skipper David Bell to reduce the arrears. Local dignitary Colonel Harold Hooper presented the cup to a delighted City skipper Norman Low. Norwich's match-winner Hold, incidentally, would later follow in the footsteps of his manager Lochhead by managing and coaching a string of clubs abroad.

By the end of the 1940s it was clear the balance of power was slowly shifting in East Anglian football. More than two years for Norwich at the bottom of the League had coincided with a steady rise in Ipswich fortunes. Gates steadily improved at Portman Road and Town were a fixture in the top half of the Division Three (South) table. There seemed little prospect of Norwich managing a quick return to their former status as a Division Two club, while Ipswich's chances of promotion looked far more realistic, even though they'd only completed a handful of seasons as a professional club.

The 1948-49 season got off to a dramatic start at Portman Road, with a number of records being broken. The opening games saw Town in irresistible form, cracking an astonishing sixteen goals in their first three games. The excitement of winning 6-1, 5-1 and 5-1 in an eight-day period seemed to prove too much for them, however, for a mere ten days later they tumbled to a club record 2-9 defeat at Notts County, where the celebrated Tommy Lawton banged in four goals. Scorelines like these were heady stuff for the spectators and, not surprisingly, the visit of Norwich in October 1948 attracted a League record 24,569 crowd to Portman Road.

By now, City were looking in better shape, and the meeting saw both clubs in mid-table. Interest in the clash meant that British Rail sent three special trains from Norwich Thorpe Station, and the Eastern Counties bus company reported 'record business'. Keen not to be locked out, spectators arrived early and 20,000 were thought to be inside the ground a full hour before kick-off. The fans' favourite, lively Oscar Hold, had left the Canaries recently to join Lawton at Notts County, but there were high hopes for his replacement, a versatile 22-year-old from Cambridgeshire called Ron Ashman.

Town, whose average age was far higher than their opponents, dominated the early stages and were rewarded when Jackie Little set up John Dempsey, who swerved round Ivan Armes and went down the middle before placing a fine shot past debut-making George Ephgrave in goal. It was a nerve-wracking time for the lanky keeper, who played despite his wife being seriously ill in hospital. Captured in Crete during the War and imprisoned in Odessa, Ephgrave cut an imposing figure between the sticks, and City fans used to joke that the shadow created by his huge cap covered half the field. Undaunted by Town's strong start, and the referee halting the game because of a phantom whistler in the crowd, City hit back when Ashman headed home George Morgan's corner before the interval. Exchanges were even after the break, but it was young Ashman who became hero of all Norfolk when he seized on a Les Eyre pass and burst down the middle at high speed before firing home. The refrain 'On the Ball, City' rang round the ground lustily over the final fifteen minutes as the visitors held on for two points.

Following the record gate at Ipswich, another record was created for the return in March 1949 at Carrow Road – and the 35,361 turnout would stand as the biggest for a League meeting between the clubs well into the 21st century. Clearly interest in the derby was increasing, helped by Norwich's improved form and the fact that both sides still harboured an outside chance of promotion at this stage. A week earlier, City had gone down 1-2 at Notts County, when an estimated 6,000 of their fans made the trip.

These fans remained in bullish mood and predicted the ageing Ipswich side, among the oldest in the country, would be brushed aside. Due to the demand for tickets in Norwich, it was revealed that far fewer Town followers would be at Carrow Road than might have been expected. The now-familiar trek along the winding A140 of visiting supporters got underway early in the day and all forms of transport were in evidence, including a number of bicycles doing the forty-mile journey. Despite the grey, drizzle-laden skies, the atmosphere in the ground was electric and City fans were in uproar when a group of Ipswich fans decided to take to the field before kick-off to tie blue and white ribbons around a goal-post. They were escorted off by 'an exceptionally large policeman', according to one report. Spectators sitting perilously on top of the Barclay Stand roof were asked to come down for their own safety. Inevitably, the game proved to be a helter-skelter affair, with City desperate to regain winning ways and Town protecting a lengthy unbeaten run. In a whirlwind start, City went ahead on seven minutes, Ashman converting a Dutton pass in front of an ecstatic Barclay End. Town responded well and the game developed into an exciting end-to-end affair, the visitors having two goals disallowed before Les Eyre clinched victory for Norwich after a swift breakaway raid.

The result pushed City to fourth in the table ahead of Town, but for the remainder of the season they were neck and neck on the fringe of the promotion race – and Town ultimately finished a point ahead in seventh place. The 1948-49 season ended with City's crowd figures (a League average of 23,580 and 6,012 for reserve games) thought to be the best in the country in relation to the population catchment area. Town's average League gate was some 10,000 lower at this point, but interest was growing in Suffolk too. The campaign ended with the now-regular meeting for the Norfolk Jubilee Cup, and City completed a hat-trick of wins, Albert Foan ramming home the only goal of an unremarkable game at Carrow Road, and also missing a penalty.

# 4

# COLOURFUL CONVOYS
# ALONG THE A140

(1949-59)

Three British Rail 'specials' jam-packed with excited Canaries fans chugged into Suffolk on Saturday, 15 October 1949, on an unseasonably fine and sunny day. Most of the yellow and green-bedecked passengers had paid 6s 6d for their tickets – not cheap when the average wage was less than £10 per week. Discounts had been offered from Yarmouth, Lowestoft, Saxmundham, Bungay and Diss and there was no shortage of takers.

Although the trains were packed, it was noticeable along the A140 trunk road that more supporters were travelling to derby games by motor car these days. Nearly one in seven East Anglian families owned a car in late 1949, despite the austerity of the times. The local papers once again made much of the colourful sights to be encountered along the Norwich-Ipswich road during the morning of the game – there was even an invalid chair to be seen among the convoy of vehicles trundling south. Some villagers who lived along the route – at places like Claydon, Stonham, Scole and Long Stratton – had come to look forward to matchdays, enjoying the colourful carnival parade which passed through their sleepy villages and often exchanging banter with occupants of the charabancs. Norwich's yellow and green favours in particular created a splash of colour in these grey post-War days.

On the Wednesday before the game Town fans had begun queuing at 7am for tickets due to go on sale at 9, and those who arrived late missed out. The attendance would subsequently be announced as 26,161 – by some distance the biggest yet for a Portman Road derby and a Town record for a Division Three game. Inside the ground before kick-off a small boy dressed in yellow and green entertained the crowd on the pitch with a ball until police cleared the field for the players.

Compared to Norwich – a Football League club for thirty years – Ipswich were still mere greenhorns. Although the Canaries had seemed genuinely pleased to see their neighbours Ipswich achieve League status, they'd clearly never expected the upstarts from Suffolk to swiftly overtake them and finish higher in their first four seasons at this level. The old order would be restored in the 1949-50 season, with Norwich once again claiming their place as the region's 'senior' club by finishing higher up the table. In contrast to the previous campaign, Norwich had got off to a fly-ing start in the autumn of 1949, and Ipswich slumped badly in the open-ing weeks. When the sides came together at Portman Road in October, City were lording it in fourth place, with Town down in the dumps in 21st. In a bid to halt their slide, Town sprang a surprise by calling coach and assistant-manager George Smith, 34, out of retirement and played him at centre-half. It was a move that smacked of desperation and pro-vided more ammunition to those who had recently taunted Ipswich as an ageing team of has-beens. Gleeful Norwich recalled that Smith's last game against them had been for QPR when the man he marked, Roy Hollis, bagged three goals. The experiment would prove a failure, for Smith would subsequently quit Ipswich altogether after an unseemly row in which he publicly criticised the club's management.

In-form City were hot favourites to beat Town on this sunny after-noon, but the *Pink 'Un* warned: 'These derbies have a habit of develop-ing into cagey affairs with nerves deciding their issue as much as any-thing.' Sure enough, the formbook was turned upside down and the match would prove the finest hour of veteran winger Jackie Brown, a 34-year-old former Irish international who'd been rescued by Ipswich from non-league football. An affable little fellow with a receding hairline, Brown cracked a wonderful hat-trick to give Town a surprise 3-0 win that they fully deserved for a fine display. His first was a cross-shot which swirled into the net over Ken Nethercott on seventeen minutes, and the second, shortly after half-time, was a sensational goal that older Ipswich fans would still recall fondly decades later. He gathered the ball from Dave Bell out on the right flank, got free of Maurice Tobin's attentions, sprinted thirty yards, and let go a thundering drive which cannoned in off the underside of the bar. Brown's one-man show continued and he tried a free-kick 'special' soon after but Tobin got his head in the way and was nearly knocked out. Brown's third was a late left-foot drive after Joe O'Brien's centre had been only half-cleared. Despite the din from home fans, reporters claimed they heard Brown's whoop of delight as the ball went in.

A day or two after this crushing defeat, City boss Doug Lochhead decided to take a couple of months' sick leave, the legacy of injuries he'd received in a road accident a few weeks earlier. Skipper Norman Low took over team selection. Lochhead's health would continue to trouble him over the subsequent months and, by mutual agreement with the club, he sadly left his post for good the same weekend as the return match with Ipswich in March 1950. By this time, City were fifth in the table and

Town were hovering dangerously in the re-election zone, their first experience of life in the League's trapdoor area. To try and spark a revival, Town had plunged into the transfer market and one of their new boys was Norwich centre-forward Allenby Driver, who was over thirty but still quite a handful for Third Division defences.

'Exile' of the *Pink 'Un* demanded that City went into this game with 'fire and zest' to avenge the 0-3 defeat back in October, and he warned that Ipswich should not be under-estimated despite their League position. He said City shouldn't pay too much heed to the word from Nottingham Forest a week earlier that Ipswich had been the worst side to visit the City Ground all season. 'Exile' admitted he was glad for some football excitement to write about, following all the recent hullabaloo attending the election of the Government (Clement Attlee's Labour Party had clung to power with a tiny majority of five seats).

A colleague of 'Exile' in the *ECN* offices reckoned that if Norwich were to announce the name of their new manager to succeed Lochhead, it would cause more fuss than the election results – but 'Exile' thought that might be stretching things a bit far. On the morning of the derby match, a statement from City chairman James Hanley appeared in print, thanking Lochhead for his twenty years of loyal service. Craggy Norman Low, a dependable Geordie with slicked-back wavy hair, continued without fuss in his triple role of centre-half, skipper and caretaker manager.

Town gave a debut at Carrow Road to their two new men, Jim Feeney and Sam McCrory, the result of a double swoop on Swansea, whose fans were said to be furious at losing them. Harry Baird was recalled and hat-trick hero Jackie Brown dropped. The changes worked well and the heavy going suited lowly Town, who delighted their huge following among a bumper crowd of 32,357 by winning a point. City had also reshuffled their side and played forward Ron Ashman at left-half, a position he would come to occupy for many years. City took the lead with an angled drive by John Church in the early stages, but Stan Parker's clever lob pulled Town level after the break. The equaliser seemed to provoke ill feeling and City pair Les Eyre and Cliff Birch both needed treatment after bad tackles. Debutant McCrory received a stern lecture from Beccles referee Mr Willis Everett. Driver almost grabbed a late winner but hit a City post. The noisy crowd included a number of dignitaries, notably the King's Lieutenant of Norfolk, Lt Col Sir Edmund Bacon, the Lord Mayor and Lady Mayoress of Norwich, and Peter Baker, the newly-elected MP for South Norfolk.

By the time of the two clubs' annual Norfolk Jubilee Cup meeting in May 1950, City were still managerless, having failed in a highly ambitious plan to break the bank and give Arsenal's Tom Whitaker the job. They'd been prepared to pay him £2,500 – a huge salary for a Third Division club – but Whitaker eventually decided to stay at Highbury. Meanwhile, having beaten Port Vale on the season's final day to narrowly escape the need to apply for re-election, Ipswich were in a more buoyant mood than Norwich and it was no surprise when Town won the cup 2-1 at Portman Road. Les Eyre's headed goal for City was cancelled out by goals from John Elsworthy and Stan Parker.

With Norman Low given the City manager's job on a full-time basis and quitting as a player, Norwich enjoyed a fine season in 1950-51 with a settled side going on a run of 23 unbeaten games. Only Nottingham Forest could keep pace with them at the top and in a fine FA Cup run Liverpool were humbled 3-1 at Carrow Road. Town also found some improved form and by the time the two clubs met in the League – both games in the spring of 1951 – it seemed that with a fair wind both could finish in the top six. The first clash was at Portman Road (still without floodlights) on a fine Wednesday afternoon with a 5.20pm kick-off. Many of the 24,239 crowd had to leave work early to make the start, and they witnessed a game in which Town did everything but score. Four minutes from time centre-half Reg Foulkes strode forward to head home Tom Docherty's corner and Norwich pinched a fortunate victory.

Foulkes explained afterwards: 'It was all or nothing if we were going to get that promotion rise, so I shouted to Don Pickwick that I was going up. When I saw the ball coming over I could see a nice vacant spot and I only had to turn my head.' Desmond Hackett of the *Daily Express* reckoned the Norwich boys should give big Reg the team's entire £22 win bonus. Foulkes was one of several men experiencing his first East Anglian derby, another being Town's new signing from Millwall, Len Tyler. This seasoned full-back knew all about performing on a big stage, for he'd been involved in the entertainment industry and had recently been engaged as a stand-in for the comedian Tommy Trinder. Back in goal by now was Town's old-stager Mick Burns, recalled to the side at the grand old age of 42. It may be due to the hairstyles of the era, but in the team picture for 1950, it has to be said that Burns looks even older than that!

Many pitches across the country at this time were cutting up badly and some put this down to the fact that Third Division clubs now had to play 46 games in a season, following enlargement of the League (fellow East Anglians Colchester United were among the new boys). Norwich City blamed their recent defeat at muddy Port Vale on the 'Burslem farmyard' and had looked forward to playing on Ipswich's famously true surface, which benefited from the fact that its hosts didn't train on it. Their win kept City in the promotion chase but the *Pink 'Un* noted that it came after spells of 'panicky apprehension' during the game, with everyone afraid of making mistakes. The paper also noted that City's fans, outnumbered by at least four to one, made far more noise than the home contingent.

Defeat at Plymouth ten days later meant City's last realistic chance of promotion hung on them beating Ipswich in the derby return on Saturday, 28 April. Battered and bruised from recent games, City went for Town's throats in a fast and furious battle under overcast skies. More than 30,100 filled the ground and the levels of tension were probably the highest yet for this fixture. Town weathered the first-half storm and took the lead two minutes after the break when Foulkes brought Sam McCrory crashing down, the latter firing the penalty high into the net. City hit back with relentless attacking but missed a golden opportunity when Foulkes' penalty was easily saved following a trip on Les Eyre. The weak spot-kick was symptomatic of City's anxiety, but their hopes rocketed when Roy Hollis finally got the ball in the net five minutes from time. In a dramatic finale, Foulkes was carried off after blocking a Jackie Brown thunderbolt with his head. Then Town surged forward and added two late goals through McCrory and Peter Dobson to make it 1-3. City's gloom at missing the promotion boat was made all the worse by the fact that their local rivals had been the party-poopers.

For the first time since the War, the 1951-52 season saw the fixture-makers instruct City and Town to meet twice over the Christmas period. Although it meant a short journey for City fans for a 10.45 kick-off at Portman Road, the experiment wasn't a huge success as the turnout was a disappointing 15,821.

Local paper cartoonist 'Twist' reckoned some Norwich fans had turned up so early on this crisp and sunny Christmas morning that they must have hitched a lift on Santa's sleigh the night before. On the field the pattern of the previous two campaigns was being repeated – for City were East Anglian top dogs again and well ahead of Town in the table.

City keeper Ken Nethercott proved to be the busiest man on the pitch and was highly relieved when referee Mr Willis Everett – a regular at these fixtures – ruled out what seemed a perfectly good goal by Driver. After going ahead through Alf Ackerman, City's luck continued, to the fury of home fans, when a challenge by Jim Feeney on Ackerman led to a penalty, even though it looked to have been well outside the area. Noel Kinsey converted the kick for 2-0, and Town were held at bay for the remainder, although twice hitting the woodwork. The return took place a little over 24 hours later at an overcast Carrow Road. Roared on by a crowd in excess of 32,000, City repeated their first-half double strike of the previous day, Ackerman and Hollis beating Town's Welsh goalkeeper Jack Parry. The same 22 men had performed in both games and it was hardly surprising that tired legs led to a drab and lifeless second half. The crowd became unusually subdued and were probably glad to return to their yuletide firesides. With both clubs getting 20 per cent of the away gate as their take, Ipswich came out of the period much the better off. City's current average gate of around 26,000 showed there was no sign in Norfolk of the sort of slump being seen elsewhere in the country. Two days after the Ipswich double-header, City chalked up a club League record 8-0 win over Walsall at Carrow Road, with Hollis grabbing five. The first four came in the opening half-hour or so, and the result helped curtail the short career of the Saddlers' rookie keeper Peter Atkinson.

For a seventh successive season City and Town did battle as Division Three (South) clubs in 1952-53, but this time their meetings took place on successive Wednesdays early in the season. Another change was the appearance of Buckinghamshire referee Mr F Fiander, following six successive derby appointments for local man Everett. On a pleasant August evening, more than 21,000 filled Portman Road for a 6.30 kick-off with the main talking point being the sale a few days earlier of the popular McCrory to Plymouth for what the fans called a 'chicken-feed' fee of £5,000. The moaners were appeased after twelve minutes when Tom Garneys unleashed a cracking left-foot drive from the edge of the area which flew past Nethercott. The game developed into a thrilling affair, short on cultured football but a typically entertaining derby clash. Garneys knocked home Town's second after a scramble, but Ackerman immediately responded with a magnificent solo effort. It kept the game on a knife edge but Town kept their noses ahead.

The return at Norwich was settled within two minutes, the only goal coming from the boot of City's Tom Johnston. The remaining 88 minutes' play were packed with close shaves and fine saves and the 28,528 got good value on a bright September evening. Guilty of the worst misses was City's new signing Peter Rattray, who had 'emptied the till' when £9,000 was paid to Plymouth for him. The Scottish inside-left would ultimately have an unhappy time at Norwich, leaving after just 25 games and five goals to the land of his birth. Rattray's fellow-Scot and newcomer Johnston would have more luck at Carrow Road, despite costing a lot less than Rattray. Today's winner would be the first of eight goals in a five-match spell for him. Meanwhile, Town's star forward Garneys had few chances and found himself closely marked by rugged Foulkes. Heroic Town keeper Parry went off for treatment to a wrist in the second half and Jimmy Gaynor's spell as a stand-in marked the first time Ipswich had used an outfield player in this way in a competitive game.

Throughout the early 1950s Norwich clung to the fringes of the Third Division promotion race, but in 1953-54 Ipswich suddenly surged past them and spent a large part of the campaign at the top of the table. With the nation still celebrating the crowning of a new monarch, Scott Duncan's patient team-building paid off handsomely and Town raced to their first League title, despite having only finished sixteenth the previous year. With new signings George McLuckie and Billy Reed playing pivotal roles, a settled side made a wonderful start and attendances rose steadily as this developed into easily Town's best of nine League campaigns thus far. At the point in November 1953 when Norwich City came to town, the Blues held a six-point lead at the top, having lost just once in twenty outings.

City were fifth and certainly not overawed, and it was they who took the lead in an electric Portman Road atmosphere. Town keeper Parry fisted out a Chris Adams shot straight to Bobby Brennan, who rifled back a first-time rocket that the local press reckoned came close to bursting Town's net. Brennan was the new darling of the Canaries' faithful, a slim Irishman with excellent skills and an eye for goal who'd recently cost £15,000 from Fulham. Brennan's remarkable goal was trumped within minutes when Town hit back with a Billy Reed strike regarded as one of the best ever seen at the ground. Reed collected a pass from Neil Myles, beat full-back Bill Lewis and went on a run down the flank that ended with a majestic strike from distance which clattered in off the underside of the bar. Reed confirmed later it was meant as a shot and not a cross, for he had 'put a little extra on it' to make sure it beat the keeper.

By now cheeky chappie Reed, a little bag of tricks who'd signed from Brighton, was a big terrace favourite and was widely dubbed 'the Stanley Matthews of the Third Division'. After Reed's dramatic intervention the game deteriorated and became typical of many a local derby, with creativity stifled and defences keeping things tight. Ipswich's dour manager Duncan was reasonably happy with a draw and cracked a rare smile afterwards when he told reporters that much of Town's recent success had been down to the seven-leaf clover he'd been sent from Canada, which now hung on his office wall.

Town were hit by promotion jitters in the early weeks of 1954 and their big lead at the top was whittled away following three successive losses before the return game with Norwich at Carrow Road in March. Outspoken Alan Everitt of the *Green 'Un* criticised manager Duncan for leaving it too late to strengthen his side for the final run-in. The article angered Duncan who let rip at Everitt during a press conference. Town's recent bad form and injuries to key men had left a few long faces in Suffolk and the steady rain on derby day didn't help matters much, but there was still a significant blue and white element in the 27,061 crowd at Norwich. Many feared the worst when City winger Peter Gordon fired home a fine goal halfway through the first half, but Town hit back before long with Garneys on hand to net after Alex Crowe's header hit the bar. The goal proved a turning point, for within the next three minutes a City goal was disallowed and Town went ahead. Crowe got clear from Foulkes to score and by now the Suffolk hordes were in fine voice, cranking the volume up even further when the final whistle approached without further scoring. Both Town goals came at the River End in front of most of their fans and it was to here the players ran at the final whistle to acknowledge the cheers.

In the eleven remaining games Ipswich only lost once, finishing the season three points clear of Brighton to secure Second Division football for the first time. Norwich finished a respectable seventh. It was little consolation for their fans who now had to put up with Ipswich playing at a higher level than the Canaries for the first time ever.

Both teams would find victories a little harder to come by in the 1954-55 campaign. Ipswich, who failed to strengthen their squad for the challenge of the higher level of football, were immediately relegated from Division Two, despite a brave late bid to avoid the drop. Norwich finished mid-table again, with a perfectly symmetrical record in terms of wins and losses, and goals for and against. The fates of both clubs led to much gnashing of teeth in the respective boardrooms and in the summer of 1955 both ditched their managers. Many felt it rather harsh, but Norman Low's time was up after five years of failing to hoist City into Division Two. He was replaced by Tom Parker, returning for a second stint in the manager's chair. Shortly after this development, Ipswich announced that the ageing Scott Duncan was to step aside and become club secretary, to allow a younger man a chance. Town's choice was the dapper and quietly-spoken Alf Ramsey, the 35-year-old former Spurs and England full-back, whose playing days had just come to an end.

So, for 1955-56 both clubs found themselves together again chasing promotion from Division Three (South). The fans licked their lips with relish at the approaching derbies, the first at Ipswich on Good Friday 1956 and the return on Easter Monday. *Pink 'Un* columnist 'Nomad' discussed what might be the best way to combat Ipswich's well-executed push and run tactics, clearly copied by Ramsey from his Tottenham days. 'Nomad' suggested they fall back defensively to the edge of the penalty area and allow Town to make all the ground they wished with their slide-rule tactics, and then make sure of 'nipping out' the final pass. His other suggestion was for man-to-man marking to force Ipswich's men into hurried passes that would upset their rhythm.

These ideas must have fallen on deaf ears for Ramsey's team streaked into a 3-0 lead after half an hour at Portman Road. Garneys, Elsworthy and Parker were the marksmen as Ramsey and five of his team enjoyed their first experience of an East Anglian derby game. After the break Town winger Billy Reed injured his knee and was little more than a hobbling passenger on the flank. A sign of the times was the way in which his marker, Roy Lockwood, sportingly stood off him and refused to tackle hard when the ball arrived at Reed's feet. The injury to their star winger was bad news for Town, for Reed had looked in tremendous form and capable of beating Norwich on his own. City grabbed back some of the initiative, Ralph Hunt pulling a goal back and Elsworthy lucky not to concede a penalty for a clear handball. Wilf Grant settled any lingering Ipswich nerves with a cracking twenty-yarder to make it 4-1.

Both sides slumped to depressing defeats the following day, but got their chins up in readiness for the derby return game on a fine and sunny Monday afternoon. Special trains were chartered for fans from Ipswich, five of them leaving between 10.49 and 12.32, with the fare set at seven shillings return. The Town squad didn't travel until lunchtime, with Ramsey ordering his exhausted players to either take an extra hour in bed, or otherwise go to Portman Road to watch the Suffolk Senior Cup final in the morning, between Long Melford and Lowestoft.

Simultaneously, Carrow Road was staging the Norfolk Senior Cup final between Gothic and the Midland League professionals King's Lynn. More than 31,000 – the eighth highest in the entire Football League that day – enjoyed the music of the Newark Imperials Carnival Band at Carrow Road before City and Town took the field. They witnessed a sensational start by Norwich, with Gordon and Hunt netting shots past Town's bemused defence in the first five minutes. It was a nightmare start for Town's debut-making goalkeeper Roy Bailey, a signing from Crystal Palace, and it could have been even worse but for a Hunt effort slamming the woodwork. Town's inside-right Grant was hurt in a clash with City skipper Ashman and it turned out he'd broken a bone in his ankle, but he insisted on carrying on despite instructions from Ramsey to come off. Gordon's glorious long-range effort made it 3-0 to City with thirteen minutes left, but Town surprised their hosts by battling back. Full-back Basil Acres thundered in a great shot and then Garneys made it 3-2 to set up a tense finish in which City had to work hard to hang on to the points.

Even the most ardent Norwich fan had to admit that by the end of 1955-56 Ipswich had managed to make up lost ground to match Norwich in terms of the 'status' of the two clubs. They were both by now regarded as two of the bigger guns in the Third Division, their playing staffs were pretty-evenly matched, and games between the two were generally close and well contested. The days of Norwich being the region's undisputed senior club were well and truly over. In fact, there were even signs that Alf Ramsey was on the verge of taking Town to a new level with his astute tactics and ability to get the most out of fairly ordinary players. Town had become very hard to beat and only just missed promotion in Ramsey's first season.

In his second, 1956-57, the battle at the top of the table proved even tighter, but this time Ipswich finished top of the pile, scraping home on goal-average on an exciting final day. They did the double over troubled Norwich, who slumped to rock bottom in 24th place, manager Parker being replaced by Archie Macauley a few weeks before this awful season ended. With the benefit of hindsight, the 1956-57 season of highly contrasting fortunes can be traced as the point at which Ipswich 'overtook' Norwich, going on to become East Anglian top dogs for something like thirty years.

By the time the two clubs met for the first time in 1956-57, there was less than a fortnight of the season to go. Norwich were doomed to finish bottom and their financial problems had led to a public appeal in order to pay the players' wages. Town were on the verge of promotion and experiencing pressures of a different kind. Things were so bad at Norwich that former crowd favourite Bobby Brennan returned from non-league obscurity at the age of 32 to help the cause – and very nearly became the hero of the hour in the Good Friday derby at Carrow Road. With Ipswich playing out time, a 2-1 lead under their belts, Brennan beat two defenders and smashed a fine drive past Bailey to spark an almighty roar from home fans. But the cheers turned to snarls as one-armed referee Alf Bond disallowed the goal and gave Ipswich a free-kick. It had been a brave City effort – they'd even taken an early lead through Hunt – but goals by Doug Millward and Ted Phillips either side of the break won the day.

The return at Portman Road on the following Monday afternoon was a strangely muted affair. Town fans were perhaps stifled by the pressures of the promotion chase. The normally noisy occupants of the Churchman's End failed to rise to the occasion, and were particularly subdued after Johnny Gavin headed a Norwich equaliser right in front of them, cancelling out Phillips' thunderous free-kick six minutes earlier.

Later, the balding pate of Jimmy Leadbetter glanced Town ahead and Phillips completed the scoring with his 46th strike of the season.

This proved to be Big Ted's last goal of a sensational campaign, leaving him just one goal short of Derek Dooley's post-War League record. The League table published in the next morning's papers showed Town on top for the first time that season, with Norwich now mathematically certain to finish in the re-election zone. The depth of feeling surrounding the derby games certainly surprised Norwich's new boss Macauley and the turnout of almost 29,000 at Carrow Road prompted him to say that when he returned to Scotland and told his friends how many came to watch his bottom-of-the-table club they wouldn't believe him.

One of the most excited Ipswich fans at the Easter Monday game had been Ron McKinnon, newly demobbed from his National Service with the Gordon Highlanders in Aberdeen. He'd been following Town's promotion push from afar with mounting excitement in recent months, and was delighted to get his demob papers in time for the big derby match. The weekend before he'd also managed to secure an unexpected 48-hour weekend leave and, incredibly, used this short break to head to Exeter from Aberdeen to see Town's vital game at St James' Park. He left Aberdeen at 3pm on the Friday and got back at midday on the Sunday – a 45-hour absence, 41 of which were spent in various trains, covering around 1,440 miles. The football club heard about this devoted act and gave him a complimentary match ticket.

Town may have been a division higher than Norwich in 1957-58, but the rivalry was kept alive by two friendly encounters arranged for the tail-end of the campaign. The fans obviously didn't regard these meetings as meaningless, for the combined attendance at the games was just under 28,000. City supporters were delighted by the performance of new signings Derek Lythgoe and Terry Allcock in the first game, a 2-2 draw at Carrow Road. Lythgoe and Maurice Milne scored for City, Doug Millward and Garneys for Town.

The second of the friendlies was a somewhat hastily arranged affair which saw Norwich step in to replace Manchester United as Town's opponents in Scott Duncan's testimonial at Portman Road. United had pulled out in the aftermath of the recent Munich air crash. It was disappointing for Scott Duncan, who'd managed United earlier in his career, but understandable in the circumstances. The game with City was a very drab affair, the only highlight being the sight of the ageing Duncan skipping across the turf in his smart grey suit to take the kick-off. A Nethercott own-goal put Town ahead, a disputed penalty levelled matters and Millward tucked in the winner despite looking offside. According to the *EADT*: 'Numerous appeals from the terraces for things to be livened up were made, but they fell upon deaf ears.' By all accounts this game went down as the least exciting of the 52 East Anglian derby games so far staged.

Re-organisation of the Football League in 1958 saw regionalisation scrapped. Norwich, having finished eighth in the Third Division's southern section, comfortably made it into the new-look 'national' Division Three. Ipswich were by now establishing themselves in the Second Division, but their proud title as 'Unofficial Champions of East Anglia' took a shaking in 1959 when Norwich embarked on a sensational FA Cup run stretching from the first round through to a semi-final replay. The eyes of an enchanted nation were on the chirpy underdog Canaries as they beat Ilford, Swindon, Manchester United, Cardiff, Tottenham and Sheffield United before being shaded in a semi-final replay by Luton Town.

Thus, instead of an FA Cup final appearance against Nottingham Forest at Wembley, brave City had to settle for a Norfolk Charity Cup game with Ipswich at Carrow Road. Town won it 4-2, perhaps hardly surprising given that City's Cup commitments had required them to play no fewer than eleven League games in the final month of the season. Having just missed out on promotion to boot, they must have been totally exhausted by now. Nevertheless, the charity game was a fine spectacle and after Matt Crowe and Jimmy Hill put the Canaries ahead, Town hit back to win 4-2 with goals from Phillips (2), Ray Crawford and Reg Pickett. Nearly 21,000 turned out for a game that was far more entertaining and hard-fought than had been expected.

# 5

# The Year the League & League Cup came East

## (1960-64)

Although it is undoubtedly a myth that the swinging '60s were one long rave-up, the decade certainly started with Norwich City in party mood. A year after getting within a whisker of Wembley as a mere Third Division club, City clinched promotion to the Second Division in April 1960. It not only meant a return to this level after 21 years, but also competitive action against local rivals Ipswich after a three-year wait.

Shortly after promotion was confirmed, the buoyant City squad travelled to Portman Road to contest the revived Ipswich Hospital Cup under Town's recently-unveiled floodlights. Almost 15,000 saw Town's Dubliner centre-forward Dermot Curtis bag the game's only goal in the opening minutes.

The scene was set for Boxing Day 1960, when the two clubs met at Carrow Road for the first time in a Division Two fixture. City, unbeaten at home for a year, were desperate to put one over their rivals after having only won one of the previous ten meetings. Sadly for the yellow and green hordes, Town showed little Christmas spirit and their ultra-efficient approach resulted in a clinical 3-0 win. Norwich had the majority of play – they hit the post twice and forced fifteen corners to Town's one – but Alf Ramsey's men always looked in control. Razor-sharp Ray Crawford beat City's South African keeper Sandy Kennon either side of Ted Phillips' making the most of a sloppy back-pass. The result was vindication for the Ipswich fan who had bravely travelled up the A140, taking all sorts of abuse as he waved a huge banner proclaiming: 'We will pluck the canary of its feathers.'

The win moved Town up to second in the table, four places ahead of Norwich, and the lethal partnership of Crawford (25 goals in 23 matches) and Phillips (fifteen in 23) meant they were serious promotion contenders. But there was far more to Ramsey's side than two in-form sharpshooters. The future England manager, still a few weeks short of his fortieth birthday, had fashioned a hard-working side that bamboozled opponents with a simple but highly effective ploy. Town usually played with wingers Jimmy Leadbetter and Roy Stephenson withdrawn deep, where they would invariably escape their markers and find space to engineer a supply service to Crawford and Phillips, usually by means of diagonal balls into the inside-forward channels. Apart from the astonishing shooting power of Phillips, and the flair of Crawford, Town didn't look blessed with a hugely talented team, but Ramsey knew how to get each of them to do a particular job in efficient fashion. The goals and points racked up over the Christmas period would prove to be a launch-pad for Ipswich's remarkable achievements over the next eighteen months, and those of Ramsey on the international stage later in the decade.

To be beaten so comprehensively, despite having so much of the play, had a demoralising effect on Norwich and left them feeling they'd been mugged. The return game at Portman Road was the following afternoon, and 24 hours was simply not long enough for them to recover. Hopes were briefly raised when Jimmy Hill converted Terry Allcock's lobbed pass, but Ipswich settled down and soon took charge. After Barry Butler handled, Phillips maintained his 100 per cent record from the penalty spot, Kennon perhaps secretly grateful he hadn't got in the way of the thunderbolt which flew in off the underside of the bar. Crawford then bagged a brace from close range and the often under-appreciated Doug Millward hit a fine fourth to round off Ipswich's 4-1 win. It left them top of the table and the 23,321 attendance would prove their largest of the campaign. The crowd of 30,884 at Norwich the previous day would likewise be City's best of 1960-61.

Alan Everitt, sports editor at the *Green 'Un*, noted with surprise that even the calm and collected Ramsey had been up-beat about the four points won against Norwich: 'Even our ultra-cautious manager is now forecasting success,' he exclaimed. It was also reported that Norwich's new manager, Bill Reid – a replacement for Archie Macauley who'd joined West Brom – had been effusive in his praise of veteran Leadbetter, describing one particular long pass to Phillips at Carrow Road as 'stupendous'. Leadbetter's form was timely, for at the Portman Road game a benefit collection was taken for him: the fans were invited to lob coins into a blanket that was carried around the pitch.

Another major feature of the return game had been an excellent debut by Ipswich's young Scot Bill Baxter, who stepped in to replace Ken Malcolm at full-back and coped with the occasion like a veteran. Cool and decisive, he would go on to make more than 400 League appearances for the club, but in these early days he was doing his National Service in the Army, only playing when his commanding officer gave permission. The *Green 'Un* said Ramsey always knew that Baxter wouldn't let him down, although it had been a relief that Norwich had dropped their wily old winger Errol 'Cowboy' Crossan for the game.

With Crawford staying ahead of Middlesbrough's Brian Clough as the League's leading scorer, Ipswich went on to claim the Second Division title in 1960-61. They clinched an historic promotion with a 4-0 home win over Sunderland, on the same day that City, not far behind in fourth place, surprisingly went down 0-1 at relegation-haunted Leyton Orient in front of 2,000 disappointed travelling fans from Norfolk.

Norwich looked on enviously as Ipswich celebrated promotion to the top flight after just sixteen seasons in the League, while their other 'neighbours', Peterborough United, celebrated promotion from Division Four at the very first attempt. Said the *Pink 'Un*: 'Perhaps the bitterest pill of all for many Norwich supporters is the fact that Peterborough owe so much of their success to the strong shooting of former Canary Terry Bly, 50 goals in 1960-61. [Ipswich and Peterborough's] outstanding performances both owe a great deal to their teams being particularly strong where the Canaries have been particularly weak – in scoring goals.' At least Norwich had ended the season with a bang, snaring £440 'talent money' for finishing fourth by thrashing Southampton 5-0, with popular skipper Ron Ashman (nearly 600 games to his credit) firing home his only goal of the season. City thus achieved their highest League placing yet, but it was almost completely overshadowed by Ipswich's success.

Brian Clifford, who covered Norwich for the *Pink 'Un*, was anxious to apologise for underestimating Ipswich: 'I'd better start by getting on my knees and throwing a couple of "salaams" out Ipswich way. "Sheffield United for the championship" and "I just can't see Ipswich beating Derby" were the written gems that I cast for your approval almost a month ago. Of course you don't need me to remind you what happened. So with due humility I'd like to hand out my congratulations to Ipswich and to say here and now that I'm not one of those journos who think Town will come tumbling back into the Second Division again. Still, if my tips are anything to go by (which they are not), Ipswich have straight away got an additional burden to carry in the first division.' Unlike most partisan City fans, the *Pink 'Un* was generous in its praise for Ipswich: 'It's been a wonderful season for East Anglia generally. Top credit marks have gone of course to Ipswich Town on their great achievement in becoming the first side from the area to earn a place in the First Division.'

There were genuine worries in Norfolk at this time that some City followers might be tempted to switch allegiance, now that Ipswich had won the race to play in England's top flight. But Norwich fan Mrs Vivian Willey of Bury St Edmunds scoffed at such speculation: 'Living so much nearer to Ipswich than Norwich, it has been suggested we Norwich supporters will forsake them in order to see First Division football next season. I say "well done Ipswich and good luck next season" but to me and countless others in this area, Norwich are the team. City have done remarkably well in their first year [back] in Division Two and we know it is only a matter of time before we will be seeing First Division football at Carrow Road,' she wrote.

Ipswich's great adventure in 1961-62 got off to a fine start and things were still going far better than expected when FA Cup distractions came along in January. By the time Ramsey's men tackled Second Division Luton Town in a third round tie, needing two replays, the halfway point of the League season had come and gone and Town were in the top four. Norwich found themselves halfway up the Second Division table and consequently the FA Cup presented them with a far more welcome distraction. So it had been a tense dressing room at Carrow Road at lunchtime on Monday, 8 January, when the players huddled around a radio to listen to the FA Cup fourth round draw. There was a roar as the announcer's voice crackled: 'Norwich City or Wrexham will play Luton Town or Ipswich Town.' With City and Town both favourites to win their ties, it quickly dawned that the very first East Anglian FA Cup derby was on the horizon. Norwich duly beat Wrexham 3-1 two days later and Ipswich did their part the following week, overcoming Luton 5-1 in a howling gale, watched from the stands by the entire Norwich squad.

Neutral onlookers might have thought Ipswich's unexpected involvement in the First Division title race would see them relegate their Cup-tie with Second Division Norwich to a matter of secondary importance. This was a long way from the truth, for the cup clash created huge interest across the region. Indeed, it was beginning to seem that every time the two clubs met competitively, the occasion was treated as more important than ever before.

The week before the big game both City and Town played poorly and were beaten. Norwich went down at home to Rotherham – their fourth League defeat in a row – but had their gate boosted by at least 50 per cent due to Cup-tie tickets being on sale in the ground. Skipper Ashman missed the Rotherham game, after a run of 145 successive appearances, to ensure he would be fit to play against Ipswich after pulling a muscle in training. Norwich's new manager Bill Reid had spent many years at homely St Mirren and must have been surprised at the intensity of feeling surrounding the Ipswich Cup-tie. But he thought his side would at least hold their own against a Town outfit that flopped 1-3 at Birmingham in the preceding week, wearing an unfamiliar red-and-white change strip.

The *Pink 'Un* excitedly built up the tie as the 'Cock of East Anglia Match' and one supporter felt it necessary to write in and call for calm:

'Every match with Ipswich is like a cup tie anyway, so this may not be much different.'

The *Pink 'Un*'s man said the City squad were in good humour and had told him they were planning special tactics to stop Ipswich. These included 'boarding the goal up' and stopping James Leadbetter ('winger without portfolio') by sending him a flu germ, or failing this, by 'standing on his feet, saddling him and climbing on his back!' Bill Reid said he was pleased at all this daft banter, for it showed his players agreed with one of his main philosophies, that you cannot play football without a sense of humour.

After the two teams emerged on a fine and bright afternoon at a packed Carrow Road to a deafening welcome, a hearty rendition of the anthem 'On the Ball, City' struck up – the first time it had been properly sung this season, according to the *Pink 'Un*. The ground had been full long before kick-off and the sea of flat-capped and overcoated spectators were entertained by the rival mascots who slowly lapped the pitch swapping banter. Norwich were represented by the debonnaire figure of a cigar-toting canary in top-hat and tails, accompanied by a 'Norfolk dumpling', a figure in a country-bumpkin style smock, topped by a huge dumpling head. Ipswich's mascots were slightly less bizarre: bus conductor 'Swede' Herring with his huge blue-and-white umbrella, and youngster Ian Harvey in a replica Town kit. There were 39,890 inside the ground, easily the best yet for an East Anglian derby. The noise levels were high back in Ipswich, too, for the game was screened live on thirty TV monitors by Top Rank Vision. The venue was the Baths Hall in St Matthews Street, where the indoor swimming pool would be covered by a temporary dance floor for jazz and pop concerts and special events such as this screening.

Perhaps predictably, the first half was a stalemate, the tension in the air seeming to stifle both sets of players. The tie badly needed a goal and it came a few minutes after the interval when Derrick Lythgoe's cross was headed in by Allcock. Town were stung into a quick response and five minutes later Leadbetter swerved around Bryan Thurlow and cracked the equaliser. Crawford hit a post and another effort was cleared off the line as the action hotted up, but the game ended 1-1. Many unlucky punters inside the ground went home frustrated, not at the result but because they never got a proper view of the action, due to the ground being overfilled.

One aggrieved spectator was B Mulley of Gorleston, who complained: 'I spent the game wandering behind the terraces trying unsuccessfully to get even the smallest glimpse of the game. Add several hundred more who climbed into roof trusses, clung to advertising hoardings, climbed trees and even a few who hoisted themselves onto the actual roof of the stands – not, I hasten to add, to get a better view, but to get a view at all. There were about 2,000 frustrated, disappointed and thoroughly disillusioned fans.'

Mr Mulley was not the only one to believe Carrow Road could not hold 40,000 in comfort and safety. There were also allegations that many had got into the ground without being counted and that the marshalling had been ineffective. E Waters of Ipswich insisted that criticism of the police at Carrow Road had been out of order. If anything, they should be praised for preventing a repeat of the Burnden Park disaster, where 33 died in 1946, and the blame should be pinned on the greedy Norwich directors: 'Their sole aim was to get the money irrespective of whether spectators could see the game or not.'

Mr R Woodward of Felixstowe purchased a 3s ticket but saw nothing: 'I was behind an impenetrable wall of Goliaths in what I believe is called the South Stand. I stuck it till 4.33pm when I decided to call it a day and made for the car. I am consoled by [the *EADT*] report that the game was not worth seeing anyway.' S Taylor of Ipswich said he and his wife had queued for hours for tickets, but at the game the ball came into their field of vision just four times in 90 minutes.

Others had different causes for complaint. F Kisner of Ipswich wrote: 'I was kicked in the pants and had my hat knocked off because I suggested on the way out that it would be a good idea next time Ipswich play at Carrow Road they harvest the sugar beet from the pitch and get rid of those bumps. What a contrast to the Portman Road carpet!' City fan R Wooltorton of Ditchingham also had a moan: 'It was a good thing that [astronaut] Major Glenn was not in orbit at Carrow Road on Saturday; the trackers might have tracked Ipswich's aerial passes by mistake. Good football is surely played at ground level.'

The replay took place at Portman Road three days later on a desperately cold evening, with the pitch in a semi-frozen state. Despite the huge interest, the match was not made all-ticket. Admission was 4s for covered areas, 3s out in the open, and half-price for boys. City were allocated about 800 of the 3,200 seats, priced at 6s 6d each. Three special trains were laid on for City fans in addition to normal rail services. A stadium record crowd 29,796 was admitted, making Portman Road a noisy cauldron, bursting at the seams. An estimated 4,000-plus Norwich fans were locked out, leading to angry criticism that the game should have been all-ticket, thus saving many a wasted journey. At least the local pubs did good trade. Ipswich officials, it transpired, had not expected the demand to exceed the record 28,778 recently accommodated without tickets, for a game with Spurs. The club had also wanted to avoid the presence of ticket touts. Reports varied on how many were locked out, but it was clear that, had there been sufficient room at the two grounds, something like 75,000 would have watched the two games. Clearly interest in the East Anglian derby had reached an all-time high.

Famed for their giant-killing exploits, it was eight years since Norwich had beaten a First Division side away from home, but they fancied their chances tonight, not least because the hazardous pitch conditions could prove a leveller. Ipswich proceeded to have the majority of play but could not turn superiority into goals and paid the penalty when Allcock volleyed home with Roy Bailey looking out of position in his frozen goalmouth. Crawford hooked a Leadbetter corner high into the net at the Churchman's End shortly after the break and, back on level terms, Town went for Norwich's throat. Kennon pulled off a wonderful save from John Elsworthy, and Doug Moran hit the bar as Norwich clung on. Then, against the run of play and with extra-time just two minutes away, Gerry Mannion delivered a firm, low cross which found Allcock, who sidefooted a shock winner past Bailey.

Allcock, recalling that night more than forty years later, said: 'As the game went on the conditions seemed to get worse. With about 90 seconds to go, we were all signalling to the bench that we would need different boots for extra-time and then I managed to score. I got in front of a near-post defender and hit the ball first time. On the way back home, the coach stopped at a pub in Diss, halfway back to Norwich. It was full of Norwich fans and they lifted the roof off.' The City hero admitted they'd been very keyed up before facing Ipswich: 'They were the best team in the country. Alf Ramsey had a very balanced side, using the tactics he was going to win the World Cup with. But we were very confident. We'd beaten Manchester United, Tottenham and Cardiff – all First Division sides – in the years just before that and I was going through a spell of scoring goals with my eyes shut. We were looking forward to lowering their sails. It took two games to do it.'

Town skipper Andy Nelson was philosophical: 'Sitting in the bath after the game most of the Town players found it hard to believe we were out of the cup. Still, it is the unexpected that makes football. There would not be much point in supporters travelling miles and miles to cheer their team if the result always turned out as forecast.' Some Ipswich fans also took defeat in good part, with M Farman of Birmingham stating: 'It is easy for the Ipswich fan to tear his hair in disgust after having a high percentage of the play in the replay but let us not detract from the Norwich achievements.' The Canaries fans were gleeful, particularly about the fact that Ipswich's hot-shot Ted Phillips had been silenced. R Disdle of Wimbledon was even inspired to compose a ditty to the tune of Jimmy Dean's current smash hit *Big Bad John*:

'He stands six feet tall in his football boots
    And defences shake whenever he shoots,
Big Ted, Big Ted.
    They said that we would rue the day
When 'gainst the City he did play,
    But it didn't happen quite that way
For Big Ted.'

Ken Cage of Stowmarket wrote to the *Green 'Un*: 'Bravo Canaries, what a superb show you gave at Portman Road. I was told by the cocky, confident Town supporters to take a bucket with me to pick up all the feathers that would be flying around after the match. They all went to Portman Road to see a one-horse race. That's exactly what they did see, but the wrong horse did the leading. How the mighty are fallen!' The paper's editor said he shared the view of many Town fans: 'Norwich were lucky to get away with it, but good luck to them now that they are through.'

Norwich exited the Cup in the subsequent round at Sheffield United, but were consoled by making great progress in the Football League Cup, a fledgling competition in its second year. Victories over Chesterfield, Lincoln, Middlesbrough, Sunderland, and Blackpool took them to a two-legged final at the end of 1961-62. Their unlikely opponents were mid-table Fourth Division minnows Rochdale, and the Canaries lifted the cup with a 4-0 aggregate victory.

The season had one more shock in store, for Bill Reid decided to quit as manager to return to his native Scotland. His replacement was former Arsenal goalkeeper George Swindin, who would only last twenty games before moving on to Cardiff. By the end of 1962, long-serving skipper Ron Ashman found himself in the manager's chair, initially in a caretaker capacity.

There was far more stability at Portman Road around this time, of course, with Alf Ramsey leading the club to the First Division championship in its very first campaign in the top flight. The football world had not seen anything like it. A team of cast-offs and ageing journeymen lifted the title at the first attempt – partly through Ramsey's crafty tactics, and partly due to an end-of-season capitulation by favourites Burnley.

With Norwich having won the League Cup and Colchester scoring 104 goals to win promotion from Division Four, this was a tremendous time to be a football fan in East Anglia. In the 1962-63 season Ipswich's entry into the European Cup took centre-stage in the region, with Norwich having to take a back seat. Canaries fans witnessed the start of a rather uneventful period that would endure for several seasons.

Ipswich went into sharp decline after their 1962 championship, Ramsey leaving to manage England, and the unfortunate Jackie Milburn taking charge of an ageing side that needed rebuilding. Following the FA Cup-ties of January 1962 it would be more than two years before Ipswich and Norwich would take the field together again, by which time Town were rock bottom of Division One and heading inexorably towards relegation. Due to both clubs being knocked out of the 1963-64 FA Cup, a free Saturday occurred in February and a friendly match at Portman Road was arranged. The circumstances could hardly have been more different to the last vibrant meeting. This time Town were low on confidence and cohesion, star centre-forward Crawford had departed, and hot-shot Phillips was feeling sorry for himself on the transfer list.

One fan pointed out that although neither club was currently doing well, if they formed a combined eleven, a fine-looking line-up could be created. He suggested: Kennon, Kelly, Compton, Baxter, Nelson, Bolton, Broadfoot, Bryceland, Davies, Hegan and Punton.

Manager Milburn used the friendly to give Phillips a return to action, having dropped him after a 1-10 annihilation by Fulham on Boxing Day. Scot Jim Thorburn made his debut for Town in goal, and the game proved surprisingly hard-fought, with one reporter describing it as 'positively hostile', the local referee having his work cut out throughout. Phillips marked his comeback with two goals and Welsh ace Ron Davies bagged a consolation for City. A healthy crowd of 11,446 enjoyed the rare sight of a Town victory in these troubled times. The fans were pleased to see the two clubs playing each other, and one, R Brett of Stowmarket, wrote to the *Green 'Un* to suggest the creation of an annual East Anglian Challenge Cup, to ensure regular games between the two. It would be fourteen years before Mr Brett would get his wish, for in 1978 a competition of this nature was indeed launched, sponsored by Willhire, and involving Ipswich, Norwich, Cambridge and Colchester.

A few weeks after the friendly, Town agreed to send a side for City manager Ron Ashman's testimonial. Although the League season wasn't quite over, relegation for Ipswich had been confirmed eleven days earlier. The disheartened players were mostly just going through the motions, although some were keen to impress in order to find a new club. The

*Green 'Un* optimistically forecast: 'This should be unlike most friendlies and no end of season affair. It promises to be a battle royal.' The idea of the two managers, Milburn and Ashman, actually playing themselves was discussed but given the thumbs-down by some fans, who made it known they would prefer a 'serious' and full-blooded game, rather than gimmicks. The *Pink 'Un* backed the view of its Ipswich counterpart: 'There is no intention in either camp of making this a polite exhibition of the football arts. I doubt if the fans would let it go on at that level, at any rate. Both Ashman and Milburn have said they intend fielding a full-strength side.'

For once, in this nightmare of a season (Ipswich conceded 121 goals in 42 League games), Town's defence looked secure and City were held to a goalless draw – a rarity for a testimonial game. It was the usual feisty affair and Town inside-forward Danny Hegan was carried off with an ankle injury. The crunching tackles pleased the 11,000 crowd and the game proved an interesting taster for the Division Two clashes they now knew would be taking place in 1964-65, beginning in a few months time.

# 6

# ANGRY SCENES IN AN
# ICY GOALMOUTH

## (1964-71)

Ipswich plummeted from the First Division in the spring of 1964 like a skydiver with no parachute. No matter what manager Jackie Milburn did, results only seemed to get worse. The club was still in disarray five months later when Ipswich and Norwich resumed hostilities in the Second Division. Blues supporters found it hard to look forward to the September 1964 derby at Carrow Road in view of their team's dire form.

Seven days earlier, Ipswich were crushed 1-5 at home by Preston. The beleaguered Milburn, stressed and unwell, resigned a few days later. The squad travelled to Norwich without him, even though his resignation still hadn't been formally accepted at that point. Morale was at an all-time low with winger Joe Broadfoot saying things were so bad that he was planning to quit football to become a London cabbie. Milburn had been popular among his players and at the kick-off there was a token gesture along the lines of 'Let's win this for Jackie' – but it was not enough. Although Gerry Baker made the most of a lucky bounce to give Town the lead, Norwich hit back through cracking drives from Gordon Bolland and the prolific Ron Davies. Ipswich's woes were compounded by losing captain Billy Baxter with injury, a massive blow that put huge pressure on fellow defender Trevor Smith, a teenager making his debut. City's 2-1 win was their first in the League over Town for nearly ten years and pushed them up into second place, but left Ipswich rock bottom.

There were suspicions that Norwich reporter Bruce Robinson was being less than sincere when he wrote in the *Pink 'Un*: 'Poor Town. In the space of two or three seasons they have sampled the nectar of success and the bitterness of failure: promotion and the League championship; relegation and all its attendant worries. Now Milburn resigns and key players seek the means to leave. The injury list gets longer and longer, the huge snowball of misfortune rolls on. A more down Town is difficult to imagine.' City manager Ron Ashman sounded genuine, however, with his brief after-match comment: 'We know what it's like to be out of luck.'

By the time of the 1964-65 return, the Bill McGarry revolution was underway at Portman Road. Winston Churchill was on his death-bed at Chartwell, but the bulldog spirit was alive and well in Ipswich, thanks to the disciplinarian McGarry and his uncompromising methods. Recruited from Watford in the autumn, McGarry had been a tough little wing-half himself and he transferred his gritty style into management. The Ipswich players hardly knew what had hit them, for a man more different to the laconic Jackie Milburn was hard to imagine. But McGarry's tough-love approach got instant results and before long he'd steered the ailing club to almost mid-table.

Promotion-chasing Norwich knew they would have a battle on their hands in the January 1965 game at a semi-frozen Portman Road. What would emerge from the occasion would be one of the strangest controversies ever to envelop an East Anglian derby.

Thousands of Canaries fans ventured south, creating a great atmosphere with the ground looking full half an hour before the start. Vocal wars were unleashed, particularly after the Tannoy announcer appealed for a rousing chorus of the Sir Harry Lauder song that Ipswich had adopted – 'Keep Right On to the End of the Road'. The fans obliged and their opposite numbers retaliated with a gusty 'On The Ball, City'. The floodlights were on from the start and City's Calcutta-born goalkeeper Kevin Keelan defended the icy goalmouth at the Churchman's End. Norwich were unlucky to lose inside-left Tommy Bryceland with an ankle injury early on. Down to ten men, they fell behind when Keelan slipped on the ice, allowing Gerry Baker to score twice. The 2-0 half-time scoreline flattered Town, but City fans reckoned their boys would hit back after the break when Ipswich would have to defend the hazardous frozen end of the pitch.

Naturally, then, they felt dismay when groundsman Freddie Blake and an assistant suddenly came on at half-time, heading for the icy goalmouth with buckets of sand and salt. The ice had not been treated when Norwich defended this goalmouth, and it had a played a major part in the two goals scored, so why should it be done now? All hell was let loose. The City fans were in uproar and loud booing broke out, accompanied by a chant of 'no, no, no' as Blake set down his buckets. About a dozen City followers clambered over the wall and stormed onto the pitch to push the horrified Blake and his helper away. Buckets of sand and salt were overturned and scuffling broke out. The police came on to break up the scuffles and escorted the intruders off. A shaken Blake completed his sanding duties under police escort. These remarkable scenes made front page news and many a reader must have choked on his breakfast to see pictures of poor Blake, complete with trilby and overcoat, being confronted, and of two other conservatively dressed men apparently lashing out at each other in the goalmouth.

Norwich fans clearly thought they were suffering a huge injustice, but referee Mr Wells of Luton explained later: 'The goalmouth was playable at the start, but as the temperature dropped, the surface got worse. I ordered the salt and sand to beat the ice.' City supporters felt the referee had caved in to pressure from Ipswich boss McGarry, who clearly didn't want his own goalkeeper, Ken Hancock, to suffer the same ordeal that Kevin Keelan had endured. Several supporters later wrote to the *Pink 'Un,* insisting that Keelan's 'antics' in the pre-match warm up suggested conditions were bad from the very start, so why hadn't Norwich called for sand then? It was no good complaining after Ipswich did so at half-time. D Jones of Heacham blamed the referee for deeming the pitch playable while Keelan was clearly slipping around, but changing his attitude when it was Hancock's turn at 3.45. The almighty row overshadowed the fact that Ipswich won the game 3-0, their third goal – a Broadfoot rocket on the hour – having nothing to do with the state of the pitch.

With hindsight, the farcical events of the first half proved a turning point in Norwich's season. From challenging for promotion to Division One, they suddenly began dropping points galore, and Newcastle and Northampton pulled away at the top. City never really recovered and ultimately finished 1964-65 sixth, one place below rejuvenated Ipswich, whose recovery under McGarry had been remarkable. It was, in fact, the closest League finish ever involving the two clubs, for they both earned 47 points and were only separated by 0.03 of a goal on goal-average. It was a disappointing outcome for Norwich, but Town followers were ecstatic, given the nightmare start they had made.

Although the complaints about the pitch sanding seemed valid at the time, some other moans and groans from the more partisan Norwich followers bordered on the ridiculous. One supporter complained that the referee should have prevented Town's Frank Brogan and Gerry Baker from wearing medallions around their necks, not so much for safety reasons, but more because of their 'nuisance value'. S Nobbs of Gorleston, meanwhile, was agitated about the fact that Norwich fans had been 'outgunned' in the singing of club anthems: 'Our great battle hymn has become an apologetic whisper. However illogical we may think the words are, it is still a great tune that means everything to the players.'

In the summer of 1965 Ipswich smartened and updated their ground by erecting a new office block and dressing rooms to replace the quaint and elderly wooden cricket pavilion previously used. The club also recruited former Norwich forward Sammy Chung as McGarry's assistant, adding to the very short list of players and officials who had served both clubs in the professional era.

The rivals made moderate starts to 1965-66, but this didn't diminish interest in the September clash at Carrow Road. In fact, the heavy traffic making its way up the A140 to Norwich caused such congestion that the Town coach only arrived at the ground with twenty minutes to spare, thanks to a police escort. On the pitch the action was fast and furious and Gordon Bolland nearly put City ahead, only to be foiled by the bar. Ron Davies then had a headed goal disallowed for a push on Bill Baxter. Just before the hour came the breakthrough, Bryceland hooking home a pass from promising young full-back Dave Stringer. It proved to be the winner and an upset Town boss McGarry appeared on Anglia TV later to heavily criticise both the referee and his own players for lack of effort.

The two sides were still languishing below halfway by the time of the return in March 1966, but Ipswich fans were buoyed by the return to the club of their hero Ray 'Jungle Boy' Crawford. The ace goalscorer had spent nearly three years at West Brom and Wolves, but was back at his spiritual home. He was delighted to get the call and said: 'I couldn't wait to get here. I would have run all the way down the motorway. In my first game back at Portman Road I scored as we beat Norwich 2-0. I used to love beating Norwich.' Crawford had been sold in 1963 for £42,500 and eventually returned for well under half that sum. The funds had been raised by the sale of Bobby Kellard to Portsmouth. Some fans called for Ted Phillips to be re-signed to link up again with Crawford, but by now Phillips was past his best and turning out for Fourth Division neighbours Colchester.

The March 1966 match would be the first East Anglian derby in which Norwich wore kit that was exclusively yellow and green. Having started life with blue and white halved shirts, City had switched to yellow and green shirts and blue shorts in 1907, later switching to black shorts. The shorts, too, became green in 1965-66 after fashion-conscious fans wrote to the local press insisting on the change.

As many as 6,000 Norwich fans were thought to be inside Portman Road for a game that began at a furious pace with tempers flaring. Mick McNeil's late tackle on Bill Punton earned him a stern lecture and constant booing from City followers every time he played the ball from then on. Minutes later he hauled Punton down again and got a second lecture but still no booking. City's fury increased when Terry Allcock had his name taken for an offence no more serious than McNeil's. No quarter was being given. Cyril Lea and Bryceland clashed heavily, leaving both men in agony. For the second successive season in this derby, Keelan blundered, allowing the returning Crawford to open the scoring. A disputed penalty was put away by Baxter to complete Town's 2-0 win.

Despite his one mistake, Keelan won praise for his display and the *Green 'Un* revealed that the keeper might have been playing for Ipswich had previous manger Jackie Milburn not been pipped at the post by Norwich's Ron Ashman in a race to sign him from Wrexham.

Ipswich supporters were delighted to stave off relegation worries at Norwich's expense and keep the Canaries' costly strikers quiet into the bargain. A notice appeared in a local factory after the game: 'Lost! Two valuable canaries, answering to the names of Davies (£60,000) and Bolland (£35,000). Last seen in the pocket of a certain Bill Baxter (who cost £10) where it is known they spent ninety minutes.'

Ipswich and Norwich would meet again in 1966, a week or two before the start of the World Cup finals, but in sad circumstances. Barry Butler, a stalwart centre-half for the Canaries since 1957, had been killed in a car crash in April. Six weeks later Ipswich sent a side to Carrow Road to assist Butler's testimonial fund. In front of nearly 6,000, Hugh Curran bagged a hat-trick as Norwich won 3-1.

The summer of 1966 was, of course, a joyous time for English football, with former Ipswich manager Alf Ramsey playing a starring role. But for Norwich City it was a depressing and forgettable period. Not long after the Butler's death, aged 31, the club's popular manager Ashman departed after nineteen years with the club. Goalscoring favourite Ron Davies was then sold to Southampton. One win from their first thirteen games of 1966-67 only compounded the misery, and attendances at Carrow Road plummeted.

The absence of the disillusioned fans meant the visit of Ipswich on a sunny afternoon in early September attracted only 19,129, by far the lowest crowd to witness this fixture since the Second World War. Still without a win under new manager Lol Morgan, things went from bad to worse for Norwich, with skipper Allcock limping off after only five minutes with a sprained ankle. Don Heath replaced him, the first substitute ever used in an East Anglian derby. When your luck is out, nothing seems to go right, and shortly after Allcock's departure a howler by Keelan presented Ipswich with the opening goal. Amazingly, it was the third season in succession that this agile and temperamental goalkeeper had gifted a goal to Ipswich. On the first occasion he could blame an icy pitch, but this time there seemed no excuse as he dropped the ball, under little pressure, straight at Crawford's feet. The Canaries weathered this early storm and Bolland levelled, heading home a Punton free-kick before the interval. However, Ipswich regained the upper hand and deservedly took the points with Baker driving home a winner following a bad back-pass by Robin Gladwin. In a highly competitive contest, Ipswich's recent recruit from Portsmouth, seventeen-year-old full-back Mick Mills, was booked for an over-physical exchange. The result saw Town riding high in the table in second place, but City slipped to bottom.

By the time of the return on a mild evening in April 1967, life had become more cheerful at Carrow Road, largely due to a thrilling 2-1 Cup giant-killing at champions-elect Manchester United a few weeks earlier. City were climbing clear of the relegation zone but required several more points to be certain of avoiding the drop. Town were up in third, but looking unlikely to catch the leading pair Coventry and Wolves who'd broken clear. The game proved an ill-tempered affair, with referee Jack Taylor having to keep a watchful eye on Mal Lucas and Danny Hegan in particular, who had a running battle throughout. City earned their first League win at Portman Road for nearly sixteen years thanks to a fine shot by Laurie Sheffield, playing in his only East Anglian derby, and an own-goal by Baxter, who headed a Bolland cross beyond Hancock. 'On The Ball, City' rang out lustily in the closing stages, with home fans sullen and quiet, many leaving early knowing their outside hopes of promotion had all but disappeared.

A *Pink 'Un* reporter wondered if Norwich's relegation rivals might think this 2-0 win had been a case of a neighbourly old pals' act, but this laughable idea held little water, and he admitted there had been occasions in the past when City had looked to Ipswich for a good turn – and had usually been disappointed. It had been a typical no-holds-barred affair and Lol Morgan's recent decision to drop long-serving Allcock in favour of Fred Sharpe – an ex-Spurs half-back enjoying a new lease of life – seemed to be paying off. Allcock scotched rumours of his retirement and said he still had plenty to offer.

The double delight of putting one over Ipswich and avoiding relegation certainly put City fans in fine voice. One of them, B Harley of the Catton Estate, Norwich, regaled the *Pink 'Un* with colourful metaphors: 'Norwich City have held the sword of Damocles over fans' heads in 1966-67 and inflicted sheer mental torture, and then just when the fans had steeled themselves ready for the big drop into Division Three have brought about a reprieve. The sword is removed and with a fine, flashing flourish plunged into the auld enemy at Portman Road, dazzling us all in its execution of our long drawn-out cliff-hanging danger, and simultaneously dealing a serious blow to the Witches [sic] hopes of finishing third in the table.'

Can there be such a thing as a goalless thriller? If so, then the game at Portman Road on a showery Saturday in September 1967 must fit that bill. City gained their first away point of the 1967-68 season in one of the most open and attacking derbies for years. It was end-to-end stuff with Keelan in fine form during a contest that seemed to lack the usual blood and thunder, fierce tackling and bad tempers. E Powell of Barton Mills reckoned it had been a pleasure to see the old rivals playing open football against each other: 'How often in the past have we seen these games reduced to a slogging contest when taking the man became much more important than winning the ball, when the baying of the over-emotional home fans had to be satisfied by fair means or foul, usually the latter?'

Norwich were delighted at winning a point, but *Pink 'Un* columnist J Phillips must have raised hackles by admitting that Ipswich were still undoubtedly the region's top dogs and he couldn't see that changing for a while. He would prove correct in respect of 1967-68, for Town gathered momentum as the season went on and became serious promotion contenders.

The return game that season would prove another thriller, only this time with goals galore. The drama started with the mid-table underdogs Norwich surging into a two-goal lead in the first half-hour. Recent signing Charlie Crickmore and Hugh Curran drove home cracking shots in front of the Barclay End, but the jubilation was stifled when Town hit back through their South African 'wonderkid' Colin Viljoen, who headed in a Frank Brogan cross. Town also had two goals disallowed and, after a half-time pep talk from the no-nonsense McGarry, an equaliser looked inevitable. It came from an unlikely source. Full-back Billy Houghton, just two goals in seventy previous appearances, took a 35-yard free-kick and his low, raking shot flashed into the net, perhaps aided by Bobby Hunt dummying the ball as it went.

Viljoen wasn't to be outdone, and he conjured up a brilliant third for Town, gliding past Laurie Brown and beating the advancing Keelan with an inch-perfect shot. The nineteen-year-old from Johannesburg completed a memorable hat-trick moments later with a clever lob to cap Town's finest display so far this season. Curran headed Norwich's third to create a hectic final few minutes, but Town hung on and the 4-3 win kept them in fourth place and in the promotion race. Due to problems obtaining residential and work permits, the hero of the hour Viljoen was temporarily registered as a gardener working at chairman John Cobbold's Glemham Hall. Whether he really had 'green fingers' was a matter of serious doubt, but there was no questioning the young midfielder's footballing abilities.

An unsavoury aspect of this seven-goal thriller, which had been watched by 29,937, were the outbreaks of hooliganism inside or nearby the ground. One Ipswich supporter reported a gang of youths had stolen his son's, and other fans' scarves and badges after the game. This was just one of a number of incidents symptomatic of what seemed to be a growing nationwide trend at football matches.

The 'football skinhead' phenomenon was starting to rear its ugly head across Britain, and East Anglia was not immune from such behaviour: a week or two earlier terrace fighting had spilled onto the pitch before the FA Cup-tie between Colchester and West Brom. It would be naive to think that the previous 42 Ipswich-Norwich derby games had been entirely well-mannered and trouble-free, but nowadays it seemed that the risk of violence was a part of the occasion.

Town's 4-3 win at Carrow Road was followed by a decisive plunge into the transfer market by McGarry. He swooped on Middlesbrough for striker John O'Rourke, and Mansfield for midfielder Peter Morris. This pair would prove the final pieces in the jigsaw and Town promptly went on an unbeaten run that saw them clinch the Second Division title a point clear of QPR. First Division football was back at Portman Road, and once again envious eyes were being cast south from Carrow Road. Having finished a respectable ninth, hopes of First Division football in Norfolk had to be put on hold yet again.

Ipswich's promotion didn't mean local derby action disappeared off the calendar completely, for the clubs were paired together in the second round of the 1968-69 League Cup. City were as keen as Colman's Norwich-made mustard to avenge that Viljoen-inspired home defeat. On a fine evening at Portman Road Norwich showed just why they had a fearsome reputation as cup giant-killers, storming to a 2-0 lead within the first twenty minutes. Curran finished superbly for the first, and Charlie Crickmore netted the second from the spot after Baxter fisted a John Manning cross over the bar.

In those days, that sort of offence didn't warrant even a talking-to, so Baxter maintained his record of never having been booked, which was remarkable given that he was a fierce competitor who never compromised in the tackle. McGarry unleashed one of his well-known tirades at half-time (the hair-dryer treatment, to use more modern parlance) and his players responded by drawing level, McNeil heading in a corner and Crawford converting a cross from substitute Charlie Woods. If those in the blue corner thought they'd saved the day they were wrong, for the deadly Curran tucked away two well-taken goals in the final ten minutes. The 4-2 win was celebrated long and loud on the return journey to Norfolk and red-faced Town were left to ponder their defensive frailties.

Norwich's League Cup march ended in the fourth round with a 0-4 home hammering by Southampton, and they would have a moderate mid-table sort of season in Division Two. Ipswich did likewise in the top flight, having coped with a change of manager in November 1968 when Bill McGarry quit, along with coach Sammy Chung, to take up similar posts at Wolves. The vacant manager's job was offered to Torquay's Frank O'Farrell, who accepted informally but then changed his mind. Echoing McGarry's parting shot, O'Farrell reckoned that there was no potential for improvement at Ipswich, a club that was already punching above its weight.

The man who eventually took the job would, after several years of toil, prove McGarry and O'Farrell very wrong indeed. That man was 35-year-old Bobby Robson, a former England international who was desperate for work having recently signed on the dole following bad experiences at Fulham and Vancouver. An interesting footnote to all this: O'Farrell chose to join Leicester instead of Ipswich and within a few weeks the Foxes had been relegated, their fate being sealed by a 1-2 defeat at Ipswich.

Town fans enjoyed the last week of 1968-69. Not only were Sheffield Wednesday and O'Farrell's Leicester beaten in the League, but they had two extra chances to watch their favourites in action via testimonials for Ray Crawford and Terry Allcock. The latter was staged at Carrow Road just 24 hours after Crawford's big night and, with many players featuring in both, it was hardly surprising that this was a fairly gentle affair as local derbies go. Ken Foggo, Allcock himself, and Clive Payne scored the City goals in a meaningless 3-1 win.

With hindsight the game has significance due to the identity of the 'unknown' wearing Ipswich's No 9 shirt in the first half. This turned out to be Clive Woods, a 21-year-old born and bred in Norwich and a keen supporter of the Canaries. He'd recently been playing for Eastern Counties League side Gothic, but was now undergoing his second trial at Portman Road, an earlier stint having come to nothing. The younger brother of Dennis, a Watford and Cambridge United player, Woods had left school five years earlier and taken a number of jobs in Norwich, including one as a Co-op bike delivery boy. He recalled: 'I was like Granville on *Open All Hours*.' Woods was on £19 a week in a shoe factory by the time Robson played him in Allcock's testimonial, but six weeks later he would sign on the dotted line at Ipswich, becoming one of the First Division's most celebrated 'late starters'. He officially became an Ipswich player on the same day as Trevor Whymark, another Norfolk lad pinched from under Norwich City's noses.

More than two years would pass before another East Anglian derby would be staged. Again it was a meaningless friendly, albeit one which pulled in a relatively healthy crowd of 9,000 to Carrow Road as a mid-week curtain-raiser to the 1971-72 League season. Admission was 50p or 30p, depending on your vantage point (10p for juniors) for what turned into an entertaining seven-goal affair. Ken Foggo and Payne blasted City into a healthy lead before Town's new signing, Bryan Hamilton, tucked home a beauty and Viljoen quickly equalised. Big defender Duncan Forbes deflected a long-range effort into his own net to give Town a 3-2 lead, but Steve Govier levelled with a header and then, near the end, Peter Silvester headed City to a 4-3 win.

It may have been just a friendly, but local rivalry runs deep and an unruly element among the big Ipswich following decided to register their disapproval by making their presence felt in the city centre. Police reported that 200 or more youths stampeded down Riverside into Prince of Wales Road, where windows were smashed. Seeing the trail of damage the next morning, Norwich's older generation must have wondered what the world was coming to – especially as that day's news bulletins told of hippies burning effigies of a judge outside the Old Bailey in protest at the jailing of the editors of the underground magazine *Oz*.

This mid-season friendly in 1964 was
watched by nearly 12,000

Norwich centre-forward Ron Davies
scored in two 1964 East Anglian derbies

Norwich goalkeeper Kevin Keelan (left) passed Ken Nethercott's
appearance record against Ipswich in 1973

Ipswich's Mark Brennan chases Norwich's Mick Channon (1985)

Terry Butcher rises above former Town teammate Keith Bertschin (1985)

The first East Anglian derby at League level took place on the day before war broke out

Winger Jackie Little starred for Town
against City either side of World War II

Ipswich's Fabian Wilnis is challenged by
Norwich's Matt Svensson (2003)

Norwich won this Division Three (South) contest 2-1 in 1948

The *Eastern Daily Press* coverage of the bizarre pitch-sanding provocation in 1965
(See page 74)

Trevor Whymark's testimonial derby game
was staged in 1979

Cover star in 1976 was Johnny Miller,
who played for both clubs

Norwich's David Jones and Ipswich's David Geddis (1978)

The *Daily Mail* promotes
the 1962 FA Cup meeting

Asa Hartford (left) tangles
with Trevor Putney (1985)

A testimonial derby game for
Kevin Keelan in 1974

A heavy police presence keeps
order outside Portman Road

Norwich players applaud Ipswich's Colin Viljoen at his 1977 testimonial

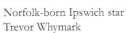

Norfolk-born Ipswich star
Trevor Whymark

The historic Milk-Cup semi-final
decider in 1985

Skippers Mick Mills (Ipswich) and Martin Peters (Norwich)
before the Willhire Cup meeting of 1978

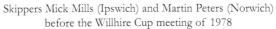

Ipswich keeper Paul Cooper fists away from Eric Gates and Norwich's Mick Channon (1983)

The Norwich Hospital Cup contest was revived in 1989

Norwich's Duncan Forbes, veteran of 13 local derbies in the 1970s

Ipswich won this 1998 contest by 5-0

Midfielder Peter Morris served both clubs

Norwich fans are escorted by police from Ipswich station to Portman Road in 2005

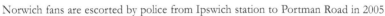

Managers Bobby Robson and John Bond appeal for calm from the fans

Wing wizard Clive Woods represented          Norwich dispelled relegation fears by
both Ipswich and Norwich                          winning at Ipswich in 1967

## THIS THREAT WAS MADE GOOD

Ipswich fans enjoyed a 3-0 win at Norwich on Boxing Day 1960

Billy Houghton scored a 35-yarder for Ipswich at Norwich in 1968

A car sticker in dubious taste. Norwich fans could buy their own equivalent

Norwich's John Deehan holds off Ipswich's George Burley (1985)

Norwich's Dale Gordon, an Ipswich fan as a boy, signs for
a young Norwich supporter in 2003

7

# Cobbold Claims Regional Supremacy

(1972-73)

It may have taken eleven years to emulate Ipswich by becoming a First Division club, but the long wait only intensified the joy Norwich fans felt when top-flight football finally became a reality at Carrow Road in 1972.

Masterminded by stern-faced manager Ron Saunders, City's promotion was clinched by a 2-1 win at Leyton Orient on a Monday evening in April. Canaries legend Ron Ashman voiced the feelings of many: 'A great feeling for everyone connected with City, especially after Ipswich's successes of recent years. But they're there at last!' Town boss Bobby Robson welcomed the news, too: 'I am delighted for East Anglia that they've got promotion. Next season there will be a keen sense of rivalry between the two clubs and it should be very interesting. It has been missing from football in the area and will be good for the game here.'

To the disdain of their East Anglian readers, some Fleet Street pundits wondered whether the region had the depth of interest and population to sustain more than one First Division side. Suffice to say, such talk did not go down well out in the 'boondocks' of eastern England. Ipswich fans, of course, could recall how the so-called experts from London had also sneered when their team joined the elite back in 1961 and then again in 1968. The club had certainly answered its critics in emphatic fashion on those occasions.

By the start of 1972-73, Robson was repaying the patience shown in him by the Ipswich board by establishing a set-up that was full of potential. Young gems like Kevin Beattie, George Burley and Eric Gates were coming through a carefully constructed youth scheme, and those fans who had called for Robson's head a few years earlier had by now gone quiet. Most Ipswich folk were satisfied their club was moving in the right direction and even felt generous enough to give a 'friendly' welcome to their old rivals from Norwich to the top division. Writing in the *Green 'Un*, Ken Rice lashed out at Fleet Street for not giving Norwich's success better coverage, and for being negative about their chances of survival:

'East Anglians in particular are renowned for their stoic nature and I'm sure like most other injustices this one will be taken in stride. Of course East Anglia can support two first division sides. At present something in excess of 1.25 million people live in Suffolk and Norfolk alone, not including the fringe areas, within easy reach of Carrow Road and Portman Road, and with the home fixtures of the two sides alternating there should be no problem of a clash. It promises to be a memorable 1972-73 and I can't wait for the release of the season's fixture list when we'll know just when and in what order the long-awaited return of the Town-City local derby will take place. Well done Norwich, great to have you with us.'

Robson admitted on the eve of the 1972-73 season that Ipswich's aim was no longer just to survive as a top flight club, but to attempt to win something, or at least go close. For the opening game he gave teenager Beattie his debut at Old Trafford, of all places, and the youngster came through with flying colours in a 2-1 win in front of over 51,000. On the same afternoon First Division newcomers Norwich drew 1-1 at home to Everton, and the scene was set for the very first top-flight East Anglian derby at Portman Road three days later.

'Norwich had better look out on Tuesday night,' warned a partisan *Green 'Un* editorial after the win in Manchester: 'East Anglian football fans have never had it so good and the rivalry is bound to be intense.' The Norwich press corps were also in bullish mood: 'Traffic from Norwich to Ipswich will be thick as flies and Town, I think, are in for a warm night in more ways than one, for if the Canaries do not pitch into their task with their accustomed toughness and bravado, then at least City's fans will help to enliven the terraces.'

To accommodate the mass invasion of Canaries, a special car park was arranged on British Rail land near Ipswich's ground and extra police were drafted in from Norfolk. Never before had a City-Town game seen the build-up this one was getting. Largely responsible for this was the amount of coverage being given by the local press. The FA Cup meeting in 1962, for example, had been a massive occasion, but received nowhere near the column inches devoted to this game ten years later.

Ken Rice, in the *Green 'Un*, said local derby fever reminded him of the story of domestic cricket's biggest grudge match: 'It's like the chap watching the Roses cricket match at Old Trafford, who applauded a fine shot. "Art thou for Yorkshire?" asked his neighbour. "No," he replied. "Art thou for Lancashire?" "No." "Then shut up, it's nowt to do with thee." Town against City is a domestic dispute and more than just the first top division encounter between the sides. The fact that few players in either team hail from East Anglia originally is of no importance, the fact is they are wearing yellow and green or blue and white. For the players it's a game like any other. Both will naturally be anxious to win and the fact that it's so early in the season when a good start can make such a differ-ence to a side's confidence and morale will give it that added edge, but for the supporters there's more to it than that. I'm certain that for the fans of the side which comes out on top, any immediate subsequent failures by their team will be far more tolerable; they'll be as happy as if they'd won the pools; industry will boom, even their wives and children will feel loved. In short, the world will be a happier place.'

On a warm evening, Portman Road was a sea of colour and tension as a near-record 29,544 crammed the terraces for an historic occasion. Ron Saunders' men looked livelier early on, and after fourteen minutes winger Terry Anderson collected Doug Livermore's flick and lobbed it neatly over the advancing Town keeper David Best. The lead lasted just ten minutes before Bryan Hamilton swooped on a rebound off Duncan Forbes to rifle a shot home.

After a first half played at full-pelt, the second was a touch more restrained, but exploded into life in the closing stages when City's Jimmy Bone squeezed the ball past Best, just three minutes after his opposite number Rod Belfitt had a goal disallowed. Ipswich desperately pushed men forward to save the game and left gaps that City nearly exploited with a third goal.

Extrovert referee Roger Kirkpatrick blew the final whistle with his customary flourish amid great scenes of yellow and green celebration. Ipswich had now won just one of the last seven derbies. It had been an emotionally charged night and some of the older observers could hardly believe they were finally seeing the two sides play each other in a First Division setting. Lifelong Town fan John Eastwood said: 'It was hard to imagine that a few years previously I had watched contests between these two sides in the Third Division South.'

During the autumn of 1972 the two teams met in the more relaxed surroundings of the *Daily Express* five-a-side competition at Wembley's Empire Pool, Ipswich beating Norwich in an early round. But it was soon back to the serious business of the First Division return game at Carrow Road in early November. Ipswich chairman John Cobbold said he want-ed revenge for the 1-2 home defeat, but added with a typical chuckle: 'But not at any cost, of course, this game is on Armistice Day.' Special trains were laid on from Suffolk with a 75p return fare for adults.

Both clubs were sitting comfortably in the top ten of the League by now, yet all was not well among the Ipswich faithful. In the build-up to the Norwich trip Robson was publicly critical of fans he accused of spending most home matches moaning and groaning and not getting behind their team. Some of these complaints had centred on Robson's decision to swap leading scorer Rod Belfitt for Everton's relatively unknown David Johnson, a move which surprised everyone but would ultimately prove a masterstroke.

The barrackers hit back at Robson by saying the Town players never responded to the chanting of their name, and that the management at the club, and the local press, were always too quick to criticise the supporters for lacking enthusiasm. The one occasion when Town fans could be guaranteed to raise the roof was the local derby, but sadly this November 1972 clash proved a real anticlimax. Stifled by the tension, the game petered out to a 0-0 draw and the near-35,0000 crowd had precious little to get excited about. Any neutrals present must have thought the East Anglian derby fever was much ado about nothing.

Fortunately, that 1972-73 season did not deteriorate for the two clubs in the way the Carrow Road derby had done. Ipswich got stronger as the campaign went on and, with the help of big wins over Chelsea and Manchester United, ultimately finished fourth and qualified for Europe. At Norwich, once the novelty of First Division football wore off, life became a struggle and they only steered clear of the drop at the eleventh hour with a 2-1 win over trapdoor rivals Crystal Palace on a memorable night at a packed Carrow Road.

Norwich's forte this season had definitely been cup football. The Canaries played in no fewer than eighteen cup-ties, reaching the final of both the League and Texaco Cups. The run to the League Cup final provided some golden nights for the fans and the final against Spurs meant City were the first East Anglian club to reach Wembley. The two-legged semi-final triumph over Chelsea was a memorable affair and proved to the nation that City had really arrived in the big time. After the usual massive build-up, the final itself was something of a flop, with some Norwich players apparently 'freezing' on the big stage. With Spurs looking strangely subdued it made for a drab game, decided by Ralph Coates' late half-volley into the Norwich net.

Just a few days later, City overcame the disappointment of Wembley to beat Motherwell 4-3 on aggregate in a two-legged semi-final of the Texaco Cup. In view of their relegation worries, the Texaco competition should really have been low on the priority list, but its importance, especially to the public, was suddenly increased when Ipswich overcame Newcastle in a later semi-final, to join the Canaries in the final.

The rest of the nation probably disagreed, but to the folk of East Anglia, the meeting of City and Town in a cup final was a mouthwatering prospect. The sponsors were rather pleased, too, for the 'local derby' aspect meant sell-out crowds at both legs of the final were guaranteed.

Sure enough, the two games would attract an aggregate crowd of 65,500. Winning would mean a jackpot of almost £50,000, Texaco having invested around £100,000 in this, their third annual contribution to British football. Their arrival on the scene was initially regarded with suspicion and cynicism, but sponsorship was by now slowly being accepted. Norwich had recently been through the ballyhoo that accompanies a cup final build-up, but it was a new experience for Ipswich and the local press gave unprecedented coverage to the games. The *Evening Star* produced a special supplement with the help of sponsors Texaco, who had recruited seventeen 'leggy lovelies' to promote their competition. Conveniently, one of these, seventeen-year-old Diane Lawrence, hailed from Ipswich and was therefore employed to 'show her colours' around Suffolk, enticing fans to the final's first leg at Ipswich by posing in a blue and white mini-skirt and other accoutrements.

Among the other attractions arranged for the game on Friday, 4 May 1973 was an appearance by the Parachute Regiment, the 314 Red Devils, to trail coloured smoke and banners over the ground. Local police knew the huge influx of fans would mean they'd have their work cut out, and they revealed some surprising statistics on the morning of the first leg: A 'league table of arrests' showed Ipswich were Division One's third-worst offenders with 238 hooligans apprehended during the season at Portman Road, although it should be pointed out that a large percentage of these had been visiting fans.

Norwich's run to the final had seen club history made on two fronts. For their first-round tie at Dundee, the Canaries had flown to a match for the first time, while the victory over Leicester in the second round saw the first penalty shoot-out staged at Carrow Road. Canaries boss Saunders, a Liverpudlian not immersed in the history of East Anglian rivalry, commented: 'I am not regarding these two games as something special just because they are against Ipswich – they are special because it's a cup final.' Town skipper Mick Mills took a different tack: 'There is more local prestige at stake than anything else.'

The two games would be staged over a 72-hour period on the first weekend of May 1973, either side of the Sunderland v Leeds FA Cup final. Ipswich would draw first blood in this long weekend battle for East Anglian supremacy, for on the night before the Texaco final's first leg, their youth team came from behind against Norwich to win a junior trophy. A number of future stars appeared for both sides on a night when Norwich were jeered for over-robust tactics.

Town's record-breaking appearance-maker, Tommy Parker, sounded wistful when he commented before the Texaco final: 'As an ex-Ipswich player I realise only too well how the hearts of player and spectators alike will be beating that little bit faster, as we are playing the old enemy.' He was quite right and the Ipswich fans were in fine voice for the first leg at Portman Road, prompting remarks about how strange it was that they should finally get fully behind their team in the very last home game of the season.

Town looked the better side throughout the first game, although Paul Cheesely went close by hitting their crossbar. A niggly game saw five men booked and an ugly brawl break out in the centre circle. Roared on by an unusually animated Portman Road crowd, Town took the lead when midfield dynamo Peter 'Diesel' Morris smashed home a gem of a free-kick from nearly thirty yards. Ten minutes later Morris, who'd only managed one goal all season before the game, bagged his second after a good cross by Mick Lambert. Town brought on sub Clive Woods late on and the winger inadvertently helped his home-town club back into the game by conceding a free-kick with his first involvement. It led to Clive Payne's header being diverted into his own net by Kevin Beattie. The game ended on a tightrope at 2-1 and trouble spilled into the streets later where gangs of fans clashed, leading to thirteen arrests.

A convoy of Ipswich fans headed up the A140 during the Monday afternoon for the second leg. Traffic was brought to a halt for a spell after a heavy cloudburst temporarily flooded the road. The majority made it for the kick-off, however, and the Carrow Road crowd nearly reached the 36,000 mark, amidst a tremendous atmosphere under the lights. City's hopes were hit after just eight minutes' play when Norfolk-born Trevor Whymark fired a Lambert cross past Kevin Keelan. It was a crucial blow and Town wrapped things up after the interval, taking a 4-1 aggregate lead when Woods scored from close range after Keelan failed to hold a Mick Mills shot.

Woods was only playing because David Johnson was unfit after taking a pounding from City skipper Duncan Forbes in the first leg. The uncompromising Forbes was booked in the second leg for the twelfth time this season. Lanky centre-forward David Cross headed in a late consolation for the Canaries, but it was Mick Mills who lifted the cup, presented to him from the Norwich directors' box.

Seeing Mills lift a trophy at the home of Town's biggest rivals was a sweet moment for the blue and white hordes. They congregated in front of the directors' box and chanted long and loud for Robson to make an appearance. The Town boss presented himself for just thirty seconds, looking rather embarrassed. Alongside him was coach Cyril Lea, who upon his return to the dressing room was thrown into the bath fully

clothed. City boss Saunders and chairman Geoffrey Watling both gra-
ciously acknowledged Town had been the better side. Match-winner
Woods, who lived a few minutes away from Norwich's ground, in Long
Stratton, said with a grin: 'It was lovely to score at Norwich.'

On the following night the cup winners paraded in Ipswich, but being
unused to such events, booked an ordinary single-decker bus, instead of
an open-topped double-decker. Players were therefore forced to clamber
through the vehicle's sun-roof in order to wave the trophy at the celebrating supporters. There was a civic reception, hosted by the Mayor of
Ipswich, Alderman Mulley, who dropped a clanger in his speech by referring to Bobby Robson as 'Mr Ramsey'. Ipswich's gregarious chairman,
John Cobbold, in his element on such occasions, said: 'This is one of our
finest nights without any doubt. It has proved – if any proof were necessary – that we are the kings of East Anglian soccer. This season has
brought magnificent achievements from all our teams. We are having to
find a new cupboard for all our cups and, of course, all of it is due to
Bobby Robson.'

Cobbold added, with amazing prescience, as it would turn out: 'The
next thing is the FA Cup and then the UEFA Cup.' Mills would later say:
'The atmosphere at Carrow Road that night was incredible. The Texaco
Cup was the first trophy of the Robson era at the club and some of us
in that side would later be in teams that won the FA and UEFA Cup.
Ipswich fans and players alike especially love to win at Carrow Road of
course. To do so and get a trophy made it so, so special.'

Sadly, a little of the gloss was taken off the achievement when reports
emerged of how Town fans had wrecked a train, putting it out of service. 'This was the first major trouble attributable to East Anglian football
fans on trains,' according to a British Rail spokesman. 'In the past Ipswich
and Norwich fans had been among the best behaved in the country as far
as we are concerned.' The list of damage was horrendous: 214 light bulbs
removed, 32 light-shades smashed, eleven fire extinguishers hurled out of
windows, slogans daubed in paint and the train stopped unnecessarily
three times via the communication cord. Another train had five windows
broken, apparently due to rocks being hurled by City fans as it pulled out
of Norwich Thorpe station. Four people, including an elderly fan, were
hurt by flying glass.

Additionally, in Norwich city centre, supporters of both clubs ran
amok, smashing shop windows and damaging vehicles. More than twenty were arrested, mostly at the game itself. Police reported that some
Ipswich followers had daubed 'Clockwork Orange-style' make-up on
their faces. This sort of episode was a sad reflection of the times, as foot-

ball generally was suffering from hooliganism on a grand scale. The *Evening Star* commented the following day: 'It seems that success induces a kind of euphoria which leads directly to an orgy of destruction – and on the other hand defeat induces a kind of rage which leads to exactly the same urge to destroy.'

But the trouble could not overshadow the decent supporters' golden memories of what had been a truly a fascinating season for both Ipswich and Norwich. In addition to all their other achievements, the two rival clubs had met in major games on four different occasions, those games pulling in a remarkable total of 129,680 people. The East Anglian local derby proved in 1972-73 that it had become a fixture on the football calendar which demanded to be taken seriously.

# 8

# 'THE DERBY GAME WITH NO SOUL'

## (1973-77)

Ipswich and Norwich may have started 1973-74 on equal terms in English football's top tier, but within a few weeks all had changed. Town were very much on the up, back in European football for the first time in eleven years, and playing consistently well in the League. City, however, in their second season in the top flight, made a miserable start and never recovered. During a dreadful home defeat by Everton in the November, manager Ron Saunders angered fans by bringing on a defender for a forward, a mystifying move that led to cushions being hurled on the pitch. After the game Saunders indulged in a shouting match with chairman Arthur South and promptly quit the club. Life was good for the blue side of the East Anglian divide, but for Norwich this would be a long, hard winter.

The Canaries were managerless for two weeks, when the bright young boss of AFC Bournemouth, John Bond, breezed into Carrow Road in his sharp suit, promising to bring colour and light to a subdued and depressed football club. Being East Anglian (he hailed from Colchester), Bond had appreciated the importance of the local derby. City fans suddenly looked forward to the game with Ipswich on Boxing Day, particularly when Bond signed ace marksman Ted MacDougall from his former club. By this time, Ipswich had established themselves as a top-six side and their fans were also excited about Boxing Day. The importance of the derby can be gauged by it being a major talking point at a time when Town were occupied by glamorous European games against the likes of Real Madrid.

Starring in Ipswich's defence was young Kevin Beattie, who remembered the period well: 'Even when we were playing Barcelona, Feyenoord and Bruges in Europe, the local derby was still the biggest game of the season. The Europe games were almost one-offs, whereas the derby was our bread and butter. Under Bobby Robson we had a nice passing side – but all that went straight out the window when we played Norwich. Whatever the gaffer told you, you forgot as soon as you got on the pitch, because the game was so intense.' Beattie admitted that his main memories of games with Norwich were of battles with City skipper Duncan Forbes, who he reckons 'hated it' when Beattie went forward for set-pieces as he could leap so much higher than the big Scot.

The Boxing Day encounter lured a bumper crowd of 30,000 to Carrow Road. Home fans leapt with joy when MacDougall crashed home his first goal for the club midway through the first period, after collecting a rebound when teenage debutant Billy Steele hit the Town bar from long range. City went close to extending the lead, but Ipswich rode the storm and, despite having to reshuffle when full-back Geoff Hammond went off injured, came back with a vengeance. David Johnson slotted home a penalty, given after Forbes grappled with him at a corner, and then Mick Lambert netted a brave winner after a flick from Trevor Whymark. Despite signs that Bond was inspiring a Norwich revival of sorts, it was a crushing defeat for the Canaries and the result dropped them to bottom place again.

Bond scoured the transfer market in a bid to improve Norwich's fortunes. One of his early targets was Ipswich's industrious midfielder Peter Morris, whose goals destroyed Norwich in the Texaco Cup final. At the time of his initial enquiry, Morris was still a regular in Ipswich's first team, so there was little chance of a move, but Bond finally got his man at the end of 1973-74, by which time Robson was placing his faith in younger midfielders like Brian Talbot. The £65,000 fee looked a reasonable piece of business for Morris, who was by now past thirty.

By that time very few had played professionally for both Ipswich and Norwich, and only one had moved directly from one club to the other. Winger John Roy and centre-half Bobby Bell made limited appearances for both, having played for someone else in between, while inside-forward Allenby Driver had moved directly from Norwich to Ipswich in 1950. In 1974, Peter Morris, therefore, became the first man to switch directly from Ipswich to Norwich, and only the second (after Driver), to play in derby matches for both clubs. Morris hailed originally from Mansfield, but was aware that signing for Town's local rivals was an unusual and controversial development, and he would recall later:

'It was a very difficult decision. Leaving Ipswich was hard enough, but going to Norwich was obviously going to add some extra spice to the move. Bob [Robson] offered me a three-year extension to my contract but Norwich boss John Bond made it clear he wanted to sign me and came up with a good deal. I felt it was the right time for a change after six years at Portman Road. I lived in Capel St Mary and had to cross the border every day to get to Norwich, so in the end I had to move, but I had no real regrets over my decision to head to Carrow Road. Norwich had a good set-up and I had two nice years there. Ipswich had the edge at that time, although Norwich got to the League Cup final twice in three years. Looking back I enjoyed my time at both clubs. Ipswich is a great club to be involved with and you will almost certainly find you will get that verdict from anyone who has played for the club over the last forty years or so. In my time there, the Cobbolds created an environment that was a pleasure to be associated with.'

Meanwhile, the second of the 1973-74 derbies took place on a sunny afternoon in early March, with City still in desperate trouble at the bottom, but Ipswich flying high in fourth place and preparing for a UEFA Cup quarter-final tie with Lokomotiv Leipzig. Lifted by new signings, including Phil Boyer (£145,000 from Bournemouth), Norwich frustrated Town with a gritty display and held firm until the 49th minute, when Bryan Hamilton netted a firm drive from David Johnson's pass. City refused to bow to what seemed an inevitable defeat and got a lucky break when MacDougall took a quick throw that was claimed as Ipswich's. The ball was whipped into the box and Boyer tucked in his first Norwich goal to equalise. City were delighted with their point, but they couldn't avoid the drop that season and watched enviously as Ipswich finished an impressive fourth behind Leeds, Liverpool and Derby and qualified once again for the UEFA Cup.

This contrasting season ended for the East Anglian clubs when they met at Carrow Road in a testimonial for long-serving City keeper Kevin Keelan, the Norwich player with the most experience of local derbies up to that point. Agile Keelan had certainly made the odd blunder in these fixtures, but had also kept Norwich in contention in others – and he had his admirers in the Ipswich camp. He'd served Norwich for eleven years and, in the Boxing Day derby six months earlier, he'd broken the goal-keeping appearances record for Norwich, passing Ken Nethercott's tally of 416 League games. Keelan was pleased Ipswich were coming to town for his benefit game, saying: 'I am looking forward to it immensely, and the fans can be assured this will be a full-blooded encounter, after all it is a local derby.' Relegated City again played second fiddle with Norwich-born Woods bagging two goals and Roger Osborne one, as the visitors cruised to a 3-1 win. Norfolk-based referee Norman Burtenshaw took pity on Keelan, disallowing a Woods goal that was thumped in after Keelan brilliantly saved a Brian Talbot penalty.

Norwich's relegation did not separate the clubs for long, because the draw for the quarter-finals of the 1974-75 League Cup reacquainted them. This would be their second meeting in this competition, adding to the solitary FA Cup-tie in 1962. Shortly before the draw was made, Norwich signed Town's locally-born winger Johnny Miller for £45,000. His presence, along with ex-Ipswich favourite Morris, would ensure extra spice, if any was needed.

Carrow Road was a cauldron on a windy night in early December for a stirring cup-tie between two sides positioned in the top three of their respective divisions, and playing with confidence and purpose. Miller started a seventeenth-minute move which saw Phil Boyer set up Colin Suggett for the opening goal. Morris, captaining the Canaries against his former club, drove City forward and they went close to extending the lead. A goal made in Norfolk broke Norwich hearts just before the break. Local resident Woods sent over the cross and Burston-born Whymark was on hand to net, although City players claimed the effort never crossed the line. It ended 1-1, and whoever won the replay would fancy their chances of lifting the trophy, for the other three semi-finalists all came from outside the First Division.

Despite flying high in the First Division at the time, Bobby Robson and Ipswich were certainly not giving the League Cup a low priority. The manager said: 'The Football League Cup has grown in stature enormously in the past few years and when a quarter-final tie is also a battle royal between Ipswich and Norwich you have something extra special on the menu.' His opposite number Bond, outspoken as usual, said coming to Ipswich did not frighten him in the slightest, but he did confess to being envious of Robson having such a strong squad that he could afford to release two players of the quality of Morris and Miller to join Norwich. They both received the inevitable hostile welcome reserved for 'traitors' when they appeared in Norwich colours and – as so often happens in these circumstances – they played a key part in the proceedings.

Just under 30,000 crammed into Portman Road, the highest for any League Cup-tie to that point, and on a cold night witnessed another fully committed performance from both sides. Morris called on all his experience to provide a steadying influence on City, but Johnson opened the scoring, deceiving Keelan with a mis-hit shot from a Mills cross. Norwich hit back quickly and it was Miller, performing well in front of his Ipswich-based friends and relatives, who stabbed home a MacDougall pass to equalise. Two minutes after the restart home fans were stunned when Miller did it again, collecting a through pass and side-stepping goalkeeper Laurie Sivell to give City a shock lead. In a hectic final forty minutes City survived penalty appeals and heavy pressure to record a famous victory that maintained their giant-killing traditions.

How ironic that 24-year-old Miller should do the damage. He'd come back to haunt the very club that gave him his chance in football and had stuck with him during miserable days when his career seemed to be going down the drain. He'd made his debut in 1968 and was tipped for England Under-23 honours, but slowly the sparkle seemed to disappear and he failed to pin down a regular place in the side. His early fire and sharpness vanished and there were concerns about his weight and fitness levels. But, instead of releasing him, Ipswich ordered him on a specific conditioning programme while the rest of the squad had a mid-season break in Majorca. He didn't do enough to displace wingers Lambert and Woods in the Ipswich side, but John Bond recognised his talents and the £45,000 fee was repaid with those goals at Portman Road. Norwich went on to reach the League Cup final in 1974-75 for the second time in three years, but in a near-carbon copy of the 1973 version, they lost by a single goal in a disappointing game with Aston Villa.

Compensation for another Wembley flop came with an instant return to Division One, with City finishing third behind Villa and champions Manchester United. Ipswich continued to build on their recent success by ending up third in the top flight, just two points adrift of champions Derby. They also came within a whisker of a Wembley FA Cup final, a narrow and controversial semi-final replay defeat by West Ham leaving a bitter taste in Suffolk mouths.

The mid-1970s was proving to be a purple patch for East Anglian football and the excitement continued in 1975-76, another highlight-packed season for both Ipswich and Norwich. Both had hit their stride by the time of the derby at Portman Road in late September. City had scored nineteen goals in eight games thus far, while Ipswich could point to tremendous wins over Liverpool and then Feyenoord in the UEFA Cup. Town skipper Mills conceded that Norwich's start on their return to the First Division had surprised him:

'Norwich have made a good start this season – better, in fact, than I thought they were capable of. I consider them better equipped to survive than on the previous occasion they gained promotion, but I must admit some of their results have surprised me. Local derbies are very special affairs but I think the meeting of the two East Anglian sides must be almost unique. It cannot compare with those of Liverpool and Manchester, for example, where the supporters and even the players are mixing and talking about the match. Here we only get together on match day, although the rivalry is just as keen as elsewhere.'

Mills wasn't the only one looking forward to Norwich's visit, for a huge crowd of 35,077 turned out, at that point the second highest for any game at Portman Road. Thirty years later, in 2005, it remained third on the all-time list and the biggest for any derby game at Ipswich. Ted MacDougall already had fourteen goals under his belt at this early stage of the season, and Town knew they would have to keep a close eye on him. Big Allan Hunter took on the role of subduing the Scot and his close attentions led to a bruised MacDougall departing at half-time. Town were by now well on top and the breakthrough came just before the hour mark when City skipper Morris conceded a corner that was floated over for the leaping Beattie to head home. Ten minutes later the points were made safe when Bryan Hamilton headed a second. The 2-0 win represented Ipswich's first home League victory against the old enemy for ten years. Many a celebratory pint of Tolly ale was sunk in Suffolk pubs that night. The only sour note had been when someone in the crowd hurled a missile at Kevin Keelan shortly after kick-off, fortunately causing minimal damage. John Bond acknowledged afterwards that his side had been well beaten, but defiantly predicted the two sides would not finish the season very far apart in the League table.

By the time of the return match, on 31 March 1976, Town were on the fringes of the top six and desperate to pick up enough points to claim another season in Europe. They'd missed Colin Viljoen's skills in midfield, losing the South African for a lengthy period due to Achilles trouble. Norwich had consolidated by now and were reasonably happy to be in mid-table in their third season in the top flight. They were without the suspended Forbes but Bond was confident enough to plunge twenty-year-old debutant Neil Davids into the side in his place. The youngster did well against the normally lethal Johnson-Whymark partnership, and it was a mistake by Davids' opposite number, John Peddelty, deputising for the injured Beattie, which decided the outcome. With just a few minutes of the first half remaining on a fine afternoon, Peddelty failed to gather a throw-out by Town keeper Paul Cooper, apparently 'freezing' for a second or two, and former England man Martin Peters seized the ball from him and cracked a low drive past Cooper. Both sides went close after the break, but Norwich remained in front and Bond was delighted to take a measure of revenge for the earlier defeat that season. In bullish mood after the game, he even suggested City had been worth several goals more on the day.

It would be nearly a year before the rivals met again, for the 1976-77 fixture list scheduled both derby games well into the second half of the season. By the time they met at Portman Road in mid-February, Town were second in the table behind all-conquering Liverpool, and Robson's dream of building a side that could challenge consistently for honours was well and truly back on track. He had replaced popular David Johnson with a man who would become an even bigger Portman Road folk-hero in Paul Mariner, and his side had a settled and balanced look about it. Bond, meanwhile, was beset by incredible bad luck as regards injury and illness.

Such was the state of Norwich's casualty list that Bond even applied to the Football League to have the February game at Ipswich called off, as he barely had twelve men fit enough to play. His bid was unsuccessful and Norwich took the field with keeper Keelan unable to take goal-kicks due to a thigh strain, and striker Kevin Reeves playing despite learning of the death of his father just hours earlier.

Keith Skipper of the *Pink 'Un* reckoned Bond's application for a post-ponement was counter-productive: 'If the Canaries had any heart for their mission – and this was in doubt after Bond's abortive attempt to get it called off – the spirit was soon weakened along with the flesh,' he wrote. After conceding a disputed early penalty, City's resolve unsurpris-ingly crumbled and their team of walking wounded crumbled to a humil-iating 0-5 thrashing. One correspondent sympathetic to Norwich's plight labelled it 'the derby meeting without soul'. Bond had made his point before kick-off in amusing fashion by walking to the dug-outs at the head of a procession of his injured players. Instead of heading for the warmth of the stand, they hobbled along the touchline like a parade of wounded soldiers. Bond's point was made, although the watching Ipswich fans were, of course, not in the slightest bit sympathetic.

John Wark shot home the twelfth-minute penalty after Clive Woods was hauled down, City furiously insisting the offence had been outside the area. Even the normally cool Martin Peters was steamed up over Mr Capey's decision and was booked for dissent. Town went on to register the most one-sided derby win for two decades and efficiently demolished their downhearted rivals. Trevor Whymark collected a hat-trick and Mariner grabbed another, the 5-0 scoreline meaning Town took over from Bob Paisley's Liverpool at the top of the League that night.

Although Bond was furious the League hadn't agreed to his request for a postponement, he had no complaints about the result and was ful-some in his praise of Ipswich: 'I wouldn't pretend to know how to put a team like that together; we were comprehensively outgunned and out-played.'

Earlier he had issued an apology to the other teams challenging for the title as he felt Ipswich had an unfair advantage by playing such a weakened side. This apology actually came *before* the game, an action that the Norwich press dubbed 'fatalistic'. Keith Skipper wrote: 'One is bound to ask how Bond expected his patched-up troops to face Ipswich with a grain of confidence in the light of such an oblique acceptance that the Portman Road encounter was a foregone conclusion. Most pundits would have tipped Ipswich to win against a full-strength Norwich anyway, of course.' Bond insisted that the game as a whole, and the championship race in particular, had not benefited from the League's insistence that the game must go ahead. City skipper Forbes admitted Ipswich were much the better team and that Norwich's passing was poor, but bemoaned the 'terrible' early penalty decision.

As the 1970s unfolded, Ipswich slowly strengthened their grip on the unofficial title of 'kings of East Anglia', but one Norwich fan urged his fellow fans to be patient in this respect. G Watts wrote to the *Pink 'Un*: 'It is up to Norwich to be patient in the wake of our Suffolk rivals' march to the top. The important thing is that there is a secure platform for the future [at Norwich]. Bond is building a youth policy and no doubt he will be rewarded from this, just as Robson is now being rewarded for his long-term work. Local rivalry is good for the game but one must get this aspect into perspective.'

By the time of the 1976-77 return game in April, Norwich's injury list had shortened, but they found themselves perilously close to the relegation zone. Every point collected in the spring would prove precious. Ipswich travelled to Carrow Road to perform in front of a lockout crowd of 30,000-plus on a fine and dry afternoon, still topping the table and desperate to stay above Liverpool and Manchester City, who were snapping at their heels.

The display Ipswich produced to win the points was what their own fans might call 'thoroughly professional' but to Norwich eyes was 'dull and negative'. After Mariner left the field early with hamstring trouble, Town edged ahead when Whymark netted from a tight angle from Brian Talbot's free-kick. The remainder of the game was tight and tense and featured precious little good football. Time-wasting tactics angered the home fans and a disappointed Bond called the game 'a complete bore'. Robson defended his men, explaining that injury problems had prevented his side playing with their usual creativity and flair. Mick Dennis of the *Pink 'Un* called it one of the flattest derbies for many a day from the Norwich point of view. He said Ipswich had suffocated entertainment just as effectively as they suffocated a below-par Norwich team. Robson admitted that sometimes to win championships you had to 'snatch 1-0 wins and give a professional performance like Leeds used to do' – a view that Dennis called 'a depressing truth'.

What Robson couldn't have foreseen at that moment was that his title hopes would take a bizarre turn for the worse just 24 hours later. Star defender Beattie, now at the peak of his powers, was badly burned in an incident at his home and would miss the rest of the season. The details of this unfortunate episode would never properly emerge, but what was crystal clear was the fate of Town's title chances when they lost three games in a row without Beattie in the team. They finished third, five points behind champions Liverpool, while Norwich ended up sixteenth, missing relegation by just three points.

The only action Beattie saw in 1976-77 after his accident was the sixty minutes he played during Colin Viljoen's testimonial against Norwich at Portman Road in May. The League season was still not quite over at this point, but Town's title chances had by now gone and there was a feeling of anticlimax in the air. Injury-plagued Viljoen opened the scoring after just two minutes, his shot rocketing past City keeper Roger Hansbury. Brian Talbot notched a second but quicksilver Kevin Reeves pulled one back as Town held on for a 2-1 win.

# A LANKY LAD FROM LOWESTOFT

## (1977-79)

The distractions of a long and glorious run in the FA Cup, plus a glut of injuries to key men, meant Ipswich suffered their poorest season in Division One for many years in 1977-78. Norwich, however, spent the vast majority of the season in the top ten, only slipping to halfway after a weak finish. The good news as far as Canaries fans were concerned was finishing above Ipswich for the first time in twelve years.

League positions didn't count for much when the sides met at Carrow Road on Boxing Day 1977, however, Norwich going into the derby in a happier frame of mind having recently accounted for Liverpool during an impressive run. Town were still shell-shocked after going out of the UEFA Cup a fortnight earlier at Barcelona, having frittered away a first leg lead of 3-0. Key men like Wark and Beattie were already out injured and other casualties would soon follow.

Youngster Russell Osman deputised for Beattie. He was playing in his first derby and it was his handling of Jimmy Neighbour's cross that gave Norwich an early penalty. John Ryan, a former Luton full-back enjoying a new lease of life in City's midfield, saw his spot-kick parried by penalty specialist Paul Cooper, but tapped home the rebound. George Burley, returning after a two-month injury absence, should have equalised but ballooned a great chance over the bar. Late on, the ball struck Roger Gibbins' hand inside the Norwich box, but to Ipswich horror the referee was unsighted. Having lost striker Whymark, carried off with a knee injury, the Ipswich fans had to accept this was not to be their day. What was generally a rather dull affair, in local derby terms, ended with two points edging Norwich into the top six, comfortably ahead of the old enemy.

The injury to Whymark was yet another blow to Robson's men. The Norfolk-born striker had hit eighteen goals so far, including a foursome in the UEFA Cup against Landskrona Bois. Aged 27, Whymark was currently at his peak and his partnership with Mariner struck fear into the best of defences. His 32nd-minute injury at Norwich would hasten his decline, however, for he had sustained ligament damage to his right knee. It would keep him out for four months and lead to him missing the most glorious day in the club's history, more of which later. As a Norfolk lad himself, he enjoyed the local derbies more than most, having friends and relatives on both sides of the City-Town divide. Perhaps his finest hour had been hitting all four goals in a 4-0 demolition of Lazio several years earlier, an achievement that saw Lazio's great local rivals AC Roma present him with a special commemorative plaque. It made a nice addition to the Whymark mantelpiece, but caused terrific ill feeling within the Lazio ranks.

Trevor Whymark hailed from Burston, a village close to the Norfolk-Suffolk border housing a healthy mix of both Norwich and Ipswich supporters. Close to the town of Diss, somewhere halfway between Ipswich and Norwich, the village had become famous not only for producing Whymark, but earlier for having staged the world's longest recorded strike. Pupils from the village primary school walked out in protest over the dismissal of two teachers and set up their own school nearby – their 'strike school' operating for 25 years. Whymark recalled his connections with Norwich:

'Like all the kids in the village of Burston I was keen on football but to be honest I preferred to play rather than watch. This meant I only attended midweek matches at Norwich. I must admit I wasn't a great Norwich fan although they were my nearest team. I suppose I've got a good scoring record against Norwich, but it's just coincidence and not because I've tried any harder than normal.'

As a promising fifteen-year-old playing for Diss Town, Whymark had once been invited for trials at Norwich, but the sessions came to nothing and he left school to work for a builders merchants, studying part-time at King's Lynn Technical College. More goals for Diss Town in the Anglian Combination followed and Ipswich swooped to secure his services. He signed for Town on the same day as Clive Woods, another Norfolk lad the Canaries overlooked and who came back to haunt them.

By the time of 1977-78's second derby, on Easter Monday, injury-plagued Ipswich had progressed to the semi-finals of the FA Cup while playing second fiddle to Norwich in terms of League standings. This would be Town's fifth match in a hectic nine-day spell. On a clear and bright afternoon, 29,989 assembled at Portman Road, one of the few occasions to date where the crowd at Ipswich exceeded that at Norwich for the visit of the other. Before kick-off Bobby Robson tried to defuse a little of the usual tension by calling for it to be played in a sporting manner: 'After all, the game is still just a sport, although somewhere along the line over the last few years it seems the sporting side has been slowly disappearing,' he reflected.

Town's defensive strongmen Hunter and Beattie warmed up for the big game by appearing at a function at Brantham Village Hall, where they apparently took to the stage and performed a duet of *You'll Never Walk Alone*.

With City's long-serving keeper Keelan having broken a bone in his hand in February, his long run of appearances in the East Anglian derby was ended. Roger Hansbury took over the No 1 shirt. Keelan's first derby had been in early 1965 when his 'slippery' display led to the goalmouth sanding controversy – and he'd appeared in every one of the 25 local clashes since. Hansbury was experiencing his first serious derby action, as was Greg Downs, making his League debut in an attacking role, although he would later become a favourite at full-back.

With Martin Peters missing, Bond's new formation was not a great success and Ipswich surged into a two-goal lead by half-time, both goals powered in by industrious locally-born midfielder Brian Talbot. Cracking goals after the interval by David Geddis and Mick Mills completed the rout, with City's best effort being a John Ryan long-range effort that hit the bar. It was a miserable afternoon for Norwich, particularly as this latest pounding came just a year after their 0-5 drubbing at the same ground. Bond knew the result probably spelt the end of his team's chances of a top-six finish and he was furious. Bond was never one to hide his feelings, but this time he really let rip.

The following day Bond read the riot act to his players. Mick Dennis of the *Pink 'Un* observed that this must have been one of those occasions when Norwich's reserves were glad not to be in the first team. The senior players had been subjected to one of Bond's 'special team meetings' at the Trowse training ground. He was in a black mood and when the long meeting finally broke up his anger was only partially abated and he admitted to reporter Dennis he wasn't even sure his harsh words had done any good.

Some observers reckoned Bond's outbursts were not always helpful to the cause, but there did seem to be a positive effect 48 hours after the Ipswich debacle, for City earned an impressive point against Derby. Bond explained: 'The players allowed themselves to be humiliated at Ipswich and I must do something about it. If I have to drop players then I will do it. If I have to sell players in the summer I will do it. We have nothing to lose now and I will not let certain players wreck this club.' He kept his word by introducing eighteen-year-old Phil Lythgoe and his son Kevin for the County game, dropping Mick McGuire and Keith Robson.

Successive hammerings by Ipswich at Portman Road was a bitter pill for Canaries fans to swallow. One of them, B Clements of Reydon, wrote to the local press to say in fifty years of supporting Norwich he'd seldom felt so ashamed. He said midfielders McGuire and Paddon looked woefully short of pace and were often brushed aside by their opposite numbers. J Woodcock of Yarmouth said he always saw Norwich versus Ipswich as 'brains against brawn' and that even in defeat he found Norwich the more entertaining footballing side. He went on to condemn John Bond for blasting his players in public and said the manager ought to take a leaf out of Bobby Robson's book by restoring their self-belief, not castigating them.

In terms of the two clubs' League programmes, the 1977-78 campaign ended on a whimper. Ipswich's attention was focused on the FA Cup, where a 3-1 semi-final victory over West Brom set up a historic day at Wembley. Their opponents would be Terry Neill's Arsenal. The 4-0 hammering of Norwich would be one of only two League wins in their final fourteen League games and they finished just three points clear of relegation.

This slump was, of course, offset by events beneath the famous twin towers on the muggy afternoon when Roger Osborne, the quiet man from rural Suffolk, scored the goal that brought the FA Cup to East Anglia. Most people's man-of-the-match at Wembley was Clive Woods, whose recent form had caught the eye of England boss Ron Greenwood. Woods was called up for the national squad for a World Cup qualifier against Luxembourg, but never made the team. The FA Cup win crowned Woods' career and convinced him he'd made the right decision when joining Ipswich instead of his home-town club, Norwich. In early 1978 John Bond had reportedly bid £80,000 to take him to Carrow Road, but Ipswich turned it down. Woods said: 'I don't know whether or not I would have moved [at that time] had I been given the chance, because I was enjoying my football at Ipswich.'

During the build-up to the Cup final, Town's injury problems allowed a nineteen-year-old defender from Lowestoft his first-team debut. Terry Butcher, who would feature prominently in many a local derby in later years, would go on to enjoy a celebrated and multi-faceted career in the game, culminating in captaincy of the national side. Butcher was born in Singapore where his father was stationed with the Royal Navy, but the family soon headed for the Suffolk coastal town of Lowestoft, from where his parents hailed. Growing up with both Norwich and Ipswich-supporting pals, Terry learned his football in Fen Park in the classic 'jumpers for goalposts' manner. He also played for hours on the excellent beaches nearby, in the evenings using the pier lights as floodlights. When he was nine, Butcher's Ipswich-supporting father took him to see Town beat Aston Villa on the club's way to promotion to Division One in 1968, and Terry became hooked to the Ipswich cause for life. Even in 2005, after twenty-odd years of high achievement since leaving Portman Road, Butcher still proclaims his undying love of Ipswich and his inborn dislike of Norwich.

By the age of fifteen the lanky Butcher had been playing in local men's league football, sometimes clocking up four games per weekend: 'I remember playing in some weird and wonderful places in those days and travelled all over Norfolk and Suffolk for away games. I remember playing at places like Southrepps and Wells in north Norfolk. Facilities were basic and we would often have to change in a draughty barn or even in the car.' He was selected for Suffolk schools and for a trial with England Schoolboys and even had the odd game for the Blundeston Prison Officers team, where his father worked. One Prison game at Lothingland Psychiatric Hospital was interrupted when bewildered patients wandered across the pitch. Thanks to the persistence of Mike Regis, the secretary of the Lowestoft branch of the Ipswich Town Supporters Club, Terry was eventually offered a trial at Portman Road. Butcher recalled:

'In the meantime I received an unexpected offer of a trial at Norwich, having been recommended by the manager of a local Sunday side. But I had mixed feelings. I was an Ipswich fan through and through and however much the idea of being a footballer appealed to me, the thought of playing for our closest rivals filled me with horror. People talk about the rivalry between Liverpool and Everton on Merseyside, and Celtic and Rangers in Glasgow, but in East Anglia feelings run just as high between the Norwich and Ipswich fans.'

Whether his antipathy towards Norwich played a part or not is open to question, but Butcher admits his trial at Carrow Road was a disaster: 'I didn't know where to play, who to pass to and couldn't wait to get away. It was a different story at Ipswich. The lads who were on trial spent up to a month at the club so the coaching staff got to know us.' In later years Norwich officials must have been kicking themselves for missing out in this way on the talents of Woods, Whymark and Butcher, England squad members all.

Despite his immense size and strength, Butcher admitted to being a shy and nervous youngster and was shocked when Bobby Robson offered him a one-year professional contract, by-passing the usual apprenticeship. Plunged straight into the youth team in 1976 he quickly reached the fringe of the first team, alongside the likes of Russell Osman and Alan Brazil. He developed into the fully committed type of player who readily identifies with the fans and loved nothing more than putting one over the local rivals: 'Victory over Norwich has always been sweet for me. As a local lad I know how important the result is to the fans. They made it clear they could forgive us for losing to anybody else, but the one team we had to beat was Norwich. The [East Anglian] rivalry soon rubbed off on players who moved to the area, and lads like George Burley and Mick Mills became as keyed up for the derby games as I was. The only player who had any problem was Clive Woods, who played nearly 300 games for us but was born in Norwich, supported Norwich and went on to play for Norwich.'

Terry Butcher epitomised the 'local boy made good' figure who enjoys a rapport with the fans due to the simple fact that he is basically just one of them, albeit lucky and gifted enough to actually get out on the field and perform. Add to this a never-say-die attitude and you have the classic ingredients for a local legend. East Anglia has never been a hotbed in terms of producing football talent, for most of the Ipswich and Norwich heroes down the years have been 'outsiders' from other regions or nations. At Ipswich, Butcher was a notable exception, heading a list that also includes Ted Phillips, Brian Talbot and Jason Dozzell. Although born in Cambridgeshire, Norwich fans always treated Ron Ashman as a local legend, and also reserved special affections for the likes of Dave Stringer and Peter Mendham, Norfolk boys through and through.

The summer of 1978 saw the introduction of the first cup competition specifically for the senior football clubs of East Anglia, sponsored by Willhire. Cambridge United, Colchester, Ipswich and Norwich were pitted against each other, the latter two progressing to the 'deciding game' at Portman Road in early August. Future Norwich boss Mike Walker had a superb game to keep Ipswich at bay when Colchester held Town 0-0 in the opening game. The 'final' with Norwich once again saw Ipswich missing several regulars through injury, with Terry Butcher among the walking wounded and disappointed not to be playing in his first derby game. In front of 7,235, Ipswich surged ahead with goals from Mariner and Whymark, but were pegged back after the break by Kevin Reeves. City failed to grab an equaliser despite piling on the pressure and had Kevin Bond booked, thus proving this was no tame pre-season affair.

City fans watched with mixed feelings, wondering if 33-year-old signing Martin Chivers, formerly of Tottenham and England, was really what they needed. John Bond had warned: 'Don't expect Chivers to run around like an eighteen-year-old,' and the big man certainly didn't disappoint in that respect. Stand-in Town skipper Brian Talbot was presented with the first Willhire Trophy, to be placed alongside the FA Cup in the Portman Road cabinet.

Once again in 1978-79 Ipswich and Norwich had a date on Boxing Day. Both teams were having sticky patches in the League although Town had the excuse of a run to the quarter-finals of the European Cup-Winners' Cup, which presented a major distraction from normal duties. Kevin Keelan, by now nearly 38 and still defying his years, had a fine game against Ipswich and even played a role in the opening goal, his long ball falling for Ian Davies who steered it past a stranded Paul Cooper. The lead was wiped out a minute after half-time when Mills headed home a corner by Woods. Butcher, and Town's new signing from Holland, Arnold Muhren, enjoyed their first taste of derby action and were relieved to see teammate Cooper make a fine save in the dying seconds from Reeves to prevent a Canaries win. The draw left the sides locked together in mid-table and the 26,336 crowd went home for their left-over turkey happy to have witnessed an engrossing contest on this overcast afternoon.

Storm clouds were on the horizon for City, though, for just a few days later they were ousted from the FA Cup by Second Division Leicester thanks to a horrendous performance at Filbert Street. It provoked another outburst from the under-fire John Bond and ultimately one of the casualties was Chivers, who – to put it politely – didn't seem to be putting his heart and soul into the Norwich cause.

The third of four derby clashes in 1978-79 followed in February when Ipswich granted Trevor Whymark a testimonial in recognition of his long service. The player, mindful of the need to drum up a reasonable attendance, wisely chose Norwich as the opposition. The game was staged two days after his farewell competitive appearance at Bristol City and preceded a move to Vancouver. Nearly 7,000 turned out to pay tribute, despite some bitter weather. Town won 2-1 with a tap-in goal by Whymark and a 35-yard screamer from Clive Woods, Keith Robson having opened the scoring for City. Whymark waved goodbye as a player, but years later would join the list of men to have served both East Anglian clubs by coaching Norwich's Under-13s in the 1999-2000 season and later performing a similar role with Ipswich's Under-12s.

In the League, Norwich's sticky patch continued into 1979 and even the team's midfield maestro, the laconic Martin Peters, pleaded for the fans to stop their barracking as it was harming morale. City had won just once in sixteen games, but with a high tally of draws had managed to cling on to a mid-table position for most of the season. For their part, Ipswich seemed to be recovering from their FA Cup hangover, for they had risen from a low of eighteenth and by the end had squeezed into the top six.

The League clash with Norwich at Carrow Road in April 1979 was notable for a brilliant display by diminutive Ipswich keeper Laurie Sivell, another who hailed from Lowestoft, and a winning goal by the skilful Dutchman Frans Thijssen, his first goal in English football. The shirt-sleeved Norwich fans on this sunny afternoon boiled with rage at the only goal, for David Geddis, apparently crouching to tie his bootlaces, was offside when Thijssen netted.

The hot weather had the usual side-effects on such a day, and there was a series of niggly fouls, erupting into an unseemly brawl in the cen-tre-circle at one point. Injured Norwich defender David Jones voiced his disapproval of the referee from the sidelines and was promptly booked by Mr Sinclair – an unusual achievement for a player who hadn't actually kicked a ball for eight months! Another flashpoint came when Kevin Beattie collapsed with his recurring knee problems. When coming on the pitch to inspect the player, Town manager Robson was hit by a missile thrown from the Barclay End. Clearly upset, his opposite number Bond went over to check Robson was not hurt. The tetchiness and disruption evident at this game seemed to sum up Norwich's season.

# ARISE THE IPSWICH 'ZOMBIES'

## (1979-81)

For both Ipswich Town and Norwich City, the end of the 1970s marked a new high point in their standing in the football world. Since the Second World War, both had steadily clawed their way up the ladder, reaching a point where they could shrug off the tag of coming from a footballing backwater. Ipswich had been proud members of the First Division throughout the decade, getting stronger year on year, and it was clear Bobby Robson had taken the club to a new level during his eleven years in charge. Norwich had reached the top flight for the first time and, apart from a single season back in the second tier, they too had consolidated in Division One by the end of decade. As 1980 loomed, John Bond was in charge of arguably the most talented squad of players Norwich had ever assembled.

Those austere post-War years when the two rivals slogged it out in Division Three (South) were by now a distant memory. The brave new world was encapsulated perfectly by a classic of a derby which took place at Carrow Road in the final week of 1979. It was six-goal thriller that simply took the fans' breath away.

Ironically, given the spectacle that was about to take place, John Bond grumpily dismissed all the usual pre-match fuss that surrounded this fixture. Reporters beavering out a new angle on a derby that had by now become a regular fixture on the football calendar got the sound-bites they wanted when Bond moaned: 'Local derbies with Ipswich are tremendous for the fans and, of course, we welcome the large crowd, but quite frankly I wish [this one] was all over. Far too much importance is attached to a single game and a single result when – at the end of the day – it will be no more important than any other First Division match we will play in a season.'

Wish it was all over? Norwich fans could hardly believe their ears. For them this was the big one, an end-of-year climax following a great start to the 1979-80 season by the Canaries, who'd perched proudly at the top of the League for the first time ever – albeit only briefly early in the campaign. Norwich had fluctuated between first and eighth between August and December, considerably higher than Ipswich, who were again struggling for pre-Christmas consistency while occupied by UEFA Cup action. Bond had won the manager of the month award, goal-poacher Kevin

Reeves won his first England cap, goalkeeper Kevin Keelan broke the club appearances record, and Justin Fashanu emerged as a major talent in attack. It all pointed to a great opportunity for City to put one over their old rivals, and City fans found it hard to understand why Bond wasn't excited at the prospect.

Amid a noisy atmosphere on a mild Boxing Day afternoon, Norwich unveiled their new £1.4 million River End stand, complete with hospitality boxes, which gave the ground a more modern and sophisticated look. Some fans wondered if the cost of the development might mean the club would have to bow to pressure to sell £1 million-rated Kevin Reeves – but that was a problem for later: today was all about beating Ipswich for the first time in seven meetings.

The game exploded into life when Ipswich, attacking the new-look River End, took the lead after veteran Keelan fumbled a Mick Mills cross and Eric Gates crashed the ball home. Eight minutes later City were level, Greg Downs' cross being flicked on by Martin Peters for nineteen-year-old Peter Mendham to head in. The roar nearly lifted the roof off the Barclay Stand as the fans heralded Mendham, an inexperienced Norfolk lad scoring his first ever senior goal. The red-haired midfielder hailed from King's Lynn and his all-action displays – he was a former county-standard cross-country runner – had won him many admirers lately. The goal cemented his growing popularity.

Ipswich hit back with a sustained burst of pressure, but derby goals often seem to occur against the run of play and so it proved for Norwich just before half-time. Skilful Dutchman Arnold Muhren, perhaps bewildered by the hectic nature of a British local derby, was flustered into making a weak back-pass. Former West Ham Cup final hero Alan Taylor was able to nip in and stab City 2-1 ahead. It was a real see-saw thriller and soon after the interval Muhren made up for his slip, scoring at the second attempt after Peters knocked his first effort off the goal-line. The game had developed into a marvellous spectacle, as good as any East Anglian derby in the past. The thrills included a superb save by Keelan from John Wark, Peters clearing desperately off the Norwich line, and John Ryan and Keith Robson both hitting the woodwork at the other end.

With under twenty minutes left, Wark looked to have grabbed the winner when he put Ipswich 3-2 up, heading home a fine Muhren cross from the left. But still the fun wasn't over, and after Bond threw on sub Justin Fashanu in place of defender Roger Brown, City made it 3-3 in a frantic finale. There were only seconds remaining when David Jones hit a fierce shot goalwards and keeper Paul Cooper watched in horror as the ball was deflected away from him by Keith Robson. Mr Taylor's final whistle brought to a breathless end probably the finest derby of them all.

The saga of missed opportunities and defensive howlers meant that it had been torture for the managers and coaches, and Bobby Robson was furious his side hadn't closed the game down after going 3-2 ahead. But from the terraces it had been exhilarating and the last-gasp equaliser sparked jubilation and was probably no more than Norwich deserved. The fans couldn't wait for the Easter return at Portman Road, although it was clear that future derbies would be hard pushed to live up to this level of excitement.

The return would, in fact, be the third meeting of the clubs in 1979-80, for earlier they'd clashed in the second staging of the Willhire Cup competition at Carrow Road. Compared to the Boxing Day thriller it had been a non-event, for even though City won 2-0 with goals from Martin Peters and Graham Paddon, Ipswich still lifted the cup, having done enough earlier to finish top of the four-team round robin. Only 3,737 turned out, reflecting the drop in attendances being suffered in all competitions by Norwich during this period.

By the time the teams took the field at Ipswich in April 1980, Town had surged past City in the League, finding their form with an impressive post-Christmas undefeated run. As anticipated, City had been forced to balance the books by selling Reeves for £1 million and had slipped down to below halfway on the back of a run of just one win in fifteen games. The form-book suggested a home banker, but for one Norwich player, at least, it was an occasion to be anticipated with relish. Winger Clive Woods, now 32, had by now switched allegiance, moving from Portman Road to Carrow Road during March in exchange for a mere fraction of the cash Norwich received for Reeves. The £120,000 fee looked like good business from Ipswich's point of view, given the player's age, but many Town fans wondered if their former wing wizard would come back and haunt them now that he was wearing yellow and green. Transferred players have a habit of scoring and playing well against their former colleagues and Woods only had to wait four weeks after arriving at Carrow Road before his first trip back to Ipswich.

Many players will express delight at the prospect of kicking lumps out of a former colleague, but Town skipper Mick Mills was honest enough to admit that he would find it difficult to give full physical commitment to the job of marking his great friend and former colleague: 'Clive and I were good friends as well as teammates during his eleven years at Ipswich and I never find it easy to be as competitive as I probably should in these circumstances. It's been the same with my other friends like David

Johnson, Brian Talbot and Bryan Hamilton, and I know they have felt just the same when we've come up against each other. Maybe it's just as well we don't have a big turnover in staff at this club, although, if we did, I don't suppose the players would become so friendly.'

Naturally Woods received catcalls as he took the field in the colours of Town's old enemy, but the hostility was nowhere near as intense as it can be on these occasions. Most fans preferred to applaud the player in recognition of his superb service since 1969 and, judging by Mills' remarks, the Ipswich players didn't give him a rough ride, either. In his time at Ipswich Woods played in no fewer than thirteen League and cup games against Norwich, only being on the losing side three times. He was a real thorn in the Canaries' flank during that time, a strange state of affairs considering he'd been a devoted fan as a boy. The opportunity to join City as an amateur had presented itself in 1965 but Woods wanted to be a pro like elder brother Dennis and turned the club down. His patience paid off when Ipswich came along a year or two later with a better offer. Throughout his years at Portman Road Woods continued to live in the Norwich area and the move to Carrow Road suited him well:

'I enjoyed my time at Ipswich but the challenge of moving on appealed to me. Norwich are ideal because I don't have to uproot my family and I'm looking forward to another couple of years in the First Division. There was no pressure on me to move from Portman Road and I might even have won back my place. But at the same time there might have been no second chance had I said no to Norwich this time.'

On a gloriously sunny day the game provided a dramatic late finish, with five goals in a hectic twenty minutes. Prior to this, the only incident of note was Wark opening the scoring from a Muhren cross in the first half. The game only sprang into life on seventy minutes when Graham Paddon and Frans Thijssen tangled and City were horrified to see the linesman indicate a penalty. Instead of delight, this was greeted with trepidation by Ipswich's players and fans – for in the previous three games at the ground there had been seven penalties and all had been missed, which must be some sort of record. However, this time Wark tucked the kick home comfortably and the sequence was broken. Town visibly relaxed and Kevin Bond took advantage, putting the Canaries back into the game at 2-1 by converting Keith Robson's low cross. Moments later Paul Mariner put Town 3-1 up from Alan Brazil's pass, and then, a minute from time, yet another debatable penalty was awarded, this time for a challenge on little Eric Gates. Wark strode up to complete his hat-trick, but still the scoring wasn't over, for Robson then headed home Bond's chip to give a final score of 4-2.

Affable Scotsman Wark would go on to score many goals from mid-field for Ipswich but this was his first hat-trick, and he was honest enough to admit that both penalties had been fortunate: 'They didn't warrant a penalty even if you added them both together,' he joked. John Bond's verdict was less light-hearted. Wark clearly recalled that day years later: 'I was treated like a king afterwards, fans wanting to buy me drinks and everything. I'd lived in Ipswich since I was fifteen so I knew how much it meant to the fans. We always did well against Norwich. We had a nice team but we also had players who could look after themselves. Our derby games were just as full-on as the Liverpool derbies I played in, as intense as any other derby, I'd say – apart from Rangers-Celtic, which is on a different level to anything else.'

The win kept alive Ipswich's faint championship hopes, although they would ultimately have to be settle for third place behind Liverpool and Manchester United, while City again earned enough points for a comfortable mid-table finish. During the subsequent summer months, Bond lost the services of Martin Peters, who had a brief and unsuccessful try at management with Sheffield United, and injury victim David Jones. As was often the case, Bond's foray into the market for replacements saw some interesting developments. His capture of former Everton and England centre-forward Joe Royle created a stir, and he followed this by spending a club record £300,000 on Yugoslav international Drazen Muzinic.

Royle was in the City side at Portman Road in August 1980 as part of the third and final staging of the pre-season Willhire Cup, in which the Canaries only had to avoid defeat to Ipswich to lift the trophy. In front of a subdued 6,000 crowd, Town surged ahead through Mariner and Kevin O'Callaghan but, inspired by Woods, City hit back late with replies from John McDowell and sub Steve Goble to ensured some silverware was on its way to Carrow Road.

1980-81 would prove to be a season of five derbies, the Willhire Cup and two League meetings supplemented by a clash in the third round of the League Cup that would require a replay. City fans paid £2.75 for their return tickets on the 'football special' train to Ipswich in September 1980, anxious for their boys to maintain an unbeaten League Cup record at Portman Road. It was a tall order, for Town were in red-hot form, topping the table and eighteen places above City. However, all was not well at Ipswich, for Bobby Robson had become frustrated by the lack of vocal backing his talented outfit enjoyed from the terraces, and in the build-up to the Norwich game he launched an attack in the press, calling the fans 'zombies'.

He explained years later that this extraordinary comment had not been an impulsive remark arising out of anger, but something he'd been thinking about for some time: 'We weren't going to win the title with our team off the field dozing away and offering little encouragement. I had to stir them up and this was my way of doing it. [Director] John Cobbold thought the comments were inappropriate and the local press went to town on it, with angry letters from fans pouring in. For the Norwich game some fans arrived wearing badges 'I'm a Robson Zombie' and chanting zombie slogans. It all helped stir up a superb atmosphere.'

What had seemed at the time to be a 'PR blunder' had quickly turned to Robson's advantage, for the home crowd did indeed seem a lot noisier than usual against Norwich – even allowing that this was a local derby. Randall Bevan, director of recreation at Ipswich Borough Council, and a man adept at attracting publicity when he needed it, was impressed by Robson's canny move, and told him: 'You were spot on. You've got what you wanted. It was great bit of PR. Next time I want to get something across to the public, I'm coming to you for advice.'

Robson got the atmosphere he wanted, but not the result. Thanks to a brave late rally Norwich pulled off a heroic draw and celebrated as if they'd won the cup itself. Robson said the result was a tribute to John Bond and the good work he'd put in on limited resources in building a club worthy of competing with the best in the country. City keeper Roger Hansbury had kept Ipswich at bay almost single-handedly at times but could do nothing about Russell Osman's powerful header from a Mick Mills corner. With new signing from Everton, Ross Jack, enjoying an impressive debut in City's midfield, the visitors clawed their way back into contention and there were scenes of delight when Justin Fashanu headed them level six minutes from time. Malcolm Robertson of the *Pink 'Un* called it one of the great local derbies of recent years.

Ipswich fans who travelled to Carrow Road for the replay a fortnight later were greeted by the unexpected sight of old-time Norwich mascots 'Canary and Dumpling', a bizarre couple in fancy dress, who had been dusted off and brought back after a 21-year absence. There was no shortage of noise from the Ipswich 'zombies' on a perfect dry and fine night for football. Ipswich shone under the Carrow Road floodlights, showing exactly why they were currently top of the League.

Robson remembered the display some time later: 'This one was on TV and we showed the country what we could do. Muhren and Thijssen were brilliant. I was beginning to worry however, as I could see a fixture pile-up looming. Some clubs, like Leeds, have been accused of taking a dive in the League Cup so as not to overload their fixture list, and although I could never do that, I must say I wouldn't have been too unhappy at being knocked out.'

Town surged to a 3-1 victory, Paul Mariner's volley fizzing into the Norwich net in front of a snarling Barclay End. Tony Powell equalised just after the interval, but the game's turning point came on 76 minutes when the 24,523 crowd witnessed arguably the best goal ever seen in an East Anglian derby. Frans Thijssen weaved past several defenders before rolling a perfect pass to fellow Dutchman Muhren, who waited for the right moment before curling an inch-perfect shot into the net. Three minutes later Mariner added a second to make it 3-1 and the game was over. While Robson purred about his marvellous Dutchmen, Bond saw things a little differently and questioned why his team had wilted after fighting back so well after Mariner's opener.

He may have felt down at the end, but Bond's attacking outlook won him praise from both Robson and the England boss Ron Greenwood, who said Bond's tactics, often involving a formation of just three defenders, was courageous and good for the game in England. Bond modestly responded: 'I don't think it's courageous at all, for I firmly believe that's how the game should be played. We are in this business to entertain crowds and you don't do that with blanket defences.'

Bond's work was being admired by Manchester City, who were seeking a replacement for Malcolm Allison and, after the televised Ipswich game, they applied to Norwich for permission to approach Bond. Within a few days he was heading for Maine Road, his exit from Norwich at first seeming quite amicable, but quickly degenerating into a row over the backroom staff he wanted to take with him. Bond's stay at Carrow Road had been filled with incident and controversy, so it was probably a fitting end to an exciting and fascinating era in Norwich's history.

Ipswich and Norwich met again at Portman Road again on Boxing Day in the League, by which time coach Ken Brown had been promoted to fill Bond's seat. Genial Brown had the tough task of getting Norwich out of the bottom three. Some Norwich fans had hoped for a bigger name, but most had confidence in the new man. He'd helped inspire five victories between mid-October and Christmas but City remained in the relegation zone and their task to defy an Ipswich side at the peak of its powers on Boxing Day 1980 was stiff. City had ex-Liverpool centre-back Dave Watson making his debut, but their new-look defence succumbed to well-taken goals either side of the break from Alan Brazil and Wark. City fought hard in an entertaining game but were always second best. Clive Woods appeared as a Norwich sub near the end for what would be his seventeenth and final competitive local derby appearance.

Bobby Robson gave his verdict: 'Ken Brown made Norwich fight hard and it was a tight game. Ken is a nice man, down to earth and very sensible. He was clearly still feeling his way as boss, but I thought he would make the grade.' Brown was certainly the sort of character not to get involved in slanging matches or controversy, but the pressure of getting out of relegation trouble seemed to have an effect even on him. Invited to appear as a guest at a meeting of the Capital Canaries fan club in London, Brown originally accepted but then stayed away in protest at what he called 'persistent and unconstructive' criticism of the club in the Capital Canaries' newsletter. The snub was out of character and stirred up a lively controversy for the local press.

Easter 1981 arrived with very different priorities occupying minds at Ipswich and Norwich. A recent FA Cup semi-final defeat by Manchester City meant Town's ambitious bid for a 'treble' was now gone, but they were still chasing a League and UEFA Cup double. Norwich, meanwhile, needed every point they could get to avoid dropping out of Division One. Town's talented squad was showing signs of wear and tear after a gruelling season and the Easter derby at Carrow Road was just 48 hours before the second leg of the UEFA Cup semi-final in Cologne.

This fixture congestion would gain no sympathy from Norwich, of course, and one young man desperate to sabotage Town's glory mission was eighteen-year-old pint-sized winger Mark Barham, playing in his first local derby. Years later he would recall: 'For us the two games against Ipswich were the be-all and end-all of the season. It was all 'beat Ipswich, beat Ipswich'. You knew the game meant more to the fans than any other. And especially if Ipswich were doing well, you'd always treat it like a cup final. If we lost to them we were just distraught. You didn't want to speak to anyone for days; you knew the fans would be going on about it for the next six weeks.'

Town tackled a fired-up City without the injured Burley, Beattie, Mariner, Gates and Thijssen, knowing that defeat would probably hand the title to Aston Villa. Kevin Steggles, Tommy Parkin, Robin Turner and Mich D'Avray were among the stand-ins bravely attempting to fill the breach, but it was a tall order. Norwich went into the crunch game on the back of three successive wins, inspired by Brown's new signings – Martin O'Neill from Nottingham Forest, Steve Walford from Arsenal and goalkeeper Chris Woods from QPR. Not surprisingly the derby would prove as tight and tense as any of the previous eighty. Veteran Joe Royle was prominent in the early stages, testing Paul Cooper with a stinging drive and then clearing a Terry Butcher effort off the Norwich goal-line. Both sides went close before Justin Fashanu made the all-important breakthrough on 62 minutes, cracking home from a tight angle after a long ball from Greg Downs, when the defence appeared to be expecting a cross. It proved to be the winner.

Any defeat by Norwich hits Ipswich hard, but this one felt like a catastrophe to Town's management, players and fans, because it almost certainly killed the title chase. Bobby Robson had been desperate to win the League with Ipswich and must have felt this was his final chance disappearing before his eyes. He called the final whistle 'the lowest hour of my managerial career', adding mournfully 'we lost the title today', which was a rather surprising admission, given that it was still mathematically possible for Town to finish top. Visibly upset, he said the goal had been an unnecessary gift, and explained: 'This infuriated me because of the unprofessional attitude of our defence at the end of a season when they had played so brilliantly.'

In spite of his distress, Robson did add: 'If anyone had to beat us, I am glad it was Norwich, for I hope they stay up, as it would be good for East Anglian football.' Always a man to wear his heart on his sleeve, Robson even talked about leaving the club and starting again elsewhere, but qualified this by adding that if they won the UEFA Cup he might feel differently. His sentiments shocked many and skipper Mick Mills was moved to react publicly, saying that Robson had put unfair pressure on the players with such talk. Robson would hit back later: 'Too right I did! I did that calculatingly because I wanted them to feel pressure. I wanted them to feel they had to win the UEFA Cup. But whether I remained or went had nothing to do with [Mills]. Players think they are under pressure but they aren't – it is managers who are under the real pressure.'

Perhaps inevitably, this highly charged match had involved trouble on the terraces. A group of Ipswich fans somehow obtained tickets for the River End and made their presence felt to the discomfort of home supporters around them. Glenn McColl of Norwich wrote to the *Pink 'Un* to ask why the police couldn't have transferred them to the away enclosure at the Barclay End. He also complained about some Ipswich fans being moved from the police room right through the Norwich crowd and into the away enclosure, and nearly causing a riot in the process. The police clearly had their work cut out on occasions such as this, but the Carrow Road segregation policy was hardly a model of effectiveness.

Robson's fears were confirmed over the next couple of weeks as the title slipped away, compensation coming in the shape of UEFA Cup victory, a 5-4 aggregate triumph over AZ Alkmaar in the two-legged final. Although the win over Ipswich left City fans convinced relegation would be avoided, a disastrous and unexpected last-day home loss to already-doomed Leicester proved Norwich's undoing and they dropped down after six years in the top flight.

A fascinating season of ups and downs ended in East Anglia with wild celebrations in Ipswich town centre as the UEFA Cup was paraded before thousands of revellers. There was little to smile about forty miles to the north, although many City fans took consolation from the fact that their club had played a part in preventing Ipswich winning the League.

# 11

# Canaries Fly towards Higher Ground

(1981-84)

Ken Brown was determined to take Norwich back to Division One at the first attempt in 1981-82, but the man he chose to fire the bullets didn't meet with universal approval among the Carrow Road faithful. Keith Bertschin, who signed on his 25th birthday, seemed to fit the bill perfectly for he was a strong, direct striker with several seasons' experience of scoring goals in the top divisions. There was just one problem: he used to play for Ipswich. Bertschin arrived at Norwich with a tainted past so far as many fans were concerned, and he would need to work twice as hard, and score twice as many goals, to convince the barrackers he was worthy of that yellow shirt.

'Bert Skinner' as he was known by his old Ipswich teammates, was a North Londoner who'd joined Town as an apprentice in 1973 and scored with the very first kick of his debut at Arsenal less than three years later. He won youth and Under-21 caps and after 33 appearances and eight goals moved to Birmingham City for £100,000. In four seasons at St Andrews he bagged 29 goals in 118 games and Norwich had to pay £200,000 for his services. Looking back, Bertschin says he didn't find it difficult being an ex-Ipswich man and always got on well with the crowd. Today he recalls his time at Carrow Road with fondness, his good memories overshadowing those early weeks when the goals failed to come (just two in his first sixteen games) and the unforgiving fans gave him the bird. His was a story that would have a happy ending, but more of that later.

Exiting the First Division in 1981 led to Norwich losing the services of arguably their three best players – goalkeeper Chris Woods, striker Justin Fashanu and midfielder Martin O'Neill. And in the first half of the 1981-82 season there were few signs that they could recover from this and make a serious bid to return to the top flight. By Christmas the side was twelfth in the table and promotion looked a distant dream. The icy cold day that proved a turning point in Norwich's fortunes was a Tuesday in late December and the unlikely backdrop was the semi-deserted seaside resort of Great Yarmouth. Due to the big freeze that was disrupting the football programme, Ken Brown was desperate to give his men match practice. He had to trek to the seaside to find a pitch that was anything like playable in Norfolk. He persuaded Ipswich boss Robson to send a team up to play a friendly and then called West Brom about taking their striker John Deehan on loan. He wanted a new face to partner Bertschin in attack and thought the friendly with Ipswich was an ideal chance to take a look at Deehan.

Looking out at his snow-covered native Midlands, John 'Dixie' Deehan was amazed to hear what was being proposed: 'I couldn't believe it when Ken told me he wanted me to play in a friendly. We were virtually snowed-in up in the Midlands but he told me the weather wasn't quite so bad in Norfolk and the pitch at Great Yarmouth was okay and he had arranged a friendly against Ipswich. Things weren't going too well for me at West Brom so I told him I would love to come over.'

What happened next changed Deehan's life and started a trail of events that would lead to the player carving an important niche in the history of East Anglian football. In the friendly, Deehan scored no fewer than four times in a 5-1 hammering of Ipswich, his opening goal coming in the very first minute. Brown was quick to confirm his loan move and put him straight in the side for a debut against runaway divisional leaders Luton a few days later. Deehan scored in that game too, and before long a fee of £175,000 had been handed over to West Brom and the Bertschin-Deehan partnership was firing on all cylinders. Twenty goals later and a fine run of victories saw Norwich rise from twelfth to third in a matter of weeks, securing promotion against all the odds.

Deehan and Bertschin's careers might have been taking off at City, but three East Anglian legends were moving in the other direction and bringing an end to their wonderful playing careers. Winger Clive Woods played his final senior game after thirteen years with Ipswich and Norwich, while Town defender Kevin Beattie had received medical advice that his career was over at 28, and City centre-forward Joe Royle heard similar news about himself, aged 32.

For Woods, it meant finding himself a job outside football while continuing to play for his local amateur side Newton Flotman. His love affair with the game continued and his fiftieth birthday came and went with those magic boots still yet to be hung up for good. For Royle, after ten goals in 47 Norwich games, and three appearances in the local derby, knee trouble meant an end to a fine career at the highest level. It was time for Big Joe to start sending out letters of application for coaching and managerial positions. An opening would soon crop up at Oldham Athletic and the managerial path would subsequently lead Royle back to East Anglia.

Beattie had to accept the inevitable, that his career was over after his umpteenth attempted comeback failed. He was granted a testimonial against Moscow Dynamo in March 1982 and among those who paid warm tribute was former Norwich supremo Bond, now at Manchester City: 'When I was manager at Norwich I saw Kevin play often, and was always happy when he was out of the Ipswich team whenever we were in opposition.'

A few weeks after his testimonial, Beattie's contract was paid up by Ipswich and he was apparently disappearing into retirement when word reached Norwich's Ken Brown on the grapevine that 'The Beat' might still have a few games left in him. Beattie recalled: '[Ken] got in touch and asked me down to have a trial. It all went really well but when I was about to sign for Norwich, Ipswich chairman [Patrick] Cobbold stopped it. He got on the phone to the Norwich chairman and said they couldn't allow it to happen – in fact I think it was probably Bobby Robson behind it. Now a lot of our players had gone to Norwich during the 1970s – but hardly any the other way, we were generally more successful than them – but the club obviously regarded me a bit differently. I offered not to play in the derbies but [Ipswich] were having none of it. I went to Colchester instead. Of course I don't hold that against Sir Bobby. He was like a father to me and my generation at Ipswich, but I've always wondered how I'd have got on in the yellow and green. I know I'd have got a lot of stick playing for Norwich but I'd have done my best for them. Having said that, these days, I wouldn't have anything green or yellow in my house.'

Frustrated at being unable to join the Canaries, Beattie linked up with his former Ipswich defensive partner Allan Hunter at Colchester, but only made a handful of appearances for the U's before accepting an offer to try his luck with Malcolm Allison at Middlesbrough. The state of Beattie's knee meant this was a short-lived arrangement, although he did well for a time as Boro's skipper. In later years Beattie eventually worked for Norwich, carrying out scouting duties for manager Mike Walker between 1996 and 1998.

The consistency of Russell Osman and Terry Butcher meant Ipswich could cope defensively without Beattie and with players like Paul Mariner, Alan Brazil, Eric Gates and John Wark by now at the peak of their powers, another title challenge was made in 1981-82. Disappointments in the UEFA Cup (an early exit to Alex Ferguson's Aberdeen) and in the League Cup (a semi-final defeat by Liverpool) were brushed aside as Town chased hard in a bid to topple Liverpool in the League. They signalled their intentions when Alan Brazil smashed five goals past high-flying Southampton in February 1982, but thirteen wins from their remaining

21 fixtures wasn't good enough, at least not compared to Liverpool's superb run-in.

Although he'd established Town as one of the most formidable sides in Europe, Robson left the club in the summer of 1982 to manage England, with a tinge of sadness at not having won the big prize – the League championship. Town's chance had come and gone and the fans were left fretting what the future might hold without Robson. Coach Bobby Ferguson was promoted to manage a side that, while still full of talent, was perhaps losing momentum and motivation.

At least Norwich's 1982 promotion meant derby games were back on the agenda – and the clash on Boxing Day 1982 proved another memorable event, packed with tension and unexpected twists. And starring at the centre of the action was the unlikely figure of Mick Channon, a 34-year-old former England forward who had recently been playing part-time with Bristol Rovers. He had been persuaded to sign for City on a non-contract basis earlier that week by chairman Sir Arthur South, who liked the cut of his jib and talked manager Brown into giving him a shirt. Would this hero of yesteryear, severely lacking in match fitness, give lowly Norwich the boost they needed on derby day, or would he prove an embarrassing mistake? Channon – at a crossroads in his career – gave an emphatic answer. This was a new lease of life and he had plenty to offer. He was re-energised by the atmosphere at Portman Road and had a debut to remember, inspiring his new colleagues in a cracking game.

Norfolk's own Peter Mendham was another hero of the afternoon, and he recalled: 'I had been out of the side for some time and had not expected to play, but as we got off the coach Ken Brown told me I was playing in place of skipper Mick McGuire. My future wife Gabby and step-brother Craig were there to see the game, and it was the first time they had seen me play. I recall Mark Barham setting me up for the first goal. It was such a good cross that I only had to put my head to the ball to score.' Osman levelled for Town with a close-range header, but it was surprise packet Mendham again, just after the hour, who put City into a 2-1 lead: 'My second goal was one of those hit-and-hope volleys. I knew as soon as I hit it that it was a perfect strike. The ball hit the underside of the crossbar and for a split second I wasn't sure if it had gone in or not, but it bounced into the roof of the net. I remember running to Gabby to celebrate.'

There was more drama to come, for sub Trevor Putney supplied Gates, whose cross was headed in by Mariner for Ipswich's second equaliser. Then Putney, a newcomer to the side, brought down Paul Haylock just outside the Ipswich area. Martin O'Neill, by now enjoying his second spell at Norwich, curled a 25-yard free-kick into the Ipswich net with just seconds remaining. The 3-2 win vindicated Ken Brown's wholesale team changes and went down in Canaries folklore as one of the most enjoyable triumphs against the old enemy. Ipswich sub Putney remembers it well some 22 years later:

'This game is one of my outstanding derby memories as it was only a few weeks after my debut. There was an incredible atmosphere. You could tell the rivalry ran deep. The fans were in a frenzy and made it a great occasion. The atmosphere made it different from a run-of-the-mill game, and as a player you get out there and make your first tackle and you make it count – that gets the crowd on your side and sets the tone. This game was a great battle and I remember Martin O'Neill's curling free-kick well – because I was in the wall!'

As glum-faced Town supporters among the 29,596 crowd left the ground, apportioning blame as losing football fans are wont to do, one in particular had to make a supreme effort to keep his views in check. This was Supporters Club official Bryan Knights, the man operating the PA system at Portman Road, whose words of wisdom hadn't always been appreciated in recent times by Norwich fans. News of the fans' disapproval had reached Bryan, who said: 'I have in the past been accused of perhaps saying some unkind things about Norwich City, so may I take this opportunity to put the record straight. Sincerely, it's great to have our neighbours back in the First Division to bring an occasion such as today. Anything I have said in the past or may say on future occasions over the PA system concerning Norwich should be taken for what it's meant to be, only a bit of fun.'

With Ipswich toiling in mid-table in early 1983 and Norwich battling to escape the drop zone, the draw for the fifth round of the FA Cup brought welcome excitement when the balls came out and paired the two rivals together. The Carrow Road meeting in February would be only their third clash in this competition, and the first since those classic ties back in 1962. Even though they'd played each other very recently in the League, interest in the Cup-tie was enormous. Norwich licked their lips at the prospect of record gate receipts, knowing their previous record of £56,894 (for the 1980 League Cup-tie with Ipswich) was likely to be overtaken. Secretary Neil Pleasants seemed rather miffed, however, that the sum would have to be shared between the two clubs and the FA, meaning Norwich would probably pocket less than £20,000 at the end of the day. The match would be screened live to many thousands of viewers in Scandinavia, where both clubs, Ipswich in particular, had built up a loyal following in recent years. This was a worry for the omen-seekers, for City had been screened live over there five times before, and had not scored in any of those games.

Demand for tickets was huge and many fans from rural outposts had difficulty getting hold of one. One fan living in Hunstanton missed work to make a 140-mile round trip to get a ticket from an outlet in Lowestoft, unaware that a travel agent in nearby King's Lynn had some on sale that day. Ken Brown reckoned there was an interest in this game that went way beyond any previous derby and he wondered whether we were seeing a return to 'the good old days of football' – for he sensed none of the 'bitterness and nastiness' of a couple of years earlier: 'If I hear plenty of 'On the Ball, City' and no swearing then I'll be delighted. The build-up for this game and the interest shown in it has been bigger than anything I've known since I've been here.'

Norwich urged fans to arrive at the ground early, saying the gates would open soon after midday and that extra police would be drafted in to prevent trouble. There were several publicity stunts in the build-up to the tie, including a local jeweller presenting both managers with a special 'golden goal' wristwatch. This was particularly good news for Ken Brown, who revealed that his current watch had seen better days and he was having to borrow his son's. Then a city wine merchant visited Carrow Road and dished out champagne to the squad as a publicity stunt, although Brown put his men under strict orders not to touch it until after the game. Instead of quaffing fine wines, the squad wisely chose to visit a dance studio and jacuzzi in the days before the game, to relax and prepare themselves.

Meanwhile, forty miles to the south, Bobby Ferguson scoffed at talk of 'special' preparations for this tie: 'To talk of a special routine for a match at Norwich is ridiculous. We have been going through the usual week's training. We have never in the past done anything special like take the players away. The wives can look after them better than anyone else.' Fergie's one concession to the 'big-match build-up' was to agree to the traditional 'special lunch' the players had enjoyed before every FA Cup-tie since the trophy was won in 1978.

With a full house of 28,000 squeezed in well before kick-off, guest of honour Sir Alf Ramsey came on to present Greg Downs with the Colman's January Player of the Month award. Other 'special events' included Norwich couple Alan Forder and Denise Tandy pledging their mutual love out on the pitch and exchanging engagement rings. It transpired that Alan had only been able to afford Denise's ring thanks to winning the football club's 'golden nuggets' lottery prize of £1,000. Meanwhile, up in the Main Stand was City midfielder Martin O'Neill, nursing an injured arm and twitching nervously, wishing he could be out on the park.

The City players who had become used to their genial manager's laid-back ways must have been surprised by his animation before this game. He stormed: 'It's approaching a life or death situation now, and I only want people who are prepared to roll up their sleeves, get on with the job and who are prepared to sweat blood for Norwich City. Whoever pulls on the shirt will be expected to give nothing less.'

After recent goal-packed thrillers in the League, the fans were due a derby that would be a bruising battle containing little open football and few clear-cut chances. And this was it. Norwich were fast out of the blocks and, after only five minutes, Terry Butcher failed to intercept a through ball and former Ipswich man Keith Bertschin sprinted through to slip it past the advancing Paul Cooper. Cue bedlam in the Barclay. Ipswich were on top for much of the rest of the game but couldn't find an equaliser, no matter what they tried. City battled defiantly, and although it wasn't pretty, it was compelling viewing.

The game might have opened out had John Deehan got through and scored on one run, but he was crudely stopped by Butcher, a profession-al foul that only earned him a lecture from Mr Lewis. Butcher looked back at the game: 'I still have nightmares about that game now as it was my mistake that set up the only goal. I tried to get in front of [Bertschin] to cut the pass out but completely misread the bounce. The ball went right over my foot leaving Bertschin free to run through unchallenged and score. It was a stupid mistake and Fergie gave me so much stick after the game.'

Norwich were through to the last eight of the competition for the first time in twenty years and the jinx on home sides in local derby cup-ties had been laid. For match-winner Bertschin, this was one of the high-lights of his career. He said in 2005: 'My best local derby memory of all was scoring that winning goal, and the worst was getting kicked all around the pitch by Osman and Butcher in return.' Ferguson was livid: 'There was only one team on the pitch and that team lost. We got into great killer positions but just couldn't finish. They had one chance all game and took it.'

Before and afterwards there were skirmishes in the city centre and at the ground involving rival gangs of fans and forty arrests were made. One Ipswich fan was attacked with a Stanley knife outside Anglia TV's offices, but escaped with minor injuries. There had also been regular out-breaks of trouble in the Barclay End during the afternoon. The scenes of triumph and trouble inspired the *EDP* leader writer to eulogise:

'Whatever contemporary brutalities were taking place outside the ground, the spirit of Nethercott, Bly and Allcock were being invoked inside, to remind people how this essentially straightforward and exhilarating game used to be enjoyed. 'On the Ball, City' is an anthem of the proud under-dog conscious of the power of the human spirit and the potency of racial memory. It rang out once again in great waves across the terraces and stands on Saturday and before its sound the pedigree of Ipswich struggled and finally submitted.'

Six weeks later Ipswich had to return to Carrow Road for the 1982-83 League clash, by which time Norwich had been ousted from the FA Cup by Brighton at the quarter-final stage and were now concentrating on one thing – avoiding relegation. Compared to previous adventures under the departed Robson, this was proving a non-event of a season for Ipswich, however, who were ticking over in mid-table.

From a Suffolk point of view the April 1983 League game was notable mainly for the fact that Frans Thijssen was making his much-heralded farewell appearance, having agreed to take his intricate ball skills to Vancouver. Thijssen was joining a steady exodus of Ipswich's top play-ers, and the club was inevitably finding it tough to replace the departing members of Robson's all-star line-up. Thijssen was unable to sign off with a goal at Carrow Road, and other chances went astray, the Ipswich crossbar and both goalkeepers largely responsible for the resultant 0-0 draw. The single point helped City claw their way to safety from relega-tion and the season ended with them in fourteenth place, four points behind Ipswich.

The obsession of both sets of fans about finishing higher than their rivals was something that failed to find favour with one particular exiled Norwich fan. In a letter to the *Pink 'Un*, Don Stangroom of Glamorgan wrote: 'As a Norfolk man, proud of being Norfolk bred and East Anglian in outlook, I felt saddened at reading [in the Richard Futter column] of Canary supporters so parochial as to be satisfied when Ipswich are lower in the table than City. When Ipswich were League champions and again when they won the FA Cup, I shared their joy and elation. Better we strive to emulate the Suffolk's side's considerable achievements than snipe at them. I would like to see City enter into a 'special relationship' with Town and do our outmost to help them, on a reciprocal basis, to aid the advancement of East Anglian football. I find [local rivalry] so petty and small-minded.'

Derby cup action was once again on the fixture list in 1983-84, with Norwich drawn to face Ipswich at Portman Road in the fourth round of the League Cup. Having met just thrice in eighty years in the FA Cup, the clubs had now clashed six times in the considerably younger League Cup competition. The tie took place on a cold and crisp November evening, with both sides occupying mid-table positions in the League, but in terms of current mood and form Norwich were in better shape. It was a miserable night for Town fans, who watched their players turn in the least-committed derby display in living memory. Norwich had lengthy periods on top and deserved their 55th-minute winner, which was set up by nineteen-year-old Louie Donowa, a newcomer to the team who, ironically, grew up on the Whitton housing estate on the edge of Ipswich. Donowa headed Mark Barham's pass to 35-year-old evergreen Mick Channon, who tucked the only goal past Paul Cooper.

It had certainly been a disappointing display by Ipswich and it was no surprise when Ferguson ordered them in for extra training the following day. At least skipper Butcher had an excuse for what he admitted was the club's 'worst display for years'. He'd hardly slept the night before the game, having stayed up to care for his pet labrador, who gave birth to nine puppies: 'It was a marvellous experience to watch these nine little creatures come into the world and I wanted to make sure Sadie didn't roll over and squash any. I thought it was a good omen [for the derby game], but Mick Channon scored the only goal.'

With some justification, Norwich folk had by now sensed a shift in the balance of power in East Anglia. Ipswich were beginning to look like a spent force following the departure of Bobby Robson in 1982. Malcolm Robertson of the *Pink 'Un* reckoned the manner of City's performance in the League Cup-tie suggested things were changing after years of Ipswich superiority, with City set to become the real force now: 'Many of Town's big stars are still in the side but the heart seems to have gone. Ipswich are beset by internal squabbles, uncoordinated and unsure. City looked much more confident.'

It had certainly been a great night for young Donowa and a dream debut as far as local derbies were concerned. Plucked from under Town's noses, he'd turned professional in 1982 and was part of Norwich's fine FA Youth Cup-winning side of 1983. He would make his name with eighty appearances in Norwich's first team as a pacy attacker, but his later career turned into a relentless journey of short stays at different clubs. After playing for Deportivo La Coruna and Stoke City, he would have a spell of 23 games in Ipswich colours in 1989-90. He failed to make a big impact at his home-town club, however, and his travels continued to Bristol City, Birmingham, Burnley, Crystal Palace, Shrewsbury, Walsall, Peterborough and Ayr United. After this he continued at various clubs in non-league football.

Ipswich's general malaise naturally provoked great glee in Norwich, and when the sides met at Carrow Road on Boxing Day 1983, Norwich's biggest crowd so far this season (home or away), of 25,679 turned out to see if City could rub the old enemies' noses in it. It proved a hard-fought affair with 43 free-kicks, keeper Chris Woods taking a buffeting from Paul Mariner, Peter Mendham hobbling off injured, and Eric Gates needing stitches in a facial wound. Ipswich had the better of things in this good old-fashioned British rough-and-tumble, but the few clear chances that cropped up were frittered away and it ended goalless.

As 1983 turned into the year George Orwell warned us all about, Norwich hoped they could steer clear of the oppression currently gripping their opposite numbers. The latest cause of upset at Ipswich surrounded star players and high-earners Mariner and Wark, who caused outrage on the Town terraces when their demand of 'more money or we leave' was made public.

*EDP* writer Bill Walker urged the Canaries not to fall into the traps that had helped Ipswich slip into their current slow decline: 'Do City have to pay big-club wages and incentives to keep together and satisfy a bunch of players who in turn could bring them rich pickings from successful League and cup runs? Do they have to sacrifice one to please the other? Neighbours Ipswich faced that dilemma at the [end of the 1970s]. They knew which way they were heading and decided to do everything they could to keep all the best players at Portman Road. That decision was rewarded when Ipswich won the FA Cup and UEFA Cup, bringing glory to East Anglia. But it looks to be costing them dearly now. Mariner and Wark are in dispute, wanting an increase to salaries which already would delight every one of the Norwich team. Brazil, Muhren and Thijssen had to [be sold]. The club are £1.5 million in debt. Can Norwich afford to take a similar gamble? They are at the crossroads.'

By the time of the 1983-84 return at Portman Road, Ipswich had sold their pay rebels Mariner and Wark to Arsenal and Liverpool, respectively, and they'd slipped down into the division's bottom three. Less than two years after Bobby Robson departed, only two of his all-star team (Cooper and Osman) were in the side to face Norwich in April 1984, although two others (Burley and Butcher) were out injured. Relegation had become a real possibility, but Bobby Ferguson's recent signings Romeo Zondervan and Alan Sunderland looked like they might have the nous and enthusiasm to steer Town clear of danger.

Pepped by a 3-0 win at doomed Wolves just 48 hours earlier, Town approached the Easter Monday derby with more purpose and vigour than mid-table City, and this time it was Norwich fans who were embarrassed and frustrated by their heroes' apparently lack of inspiration and effort. Only keeper Chris Woods was spared criticism after he saved a Gates penalty, but he could do little about Zondervan's crisp shot on 27 minutes and Sunderland's poached effort in the second half. The win set Town up nicely for the rest of the season, and a fine victory at Old Trafford shortly afterwards assured them of First Division football for another season. Norwich were left looking anxiously over their shoulders after Easter 1984, but picked up enough points to survive without having to press any panic buttons.

# 12

# 'So much noise you couldn't think straight'

## (1985-91)

Strengthened by the capture of defender Steve Bruce, and undaunted by a major fire which destroyed the Main Stand at Carrow Road, Norwich City enjoyed a satisfactory first half to 1984-85. There was little to smile about at Portman Road, however. Ipswich had a dreadful autumn, the shortage of fire-power in attack meaning they won only once in eleven games, and that coming against hapless Stoke who were bottom.

Before the 1985 New Year's Day derby at Ipswich, the East Anglian rivals were separated by nine places in the table, Town struggling in nineteenth, average crowds below 17,000, and relegation looking a real possibility. Although their away form was not good, City were in much better shape generally, thanks in part to the evergreen talents of veterans Mick Channon and Asa Hartford. However, the formbook often goes out of the window on derby day and it was Ipswich who prevailed on a damp, miserable afternoon, ending a depressing run of nearly 600 minutes without a home League goal. Buoyed by Eric Gates' third-minute drive past Chris Woods, the home fans responded to manager Bobby Ferguson's pre-match plea: 'Please don't desert the lads, give them the sort of support which pulled us through the bad times last season.'

That early goal restored some of Town's lost confidence and they began to believe this was their day when Mr Bune ignored loud penalty appeals after Butcher floored Channon. Locally-born Jason Dozzell, who had only just celebrated his seventeenth birthday and had a mere handful of first-team games to his name, extended the lead after the interval with a neat shot on the turn.

Following Town's 2-0 victory both sides could turn their thoughts to the cups. The following weeks featured tough-looking FA Cup-ties away at lower division opposition. Then would follow Milk Cup action, with Ipswich and Norwich both lining up in the quarter-finals, against QPR and Grimsby respectively.

Bad weather played havoc with the Milk Cup programme in January 1985, so the semi-final draw was made before the identity of the four survivors was established. The possibility of an East Anglian final at Wembley was ruled out when Ipswich and Norwich were paired in the semis – if they got there. John Deehan headed the only goal at Blundell Park to put City through on 16 January, and then, twelve days later, Town fulfilled their part of the bargain, overcoming QPR 2-1 in a stormy Loftus Road replay in which one player from either side was red-carded. The scene was set for the biggest cup-ties ever staged in East Anglia – a two-legged semi-final between City and Town. Although it was a repeat of the 'double-header' Texaco Cup final of 1973, this was a far bigger occasion because a place at Wembley and major silverware was the prize at stake.

Despite their poor League form, Ipswich were the only side in the country to retain an interest in both major cups by the end of February. The first leg of the Milk Cup showdown was staged on a heavy Portman Road pitch on an overcast Saturday afternoon amid an electric atmosphere. City and Town had both played at Wembley twice prior to this season, but the chance to win a place beneath the twin towers at the expense of the old enemy made this a unique occasion and both sets of fans were in tremendous voice.

The first leg saw Ipswich press from the start and they gained instant reward when Mich D'Avray nodded in a George Burley cross. Late-coming spectators had not even reached their seats. Ferguson's men dominated the first period but missed a host of chances. As the one-sided game wore on with the score remaining 1-0, Ipswich fans began to worry that a single goal would not be enough. Such was the extent of Town's unrewarded pressure that City players remembered it well many years later. Steve Bruce recalled: 'It could easily have been three or four because Ipswich played exceptionally well to give us a seeing-to not reflected in the scoreline.' And experienced Mick Channon remembered: 'We didn't kick a ball in the first half. We played atrociously and should have been two or three down.'

Norwich were delighted to hear the half-time whistle still just one goal behind, but the small matter of how to make the most of their good fortune in the second half would cause a major row in the dressing room. According to Channon, manager Brown instructed them to keep playing open football and press forward in the search for an equaliser. But pragmatic Channon saw this as a major tactical blunder and was not afraid to stand up and say so. He recalled: 'I said "Just a minute, we're losing 0-1. The first thing we mustn't do is give away any more goals. If it's got to be 0-1 let's keep it at 0-1, it doesn't matter how we are playing." Ken Brown went very quiet. He had wanted us to go out and play and beat them on the day, but sometimes in football you can't do that. When you're playing badly, you can't just pick it up, especially when there's a home leg to come.

So as we went out on the pitch for the second half I said to the lads: "Let's keep it tight." We were close to getting the biggest day of our lives, collectively as a team, so we scraped and battled to hold on for a 0-1 defeat.'

The result was a psychological boost for Norwich, and even their most partisan of fans seemed to accept they'd got away with murder by only losing 0-1. Everything was still to play for. Winger Mark Barham was also relieved to escape from Ipswich unscathed. Recalling the occasion, he said: 'I remember taking a throw-in at Portman Road in the first leg and there were fans on the pitch fighting all around me – they'd just spilled out from the terraces. Eventually the police came along and threw them all back in – they didn't take anyone away or anything. That's the thing, the stands are so close to the pitch at Carrow Road and Portman Road that the atmosphere is like fever pitch all the way through. And no one liked coming to Carrow Road in those days. The stand had been burned down, so we had portable changing rooms. The away team's was a really poxy little cabin with about two showers. Ours had loads of room and loads of showers. So we had a psychological advantage right from the start.'

The second leg was a night of rare drama. Ipswich looked nervous from the start as they clung to their narrow lead. Things began to slip away from them when Mich D'Avray was involved in a sickening clash of heads with big Dave Watson. After lengthy treatment he was stretchered off unconscious and it emerged later that quick action by referee Keith Hackett had prevented D'Avray from swallowing his tongue as he lay choking on the turf. Town's luck got worse ten minutes before the interval when a volley by John Deehan looped past Paul Cooper and into the net after taking a deflection. By now Norwich players were flinging themselves into tackles in uncompromising fashion, roared on by delirious home fans. The bruised and battered Ipswich players hardly knew which way to turn and Eric Gates was booked after he complained long and loud to the referee about the treatment he was getting. Fists flew on a number of occasions and many dreadful challenges went unpunished. Ipswich players seemed particularly angry towards Asa Hartford for his tackles on Steve McCall and Gates.

Both sides went close to scoring as the tie remained deadlocked at an aggregate 1-1, but the elusive winner didn't arrive until the 87th minute. Barham raced down the right flank and saw his cross deflected for a corner by an outstretched Ipswich leg. City piled men into the box and as Barham's flag-kick came over, it was defender Bruce who timed his run perfectly, finding space to bullet home a header. The net billowed, the tie was won and the ground erupted. Norwich were at Wembley and Ipswich were down and out. A pitch invasion at the end meant many players couldn't escape the field for several minutes, although very few fans were unwise enough to block the path of big Terry Butcher, who stormed off with tears of rage in his eyes.

Steve Bruce has seen and achieved much in the years since that goal, but the memory of it is still crystal clear: 'Mark Barham swung it into the crowded penalty area, it was my head that met it and Norwich were at Wembley. I think it is fair to say that my performance during the season had wiped out the memory of an own-goal against Liverpool [on my debut], but if there were any lingering doubts [about me] they were totally eradicated with that goal against our arch-rivals Ipswich in such an important game. East Anglia might not be known as an area that generated fervent support of football in the same way as some of the big cities, but it still meant everything to the supporters to win a derby match – and I was the hero of all Norfolk.'

The scenes lived long in former England international Channon's memory too: 'We were carried off shoulder high. That didn't even happen when I was with Southampton and we beat Manchester United for the FA Cup. The whole city of Norwich went wild.' Backroom boy Keith Webb, who would later become reserve-team manager, watched the game in splendid isolation from the burnt-out shell of the Main Stand: 'The last two or three minutes after that goal were unforgettable. The fans were making so much noise you couldn't think straight. At the final whistle it was chaos as the realisation of reaching Wembley sank in.' Barham remembers: 'I knew Steve Bruce would be running in and fortunately I put the ball on his head. I can still see the net bulging now as he powered it home. The noise was incredible and a few minutes later we were looking forward to a trip to Wembley. The celebrations went on into the early hours that night, I can tell you.'

This was definitely not one of those occasions when the losers took their defeat in a humble and sporting manner. Ipswich were livid, partly over their constant bad luck during the two games, and partly over the physical approach of Norwich in the second leg. Manager Ferguson didn't mince his words and certainly didn't leave the ground wishing Norwich well for the final. Skipper Butcher didn't pull any punches either:

'We were cheated out of a place at Wembley after being kicked off the park. The second leg was a nasty affair. There were a couple of Norwich players who seemed more intent on kicking the man rather than the ball. Referee Keith Hackett appeared determined to keep the game flowing and let some outrageous tackles go unpunished, especially one late challenge on Steve McCall. We had already used our substitute and Steve was reduced to a passenger for the last hour of the game. We had tried to play constructive football but some of our players had been intimidated by a few of the tackles. I was devastated. I couldn't believe that we had allowed ourselves to be kicked out of the cup. I stormed into the changing room and kicked a hole in a door, an action I regretted afterwards as I should have shown that sort of aggression on the pitch. I was still angry when I left for home and drove the entire journey on the wrong side of the road. I was so mad I didn't care what happened to me. To be so close to Wembley and lose like that, especially to Norwich, hurt me deeply.'

Butcher would later receive a bill for kicking a hole in the Norwich dressing room door. He recalled: 'We had a team that we knew were better than Norwich. But over the two legs missed chances cost us dearly. My frustration got the better of me unfortunately and my foot ended up going into the dressing room door.'

The player comforted himself with the thought that he could pay back Norwich in a League match in a month's time. Inevitably some Ipswich fans took out their anger after the cup defeat on property in Norwich and thousands of pounds worth of damage was done to houses and shops, with bricks going through windows and scenes of mayhem as gangs clashed outside the Woolpack public house in Golden Ball Street. One Ipswich victim of the many scuffles was John Bowers, who recalled: 'I was in a Morris Marina that stopped at a set of traffic lights by the Maid Marion pub in Norwich, only to be attacked by a huge posse who proceeded to panel-beat every panel on the car before it could get driven away. The most piquant part of the story is that the driver had borrowed the car for the day from his mum. It was her pride and joy and had done more than ten years of motoring – yet this incident saw it written off in about thirty seconds.'

It had been a remarkable week for Ipswich, for the exhausting Norwich game came midway through a fourteen-day period in which they had to face no fewer than six big games. This hectic spell involved two matches when the chase for crucial League points was uppermost, and three big occasions in the FA Cup, the last of which brought an exit at the hands of a late Everton goal.

The Milk Cup excitement meant Norwich's league form dipped and before long they were slipping down the table towards Ipswich. But in the meantime they had a day out at Wembley to enjoy, particularly in Steve Bruce's case, for they were up against Sunderland, the side he'd loved to hate as a boy growing up on Tyneside.

After the fierce rivalry of the semi-final, the game at Wembley soon became labelled 'the friendly final' after Norwich and Sunderland fans made unprecedented efforts to co-operate and mingle on the big day, encouraged by club officials and media attention. The game was no classic, but at least it was third time lucky for City following the 1973 and 1975 defeats, with Dave Watson lifting the trophy after Asa Hartford scored the only goal, his shot deflected in after neat work near the corner flag by John Deehan. On the weekend of the final, City were halfway up the Division One table, but the hangover from Wembley saw them win just two League games in the next twelve, a run that saw them sink to twentieth place and into the danger area.

While the Canaries were slipping and sliding in a downwards spiral, Town were making a determined bid to claw their way to league safety. The clubs met at Carrow Road on a damp but fine Easter Monday afternoon in early April 1985, league points crucial to both. Butcher was in no mood for a repeat of the cup result: 'Norwich had just beaten Sunderland in the Milk Cup final and were on a high. I noticed that they had put a new door on the visitors' changing room after our semi-final. I was still angry over that game and there was no way I was going to lose this one. Norwich seemed to think that they were on to three easy points, but we played well and surprised them.'

Butcher was the happiest man in East Anglia at 3.05 that afternoon, his fist pumping the air in celebration as his header from Gates' free-kick hit the Norwich net, right in front of the City die-hards in the Barclay End. Revenge felt sweet. Just after the interval a McCall free-kick was flicked on by Butcher and D'Avray shot low past Woods for the decisive second. City's Asa Harford was again prominent with his fierce tackling, but he overstepped the mark with twenty minutes left and a nasty challenge on Mark Brennan saw him become the first man ever sent off in an East Anglian derby. This was Ipswich's day, and most of the noise was coming from the visiting section of a disappointingly low 16,884 crowd. The 2-0 win was Town's third League triumph in a row and Ferguson's men were heading for safety.

Norwich also felt they were safe, but successive defeats to Watford, Luton and Leicester meant the danger signs were flashing. Due to cup commitments and bad weather the season ran well into May. A 2-1 win at Chelsea in City's final game left them on 49 points, above Coventry, Sunderland and Stoke, the three favourites for the drop. The worry was that Coventry, eight points adrift, still had three matches left. Three wins would send the Canaries down, but for Coventry to suddenly win three in a row at the end of a bad season looked unlikely, to say the least.

Norwich began to fret when Coventry won the first – against Stoke by virtue of a Stuart Pearce penalty on 17 May. Six days later the Sky Blues did it again, beating Luton with a goal in the game's dying minutes. Now they had just one game left – at home to champions Everton on 26 May. Everton had lost just once in twenty games and had reached two cup finals. Surely they wouldn't cave in at little Coventry? Football can be a cruel game, and Norwich fans began to fear the worst when it emerged that at least four Everton regulars would be missing. The Midlanders duly demolished an unmotivated and under-strength side and won 4-1, pushing Norwich into twentieth spot and relegation. It was a heartbreaking way to go, and the manner of it would eventually lead to changes in League policy, meaning in future seasons everybody would play their final games simultaneously.

The Carrow Road misery was short-lived, for a year later City bounced back as 1985-86 Division Two champions. Boosted by the goals of Kevin Drinkell, they finished seven points clear of runners-up Charlton. As if that wasn't enough cause for celebration, Canaries diehards could enjoy a belly laugh at the expense of their opposite numbers in Suffolk, for Ipswich were simultaneously sliding towards their first relegation in more than twenty years.

Town's fate was sealed over a three-day period when they lost 0-1 at Sheffield Wednesday on the last Saturday of 1985-86, and then on the Monday fellow strugglers Oxford overtook them by beating Arsenal. Towards the end of this fateful campaign, Town skipper Butcher came up against a young Welshman who would in future play a big role in the East Anglian derbies. Iwan Roberts was making his League debut aged seventeen for Watford, and found himself marked by the imposing figure of Butcher: 'Terry was really nice, talking to me all the way through the game. He didn't clatter into me once, as he could see I was young and nervous.'

Butcher wasn't so generous to other opponents later in the season, scrapping with all his might to save Town from the drop, but finding all his efforts were in vain. There was dancing in the streets of Norwich at the two contrasting outcomes of 1985-86. At Radio Broadland, for example, presenter Kevin Piper (a Norwich fan) won a bet that had been placed on-air with breakfast show DJ Rob Chandler (an Ipswich fan). Piper would claim years later that the despondent Chandler never paid up.

Promotion for City and relegation for Town subsequently meant the two clubs would not meet in the League for a number of years. Inevitably it also meant changes in personnel at the two clubs, and East Anglian history was made in May 1986 when Ipswich and Norwich struck a transfer deal that involved a player swap. City's popular 28-year-old sharpshooter John Deehan moved to Town after four-and-a-half years at Carrow Road, and 26-year-old tigerish midfielder Trevor Putney moved in the opposite direction after six seasons with Ipswich. Deehan was the first Norwich man to move to Portman Road in 36 years (and only the second ever) and the Ipswich fans would give him a cautious welcome, only warming to him once he'd settled and found goalscoring form. For Putney, however, things didn't go well early on. Even though he was the third ex-Ipswich man to arrive at Carrow Road in modern times (after Peter Morris and Johnny Miller), many City fans were merciless in their barracking, persecuting Putney for his Ipswich connections.

Putney recalled: 'I was a bit naïve in that I didn't expect any problems. I'd always been a crowd favourite at Ipswich and when I made my City debut I was pretty much the only player in the side with real experience at high level. In my debut at Stamford Bridge on the opening day of 1986-87, which ended 0-0, I had a decent game but got stretchered off after David Speedie did my ankle and I was out for four or five weeks. When I got fit again I couldn't force my way back in straight away because the team was doing well. When I did get a game, the fans didn't seem to want an ex-Ipswich player in the side, and they let me know it. Quite honestly it was awful. I'm a pretty strong character and I just kept working away to get through it, but some players would have crumbled. They would read the teams out over the loudspeakers and when my name was read out there would be a huge boo. It was not nice and it was upsetting for my wife and daughters up in the stand to hear this. My wife used to ask people around her why they were booing me, and one guy just shrugged and said it was because everybody else did it.

'This went on for some time and was terrible. Everyone at the club thought it was unfair and I remember one time skipper Steve Bruce came over and put his hands over my ears so I didn't hear the jeers. I had to work really hard to get through it and win them over. It did eventually get better after Steve did a piece in the match programme appealing to the fans to give me a chance. I remember after that we played Huddersfield in the cup and when they got to my name there was actually a few cheers. Me being me, I responded to this by performing a bow to all four corners of the ground. Then Wayne Biggins got suspended and I got into the team again and set up the winner at Southampton. In the next away game, at Leicester, I scored one of my best-ever goals, going on a long run and hammering the ball in. I kept running all the way back to the other end to celebrate in front of the Norwich fans. Doing all that meant I was pretty knackered for the rest of the game. But over that period the fans' treatment of me got better. It even reached the point where my name got a bigger cheer than the others. I do look back on those early days and wince though – I remember after a few weeks I phoned Kevin O'Callaghan at Millwall, who left Ipswich around the same time as me, and things weren't going great there either and we consoled each other.'

Putney was a regular in City's side by the end of 1986-87, performing well alongside in-form players such as Mike Phelan and Dale Gordon. Only eight of the 42 League games were lost and the Canaries finished in their highest-ever position, fifth in the top flight.

However, bad times were just around the corner. Coach Mel Machin left for Manchester City and 1987-88 got off to a poor start, despite the squad remaining largely unchanged. By November 1987, Norwich were in the relegation zone and in a real rut. Six months is a long time in football and, after leading the club to its best ever finish, Ken Brown paid for the bad run with his job. His exit, a bizarrely public affair played out at a press conference, upset many fans who felt Brown should have been spared and chairman Robert Chase should be the man departing. Long-serving coach and former defender Dave Stringer took over the hot seat and turned the tide dramatically, dragging City up from 21st to fourteenth by the end of 1987-88.

The following season (1988-89) saw Stringer lead the club to a superb fourth place and to the FA Cup semi-finals. He also engineered a top-ten finish in 1989-90, but the following season City slipped down to fifteenth (1990-91), a slow decline which the fans blamed on the board's policy of selling the best players. In his fourth full season (1991-92) Stringer steered City to another FA Cup semi-final and guided them clear of relegation before deciding he needed a quieter life. He quit and was replaced by former Colchester manager Mike Walker as Norwich prepared to take part as founder members of the new FA Premier League.

They would be joined in the new set-up by Ipswich, whose spell of six relatively uneventful years in Division Two ended when they won the divisional title in 1992. While out of the top flight Bobby Ferguson had been replaced as manager by former Tottenham sharp-shooter John Duncan. When Duncan failed to win promotion in three seasons, employing a style perceived as negative, he was replaced by the ex-West Ham boss John Lyall, accompanied by coach Mick McGiven. Less than two years after taking over, Lyall was lifting the Division Two trophy.

Trevor Putney remembers this era well. He was a regular in East Anglian derbies, appearing in seven for Ipswich and two for Norwich, in five different competitions. He recalled: 'The local press used to build [the local derby] up and by and large it meant a lot more to the fans than players. After all it was just three points, although of course the players did enjoy the extra atmosphere and the sense of occasion. The fans take it all very seriously but the players were okay with each other and did socialise afterwards. It was the same for any opponent really in those days, you would socialise with players from Liverpool, Norwich, whoever. We would play hard but then have a drink with them after. It was very good that way when I played for both clubs. I remember things like my little daughter going and tugging at the leg of somebody like Ian Rush and he would have to dunk her dummy in his drink for her. Sadly I don't think this socialising happens so much any more, the players seem to be more distant and keep apart. I remember one derby game in which Louie Donowa tried to snap me in half with one tackle, but after the game it's forgotten and you get on okay with each other.

'I also remember well the 1985 Milk Cup semi-finals between Ipswich and Norwich, when Terry Butcher was so upset he put his foot through a door. Mind you Butch would get very wound up over any game, but particularly for the derbies as he was a local boy. If you are brought up in the area of the clubs you are more aware of the rivalry, outsiders just don't realise. Norwich had Peter Mendham who was local and he knew the importance of beating Ipswich. These days it seems to be different, the dressing rooms are like United Nations meetings and hardly any locals seem to get a look in. I believe the atmosphere has changed at derby games too. This is partly down to the removal of terracing, but I recall derbies in my day when it was really intense with people pressed up against the fence and screaming. When I attended the 2003 Ipswich v Norwich derby on behalf of the Press Association I couldn't believe the lack of atmosphere.'

The various changes in divisional status meant there was a break in local derby league action between April 1985 and December 1992. After Ipswich's superiority of the late-1970s and early '80s, this period definitely belonged to Norwich, who were flying the East Anglian flag alone in the top flight. Local rivalry was restricted to meetings in minor cup competitions and friendlies. First up was a testimonial in March 1986 for Ipswich's long-serving keeper Paul Cooper. Only 4,476 tuned out for a game won by a single goal, a 25-yard drive from Gary Brooke, which flew past Jon Hallworth, who had come on as a sub for the semi-fit Cooper.

After all those exciting and breathless derbies in the first half of the 1980s, following Cooper's benefit the teams didn't meet for two years, the next occasion being a first-team friendly at the Gainsborough Sports Centre in Ipswich on a windy February day in 1988. Norwich came back from two down to draw 2-2 in a game that wasn't an entirely successful mid-season venture from Ipswich's point of view, because star winger Dalian Atkinson pulled a hamstring.

In the summer of 1988 the Ipswich Hospital Cup was revived. The rivals faced each other at Portman Road shortly before the start of the League season. Town won 3-1, Robert Fleck opening the scoring for City, with the home side hitting back via Dozzell, Zondervan (penalty) and Atkinson. The crowd was 6,554, a figure that was nearly tripled at the next meeting of the clubs four months later. This occasion was the second round of the Simod Cup, a much-maligned competition that rarely saw the sort of passion and commitment evident on this fine December evening in 1988 at Portman Road. An end-to-end contest was settled by a single goal in extra-time, when Simon Milton – who hailed from Thetford, midway between the two clubs – forced the ball home after a David Lowe cross. Coming well after 10pm, it remains probably the latest-ever derby goal.

1989 saw a revival of the Norwich Hospital Cup between City and Town at Carrow Road in August. The competition had last been heard of in 1960, since when a new trophy had been created. The original had been destroyed by the 1984 fire which swept City's Main Stand, boardroom and dressing rooms. Ipswich triumphed again, this time by 4-0, a boost for John Duncan's men, given City's higher league status at the time. In front of 7,416, Simon Milton, John Wark, Neil Thompson and Neil Woods hit the target. At half-time Ipswich introduced substitute Louie Donowa, the former City winger, who had recently been signed after spells in Holland and Spain. Donowa received the inevitable jeers from Norwich fans for having become a 'traitor' and also received stick in the press from Sheffield United manager Dave Bassett. The speedy flanker had apparently shaken hands on a deal to join the Blades, but had now performed a U-turn to join his home-town club. The Hospital Cup game was also notable for the appearance of brothers on either side for the first time. Andy Linighan was at the heart of Norwich's defence, while brother Dave was in Town's back four.

With the arrival of Mark Walton in 1989, the Canaries found themselves with a surplus of goalkeepers. Jon Sheffield went on loan to Aldershot and later in 1989-90 joined Ipswich as cover, but didn't make the Town first team before returning to Carrow Road.

In the summer of 1990 the two clubs met at Portman Road in front of a bumper 10,000 crowd to contest the Ipswich Hospital Cup. The kick-off had to be delayed by thirteen minutes, such was the unexpectedly large turnout. It was former West Ham manager John Lyall's first game in charge of Ipswich and he saw his new charges hold Norwich to a 1-1 draw – the Town goal from Ian Redford was equalised late by Mark Bowen.

Six months later, in February 1991, the two clubs renewed hostilities when they were paired at Carrow Road in the southern section semi-final of the Zenith Data Systems Cup. A tremendous overhead kick by Robert Fleck, followed by a Dale Gordon goal, gave City a 2-0 win. More than 16,000 saw the game, but around 1,000 Town fans were angry at being locked out before kick-off. The standing area for ticketless fans had become full. The irony of the situation was that Town had earlier returned a high number of unsold seat-tickets.

The final meeting of Ipswich and Norwich in the pre-Premier League days came in the summer of 1991 when they contested the Norwich Hospital Cup at Carrow Road. There was a huge police presence, suggesting more than 6,000 fans had been anticipated, and the Canaries eased to a 3-0 win. Scorers were Robert Fleck, expensive new-boy Darren Beckford, and David Phillips.

# 13

# THE PREMIER LEAGUE YEARS

## (1992-95)

Ipswich Town's renaissance under John Lyall and return to the top division in 1992 was timely indeed. The new FA Premier League had been created to replace the old Division One, and Town were proud to be a part of the new world, lining up alongside Norwich City, by now under the control of new manager Mike Walker. The new arrangements involved live screening of matches by BSkyB and all the razzmatazz that came with that – dancing girls, inflatable sumos, referees in green instead of black, pre-match entertainment and fireworks. It was football, captain, but not as we know it.

The BSkyB cameras and accompanying roadshow were at Carrow Road when Ipswich and Norwich clashed in the League on a Monday evening in December 1992. It was the shortest day of the year, but the biggest night for East Anglian football. The pundits in the commentary box were former Canaries manager Ken Brown and ex-Ipswich forward Alan Brazil. The latter, remembered as a talented goalscorer with wild curly hair, was these days thinning on top and widening round the middle, but his love of Ipswich Town shone through. His enthusiasm and optimism made him sound more like a fan as he and the more even-handed Brown swapped gentle banter with presenter Richard Keys. More used to the big-city derbies, Keys asked his fellow guests what the result of an East Anglian derby meant to local people: 'It means everything to both sets of fans. We may be out in the country, but it's still very intense here,' said Brazil.

Dave Allard of the *Evening Star* wrote: 'From Dereham to Debenham, from Cromer to Capel – a Norwich versus Ipswich derby brings out the partisan nature of almost everyone in the area. Every game going back to the time of baggy shorts and wooden studs has been special. But tonight's clash is doubly so. The first League derby for almost eight years is the first ever in the Premier League and, in addition, the first to be screened live in the UK.'

Pubs and clubs around the region screened the game and more than 300 Ipswich fans squeezed into the town's Indoor Cricket Centre to view it. One Town fan, 25-year-old Mark Whitehead, was so determined to be at Carrow Road that he persuaded his surgeon to delay a hospital operation by twelve hours so he could witness the long-awaited game. Ipswich were allocated 1,500 seats for this all-ticket affair, and police reported sixteen arrests arising from minor disturbances.

The occasion was particularly special for Ipswich goalkeeper Clive Baker, a 33-year-old signed from Barnsley four months earlier. Earlier in his career the North Walsham-born Baker had spent seven years as a professional on Norwich's books – mainly providing cover for Kevin Keelan and Chris Woods. He'd played in two derby games in Norwich's colours in 1979-80 and by taking the field with Ipswich this evening he became the first goalkeeper to play for both clubs in the professional era – and also only the fourth man to play in League derbies for both sides. Baker had established himself in the Ipswich side in the autumn of 1992 following an injury to Craig Forrest.

Baker recalled: 'I don't remember any adverse reaction from Ipswich fans to my being ex-Norwich. Also there were no problems from the Norwich people when I returned there with Ipswich on that night. The two clubs were very similar in most respects, both were friendly, family set-ups and I don't feel there were any real differences between them. I didn't find it strange going back to where I started my career, in fact it was enjoyable, especially as it was a local derby. The strangest thing was how different the Norwich ground looked as the main stand and dressing rooms areas had all been rebuilt since my day. The players all realised how much games like this meant to the two sets of fans, but for us the main thing affecting us was the additional media attention, especially in the few days before the game.'

Both clubs had had a useful start to 1992-93, particularly Norwich, who surged to the top of the League at the end of August and were still leading the way by Christmas, despite heavy defeats at Blackburn and Liverpool in October. Life was good at Carrow Road and with City undefeated at home the time seemed ripe to give the old enemy a hammering as the nation looked on from their armchairs. But local derbies are a law unto themselves, and some Norwich fans approached the game with apprehension. In his book *Norfolk'n'Good*, City supporter Kevin Baldwin described the pre-match build-up: 'Mum felt queasy all Monday. To stop her fretting around the house, she went to the butcher's to get her Christmas goose, but, of course, she ended up talking about the game there. No prizes for guessing the butcher's prediction of the score. [Sister] Karen didn't know what to expect at the game as this would be the first local derby she'd been to. However, she did get an idea of the passions that are aroused when her mother-in-law came round in the afternoon and pleaded with her not to go – the worry was that the excitement might be too much for her.'

In a nail-biting first half Ipswich's Steve Whitton got clean through the home defence but was foiled by Bryan Gunn. Clive Baker kept his former club at bay at the other end. City's Ian Butterworth failed to appear after the interval and Ipswich exploited City's makeshift defence within minutes of the re-start, Chris Kiwomya heading home after a Neil Thompson corner. Town worked hard to kill off the game and the result was confirmed two minutes from time when Thompson blasted home from a tight angle. This goal provoked a pitch invasion by over-excited Town fans, one of whom planted a blue and white bobble hat on the head of the celebrating Ipswich midfielder Jason Dozzell, performed a brief dance and then departed the pitch. The perpetrator turned out to be Dozzell's half-brother Tony Swallow. As the referee signalled for Norwich to kick-off again, Dozzell was left wondering what to do with the hat he'd been given.

Ipswich's Simon Milton recalled the episode later: 'Jason thought to himself "what am I doing? I probably can't play out the last ten minutes with a bobble hat on my head." It was such a weird thing to do. Tony wasn't the only fan to come on obviously – there were loads. But not too many of them were six foot two, mixed race with ginger hair. He was never going to get away with anything.' Milton was right, for the offender was later tracked down and charged by police. Dozzell revealed later that he'd thought about wearing the hat for the final few minutes' play, but eventually tucked it under his shirt. He added: 'My last game at Carrow Road had been back in 1985 when I failed to pick up Steve Bruce and he raced in and headed the winner to take City to Wembley. I left the ground like a zombie. Tonight I feel tremendous.'

Author Kevin Baldwin described the misery the 0-2 defeat caused in Norfolk that night: 'We all felt sick. Losing to Ipswich was like being kicked in the guts. Or having your home burgled. Or seeing your favourite pet run over by your neighbour. Twice. And the thought of our assailants/burglars/pet killers laughing at us all the way down the A140 just made it worse.'

The consolation for City fans would come in the form of a sharp decline in Ipswich's form after Christmas. A dreadful run of thirteen League games without a win dropped Ipswich from fourth at the beginning of February to sixteenth by the time of the return derby at Portman Road in mid-April. City's Mike Walker called the slump 'incredible'.

During this period Norwich also lost the leadership of the League under the dual challenge of Manchester United and Aston Villa, but went into the Ipswich game still holding outside hopes that the championship could be won. At least they could be expected to win against declining

Ipswich, even if the championship was slipping out of their reach. Couldn't they?

In the build up to the Easter Monday clash, the Ipswich *Evening Star* launched a search for a new club song in a bid to revive the fortunes of their ailing team. Supporter Marion Jordan sent in a songsheet dating back to 1954, which featured words by Jack Baldwin, mine host and leader of the Railway Tavern Ale Voice Choir of Burrell Street, Ipswich. Not surprisingly, this quaint ditty didn't win the hearts of the modern-day fans. One man who might have appreciated it was Stanley Matthews, who appeared at the game to present Town skipper David Linighan with a fair-play trophy.

The game was an intense affair, played at a hectic pace, and Dozzell put Town ahead midway in the first half after City keeper Gunn blundered when trying to clear a cross. Just before the interval Chris Sutton headed a deserved equaliser from Ian Crook's free-kick. Instead of the higher placed team coming good after the interval, it was relegation-haunted Ipswich who grabbed the initiative, scoring twice in three minutes through the persistent Micky Stockwell and the classy Dozzell. Norwich hit the woodwork twice while 1-3 down, but Town hung on to complete a surprise 'double', ending their own relegation worries and finally killing off Norwich's title hopes. Town manager Lyall had to follow proceedings via the radio at home, where he and wife Yvonne were both recovering from a virus.

The 1993-94 campaign saw Ipswich and Norwich again enjoy good starts, the sides going into their first clash of the season at Carrow Road in late August in great form. Norwich had just hammered Leeds 4-0 at Elland Road, and Ipswich had won three out of three, not conceding a goal in 300 minutes' play. Missing their new signings Ian Marshall and Paul Mason for the Norwich game, however, Town looked punchless in attack, despite dominating possession. Bulgarian forward Bontcho Guentchev had a quiet evening in his first local derby. Town's run of clean sheets was ended when Mark Robins cleverly set up Jerry Goss, who produced a clinical finish. Town's Geraint Williams had a goal disallowed, but Norwich ended the stronger side and only Clive Baker's heroics limited the victory to 1-0. The win helped set Norwich up for a good autumn, highlighted by a wonderful 2-1 win at Bayern Munich in the UEFA Cup.

By the time of the 1993-94 return derby at Portman Road, City were on the crest of a wave. Mike Walker's attacking outlook was producing some sensational away wins and everything in the garden was looking rosy. Only two things could spoil Christmas for Norwich fans – first, a 'bigger' club poaching manager Walker (he was currently rumoured to be in conflict with chairman Robert Chase), and second, losing to Ipswich. Both disasters would come to pass.

Played on the Saturday before Christmas, the match pulled in a gate of just under 20,000. Those who stayed away missed an enthralling full-blooded encounter, with the boots flying and adrenalin pumping. In an electric atmosphere there were five bookings and a sending-off. John Wark got Ipswich off to a fine start, netting an early penalty after Chris Kiwomya was hauled down by Butterworth. A fierce drive by Mark Bowen restored parity just before the interval. Watched from the stands by Bobby Robson, who had recently parted company with Sporting Lisbon, Town – and the fired up Eddie Youds in particular – showed fierce commitment and refused to give an inch to the more classy looking Norwich line-up. A classic derby reached a fever-pitch climax in the dying seconds. First, Norwich sub Lee Power was sent off for clattering into Phil Whelan, a punishment that looked a little harsh for a first challenge. And then, with Ipswich smelling victory, Youds strode forward and smacked a shot against a post. Into injury-time and ten-man Norwich finally crumbled and fell 1-2 behind as Neil Thompson's driven corner was headed like a thunderbolt into his own net by the unlucky and horrified figure of Gary Megson. The nature and the timing of the winning goal could not have been worse in a local derby.

Miserable Megson revealed: 'I was trying to clear the ball into the back of the stand but it flew off my forehead and into the net. I felt a challenge from the back, but as it turned out I wished I had left the ball alone, but it was a particularly good corner, whipped in at pace.' Norwich heads were well and truly bowed after such a heart-breaking climax, but years later Megson was able to recall what had happened with a smile on his face: 'It's not my fault if [goalkeeper] Bryan Gunn can't concentrate for the full ninety minutes,' he joked. 'Actually, I blame Ruel Fox for the goal. He should have headed the ball clear before I stuck it in our net. Ipswich would survive relegation by one point that season and I was one of the reasons why. But I always loved local derbies as a player and they give the fans as big a buzz. I find them a bit more nerve-wracking now that I'm a manager.' Megson also revealed that after his gaffe he received letters from Ipswich fans thanking him for winning the point that ultimately kept Town in the Premiership. Among his postbag was a £25 cheque to be given to Bryan Gunn's leukaemia appeal.

To compound the Norwich misery over the 1993-94 winter, the club had to cope with losing the popular Walker. A falling-out with his chairman and an approach by Everton seemed to coincide and he walked out on the Canaries to take charge at Goodison Park. Coach John Deehan took over, and the dissent among supporters increased, many of them wanting to see the back of chairman Robert Chase, whose main 'crimes' were seen as selling the best players to fund ground improvements and not re-investing in the team. Deehan steered the club to a mid-table finish, respectable in the circumstances, but after the brief glory of the Walker years, City fans were left disappointed.

Ipswich avoided relegation by a whisker in 1993-94 and many Town fans were also unhappy with life. Coach Mick McGiven had been in charge of team affairs lately, with John Lyall having moved 'upstairs', and the brand of football being played was negative. There was also talk of dressing room unrest at Portman Road.

In the early stages of the 1994-95 campaign, Ipswich and Norwich both hit problems and it wouldn't be long before both began looking distinctly like relegation candidates. Lyall returned to the manager's seat at Portman Road and spent big money on new players, but by the end of November his team had slumped to the foot of the Premiership. City, meanwhile, continued their policy of selling their most valuable assets (Sutton, Ekoku and Robins the latest in a long line of exports) and their quiet start hid the troubles that were shortly to emerge.

The first derby of a traumatic season came along on a rainswept Monday night in mid-September and saw Ipswich give a long-awaited debut to £1 million signing Steve Sedgley. The record signing had arrived from Tottenham in the summer but had been injured in a pre-season friendly at Southend United and was only now fit enough to resume. City keeper Bryan Gunn took the field with a shaven head, in recognition of the fact that his leukaemia research appeal (in the name of his late daughter) had funded the opening of a new laboratory at the University of East Anglia.

Town had won just one of their opening five games to date and didn't look likely to improve on that record when Norwich's makeshift striker Rob Newman slid in to score on twelve minutes. After Andy Johnson nearly made it two, striking the crossbar, Town drew level though a John Wark penalty, given for a debatable foul by Jon Newsome on Ian Marshall. There was more penalty drama after the break when Simon Milton impeded Ian Crook and the linesman signalled a penalty, even though the referee had originally indicated a free-kick. Carl Bradshaw stepped up to the spot and, after his first attempt was saved by Craig 'Giant Haystacks' Forrest, Bradshaw reacted quickly to net the rebound. Norwich probably deserved the 2-1 win, although arguments about the two penalties simmered on well after the final whistle. One bonus for

Town fans was the continued good form of their veteran player-coach Wark, unexpectedly holding down a first-team place at the age of 37.

Norwich fan Matt Hansell called this game one of the most difficult experiences of his life. Having obtained a ticket from an Ipswich source, he found himself sitting in a strictly 'blue' area of the ground and thus unable to express his loyalties verbally for fear of being lynched. 'At the final whistle I looked to my left to see the jubilant Norwich supporters celebrating and smiling in our direction. How I wanted to take off my coat, show them my Norwich shirt and celebrate with them, letting them know I was a Norwich fan. Sadly that wasn't an option and the only thing I could do was smile back.'

By the time the two teams met again, in March 1995, both were in serious trouble. Ipswich had recently suffered a Premiership record-breaking 0-9 defeat at Manchester United (Andy Cole hit five) and were looking certainties for relegation. George Burley, the former long-serving full-back had been tempted from neighbours Colchester to take over as manager from John Lyall, who quit after Ipswich dropped to bottom place in early December. Burley's task to revive the club looked enormous, and most observers had already accepted that any new dawn would only come after relegation and a fresh start. Norwich, meanwhile, were showing signs that they might accompany Town down to the Endsleigh League. Frustrated by the club's refusal to invest in a replacement for the injured keeper Gunn, Deehan and his team went to Ipswich on the back of a run of eleven winless League games. A spectacular turnaround would be needed if the drop was to be avoided.

Burley, clearly building for the future, even though relegation was not mathematically assured, decided the Norwich trip was the right time to drop the £1 million flop he'd inherited in the shape of Steve Sedgley. It later emerged that the player had been insulted by the suggestion that he should sit on the bench for the derby game, and walked out on the team. Tony Garnett of the *EADT* called Burley's decision to wield the axe 'brave but probably long overdue', and called Sedgley the sort of expensive mistake that would never have happened at Ipswich during the Bobby Robson era. The Lyall regime had been allowed by the board to invest heavily in players, but chairman John Kerr had ended up with egg on his face. Sedgley hit back in the press, saying the matter had been blown out of proportion, and he'd simply not seen the point of being sub. He felt he was being 'unfairly' singled out following the nine-goal humiliation at Old Trafford.

Given such a turbulent background it was hardly surprising that Norwich completed their first League double over Ipswich in 43 years.

The match slipped away from Ipswich just before the interval when Wark was sent off for tripping Darren Eadie in the centre circle, a decision that even Norwich players felt was harsh. The watching Sky TV pundit Bobby Gould called it 'a disgraceful decision'. Ten-man Town caved in to three Norwich goals in 21 second-half minutes, the first despatched by Jamie Cureton after he took a long pass and rounded Forrest. Five minutes later Ashley Ward swivelled and fired home. The scoring was completed when Forrest made a hash of a John Polston header and Eadie did the rest.

One of Norwich's ball-boys that day was Gary Cheeseman, who didn't realise the 3-0 win was nothing more than a false dawn in City's relegation battle. He recalled: 'After watching this demolition of our closest rivals I was able to leave for Australia in the knowledge that Norwich would be safe for another year. Having beaten Ipswich we would have to get something pathetically impossible – like a single point from a possible 24 – to get relegated. Which, of course, would never happen?'

It may have been Norwich's first win since New Year's Day, but it would also prove their last of the season, too. The next seven League games were all lost, and midway through this dreadful run manager Deehan fell on his sword, his deputy Gary Megson taking over. Relegation was confirmed when Leeds hit two late goals to sink City 2-1 at Elland Road in early May. The total of just one point from 24, as mentioned by the ball-boy above, sealed City's fate. Their final twenty games yielded one win (over Ipswich), seven draws and twelve losses. Ipswich's run-in was spookily similar – they lost fourteen of their final twenty – and the two East Anglian clubs together waved farewell to the top flight, along with Leicester.

Ipswich finished bottom, having lost 29 of their 42 games. They had used a club record 34 players during the season, fifteen of them making their debuts. Most of the damage had been done in the early part of the campaign, when Lyall had again taken a back seat, leaving coaches Paul Goddard and John Wark to run the team. Norwich had at least gone down with all guns blazing, with caretaker-manager Gary Megson inspiring plenty of fight but seeing his team run out of luck on a number of occasions. City finished sixteen points ahead of Ipswich in twentieth place, but still two points short of safety.

So ended a colourful three years (1992-95) which, to date, remains the only time Ipswich and Norwich have competed together in Premiership surroundings. Perhaps fittingly, of six meetings at this level, they won three games apiece. The new Premiership was going from strength to strength and football was becoming bigger than ever in business terms – but, for now at least, Ipswich and Norwich weren't at the party.

# 14

# GUNN SHOOTS HIMSELF
# IN THE FOOT

## (1995-99)

Relegation for both Ipswich and Norwich from the FA Carling Premiership in 1995 had undoubtedly been a huge blow, but among the fans there was consolation to be gleaned from the fact that 'the other lot' had also taken the plunge. Instead of Anfield, Old Trafford or Highbury, away trips would now feature the delights of Grimsby, Tranmere and Watford. But at least the fun and games surrounding the derby fixture could continue.

For Ipswich manager George Burley, barely six months into the job, relegation provided the chance to re-group and build a new side under a new 'hands on' chairman, the youthful and dynamic David Sheepshanks. Norwich also wiped their slate clean, appointing Wycombe Wanderers' manager Martin O'Neill to occupy the seat kept warm by Gary Megson since John Deehan's departure. O'Neill had served the club well in two spells as a player and his return was welcomed by fans who were unused to board decisions they actually agreed with.

Norwich's opening game of the new season, at Luton, was screened live via Anglia TV's new *Kick Off* show. Canaries fans had no trouble motivating themselves for the game, for Luton had strong Ipswich connections, their new manager being former Town coach Terry Westley and the Luton line-up featured ex-Ipswich men Bontcho Guentchev and Gavin Johnson. The new-look ITV coverage was great news for fans not making the trip, but City fanzine 'Cheep Shot' objected to the fact that helping present the show in the studio were Alan Brazil and George Burley, which they called: 'An Ipswich old boys re-union'. City beat the Town 'old boys' 3-1 and got their season off to a great start.

By the time of the first derby in November, Norwich were sixth, with Ipswich nine places lower and having more of a struggle to adapt to the new surroundings. The November 1995 clash pulled in Norwich's highest home crowd of the campaign, 17,862, and saw City surge into an early lead, Jon Newsome heading in a Keith O'Neill free-kick. Ipswich looked dead and buried late in the game when Robert Fleck snatched a second goal, his fourth since a much-heralded return from Chelsea a few weeks earlier. With just eight minutes to go, Ipswich got a lifeline when Rob

Ullathorne impeded Alex Mathie and veteran John Wark slid home the penalty. Minutes later Norwich hearts missed a beat when the referee pointed to the spot again, giving Ipswich a second penalty, but was then persuaded to consult his linesman. Wark takes up the story: 'Everyone went berserk when the second penalty was awarded. I'd scored one already and being a bit older, I just stood there chatting with Bryan Gunn while the ref went to talk to the linesman. Gunny said: "Where are you going to put this one?" I said: "Same place as the last one – in the net!" And then the ref changed his mind. I didn't say too much – I didn't think he'd change his mind twice.'

It was three points for Norwich and even their fanzine 'Cheep Shot' admitted Ipswich had suffered from 'unbelievably dodgy decisions' by the officials, but drew much amusement from what had happened: 'Now that's entertainment!' they chirped. Norwich's glee ended shortly afterwards when Martin O'Neill unexpectedly quit to become manager of Leicester. The rumour mill went into overdrive and City fans were convinced it was all chairman Robert Chase's fault – and that his continuing presence would mean there was no chance of the popular Mike Walker returning either. Walker was available and living locally – he even wrote a football column for the *EDP* – but to the fans' dismay the new vacancy was filled by the less popular and less qualified Gary Megson. Chase further angered fans by dithering and then pulling out on a deal to sign Dean Windass, who would surely have been a perfect strike partner for Fleck. Inevitably, perhaps, City started to slide down the table, their gloom increasing as Ipswich went in the other direction, climbing to fifth by the time of the return derby in April 1996.

A tremendous atmosphere was generated at Portman Road by the only 20,000-plus crowd of the season. Town were desperate for a win to get into the play-offs and City needed points to be sure of avoiding a second successive relegation. Ian Marshall put Town ahead after latching onto a long punt forward, but tricky Jamie Cureton shocked Ipswich with an equaliser just after the hour. The fact the ebullient Cureton was sporting a green-dyed hairstyle that day only seemed to make matters worse for the home fans. Town threw everything forward in a desperate search for a winner, and with just four minutes left on the clock came the bizarre goal which, arguably, remains the most memorable of any Ipswich-Norwich derby.

City defender Rob Ullathorne turned and knocked a routine back-pass towards his keeper Bryan Gunn. The big Scot shaped to belt the ball forward but, to the astonishment of one and all, not least himself, saw the ball deviate after taking an unexpected bounce. Gunn wildly kicked fresh air and the ball bobbled over his foot and into the net. It must have lasted for less than a second, but there was a definable moment of stunned silence before the Ipswich fans began screaming their delight. The visiting supporters, some of whom had recently been getting on Gunn's back anyway, felt sick to their stomachs. It was an appalling way to lose any match, let alone an important local derby.

Nearly 400 fine performances by Gunn were suddenly overshadowed by this moment of ill-fortune for the poor 32-year-old. He recalled later: 'It's etched in people's minds on both sides of the [Norfolk-Suffolk] border. That's the kind of thing that happens in these games. It was very unfortunate. We'd discussed it before the game – the pitch wasn't in very good condition, so I said "if you pass back, make sure it's wide of the goals". It was a tame back-pass, but it seemed to gather momentum and just as I went to kick it, it jumped up about two feet and passed me at about knee height and ended up in the back of the net. I've had to take a lot of stick for that over the years from both sets of fans. There's not too many people who can get a pat on the back walking down the streets of Norwich and then exactly the same thing when they're walking down the street in Ipswich. To be fair it doesn't worry me at all, it was a freak. Over a number of years I just fired them straight back up the pitch. I think this was a freak bobble which happened. Unfortunately it happened in that derby match. I had to live with it, but you know worse things in life have happened to me. [Rob Ullathorne] was probably too scared to say anything to me [at the time]. I saw him recently and I blamed him for ruining my career. We had a little giggle about that.'

That goal was just about the last straw for the long-suffering City fans, whose anti-Chase protests were still as intense as ever: 'The farcical defeat at Portman Road only served to rub salt into our gaping wounds,' wrote one. 'It may sound a bit pathetic, but I don't think I'll ever forgive [Gunn] for that,' reflected 'Ferry Cross the Wensum' fanzine editor James Emerson. The local paper in Ipswich later issued badges to Town fans, bearing a picture of Gunn, head in hands, and the message 'Well done, Bryan Gunn'. The keeper could hardly complain, though, because they also made a donation to his leukaemia appeal. The goal was the sort of incident that is talked about years later, often in exaggerated form. One observer – apparently a 'neutral' – described it in the *Guardian* ten years later: 'As his foot was arching through its powerful trajectory, the ball struck a tuft of the severely cut-up pitch, bobbled over his foot and trickled in slow motion into the goal, leaving the Scotland number two playing Nike air football. It was all very funny until some cretin at the front tried to drag the sorry Norwich goalie into the crowd whilst he was retrieving the ball a few minutes later. The temperature rose, seats from the Portman stand started flying from the Norwich fans, and this neutral felt it time to get his coat and slip out the back.'

One Norwich supporter who later felt able to forgive Gunn is Karen Buchanan, one-time editor of football magazine *FourFourTwo*: 'Yes, I can forgive him. The Ipswich fans sang "Let's all do a Gunny" while doing the can-can, as we were leaving Portman Road and I have to admit that was very funny. Stupid, but very funny. Anyway, I was too busy singing "Green hair! Jamie has got green hair!" in a splendidly accurate tribute to Jamie Cureton's green bonce to notice. Much.'

Although Ipswich ultimately missed the play-offs by just two points, there remained only one thing that could cheer up the Norwich fans after such a miserable season – the departure of chairman Chase. They got their wish in the final week of the 1995-96 season, his resignation leading to a huge turnout and fancy dress party in the away section at the season's last game, at Crystal Palace. Bizarrely that game was also won by a freak own-goal, this time in Norwich's favour. Later in the summer the reorganised Norwich board of directors welcomed the arrival of TV chef Delia Smith and her husband Michael Wynn-Jones, who became majority shareholders – and Mike Walker replaced Gary Megson as manager. Suddenly life was not so bad if you were a Canary.

Ipswich fans noted events north of the border with interest. The Town fanzine 'Dribble' commented: 'Chase will be dearly missed by all Ipswich.' True-blue Mark Jarman was even prompted to write to Chase, thanking him 'for all you've done for my club'. This touch of humour was lost on Chase who seemingly assumed the letter writer was from a Norwich fan. Says Jarman: 'I got a charming reply from him, and a photograph. He didn't realise how cleverly my letter had disguised my true allegiance, but he probably had so few letters of appreciation that he was grateful for anything he got.'

Chase's departure might have delighted many fans, but it reportedly left Norwich perilously close to bankruptcy. It would take the injection of cash from the new celebrity director and her husband to put things back on an even keel. Ironically, the couple lived just outside Stowmarket, an Ipswich Town stronghold, but there was no doubting their Canaries credentials. Delia Smith had met avid Norwich fan Michael Wynn-Jones in 1969 when she began writing a cookery column for his employers, the *Daily Mirror*. He took her to meet his family in Norfolk, and they went with his father to watch a match at Carrow Road. Delia caught the bug and within a few years she and Michael were man and wife, and Canaries season-ticket holders to boot. For a television personality, Delia would prove to be remarkably down to earth. The woman who had baked the cake pictured on the Rolling Stones' *Let It Bleed* album could now be found screaming her head off for ninety minutes at Carrow Road every other Saturday. By 1994 she'd been awarded an OBE recognising her talents and popularity, and in 1996 as she approached sixty, her favourite football club called her to their rescue. Reportedly, it was to the treehouse at their country cottage, deep in Ipswich territory, that Delia and Michael retired one day in May 1996, to decide whether to become majority shareholders and directors of the Canaries in return for some of their hard-earned fortune. 'What else could we do? The club needed us,' Wynn-Jones said later.

As if enough had not already happened at Carrow Road that summer, there was one more episode that would cause enormous controversy and ill-feeling between Ipswich Town and Norwich City. Just before the change of manager took place, City's midfielder Ian Crook was released by the club, one of many efforts to try and save cash in this critical period. Ipswich ears pricked up at this news and George Burley was quick to offer Crook a contract at Portman Road. The player duly signed forms and was unveiled at a press conference. On the same day, Mike Walker was welcomed back at Carrow Road for his second spell as manager. Knowing he had no money to spend on new signings, one of Walker's first thoughts was how wrong it had been for Crook to be allowed to slip away and join the local enemy. He was just the sort of player Walker wanted. At this point, somebody identified a loophole in the transfer paperwork. Crook's new contract was apparently signed and dated 26 June, although a technicality stipulated that he was a Norwich player until 30 June. Norwich and Walker exploited this to the full and were able to persuade Crook to forget the whole Ipswich episode and come back to Carrow Road. Crook was happy to return, now the new manager was in place, but he was later censured by the FA for signing overlapping contacts. Ipswich were furious, taking legal action which subsequently failed on the grounds that City had been entitled to offer the player a new contract before his old one expired. Town fans eventually said 'good riddance' but promised Crook a hostile welcome later in the season.

During this period, former Ipswich favourite Kevin Beattie found himself working on a building site in Norwich, happy to do a spot of labouring to earn a living and keep himself fit and active. Naturally his workmates loved having a famous ex-footballer on their team, and grew fond of calling out to passing Norwich fans to look at who was mixing the cement. The building site was just a couple of hundred yards from Carrow Road and this amused the man they called 'The Beat' no end:

'I had a lot of fun working for BB Brickwork and drinking in the local pubs with Norwich supporters,' he recalled.

The first East Anglian derby of 1996-97 was switched to a Friday night in October to accommodate Sky TV. The usual ingredients were all in place: heavy police presence, abusive chanting, disjoined and frantic football, fierce tackling. Andy Johnson and Robert Fleck swapped passes and the former slammed Norwich ahead with a fine shot. Before the break it was Johnson again, heading home a Darren Eadie free-kick. With Norwich currently second in Division One and Town below halfway, it was going according to form. Apart from baiting Robert Fleck with songs about his weight, the away fans in the South Stand had little to sing about until new singing Danny Sonner volleyed Town back into the game just after half-time. Hopes of salvaging a point disappeared, however, when John Polston headed home a 67th-minute corner and the 3-1 final score was a fair reflection of proceedings. Ian Crook's arrival as a substitute for two-goal Johnson was met with the anticipated cacophony of jeers, allowing the Ipswich contingent to forget the scoreline for a while. Defeat hurt, but Ipswich fans tried to put a brave face on things. The fanzine 'Those Were The Days' commented: 'These days the Carrow Road derby is of secondary importance [to Ipswich], because at home we not only usually win, but one of their players normally humiliates himself by scoring our last-minute winner.'

The return game was six months later, in April 1997, by which time Ipswich had clawed their way into the top six and looked all set to clinch a play-off place, at least. Norwich were a couple of places and points behind them and knew that victory was essential to their own play-off chances. A Friday night full-house of 22,000 squeezed into Portman Road and the 2,300-strong Norwich contingent contributed to a fizzing atmosphere. Ipswich gave their best derby performance for some time, powering forward with great confidence and purpose. Just after the half-hour mark they made the crucial breakthrough, Steve Sedgley slipping a pass through for Argentine full-back Mauricio Taricco to fire home. Just before the interval the lead was doubled amid great celebrations, Paul Mason cracking home a firm drive after an overhead kick by Geraint Williams. Town remained on top for most of the second half, one of City's few close efforts being a long-range shot by the under-fire Crook. Fleck changed his green boots for black ones at the break but it made no difference. Norwich's season was effectively over, and it didn't help the mood of their fans when they were locked in for fifteen minutes after the final whistle to allow the police to disperse home supporters. City fans' consolation would come later, when Ipswich were beaten in the play-offs, thanks to a late Sheffield United strike that eliminated them on the away-goals rule.

Delia Smith's friendship with the celebrated fashion designer Bruce Oldfield saw Norwich introduce a state-of-the-art all-yellow kit for 1997-98, but the fans did not take to it. After a poll was taken, the 'green light' was given for green to be reintroduced. The new kit had perhaps helped dazzle Ipswich under the Carrow Road floodlights in September 1997, for City notched a 2-1 win. Their previous home game had seen a 0-4 hammering by Charlton, and this topsy-turvy form would typify City's season. Darren Eadie sank Ipswich with an early goal from Craig Fleming's pass, and an unlucky own-goal by Jason Cundy extended the lead. Town pulled one back through on-loan Mark Stein's header, but it wasn't to be their day – they also lost striker James Scowcroft with a neck injury.

Although by now he'd made 85 appearances in the Ipswich forward line, this was only Scowcroft's third derby game. He'd grown up in West Suffolk, in an area split between Ipswich and Norwich supporters. His first links with Ipswich came as a ten-year-old, when he played in the Junior Blues set-up, at which time he was also training at Norwich. He recalled: 'I was playing for a Sunday side in Stowmarket. The manager recommended me to Ipswich and I went to Norwich as well for three or four weeks. I had to make a decision between the two clubs. Ipswich was far better organised – it was always going to be Ipswich.' He developed through the junior teams and, after the enforced sale of Ian Marshall to Leicester in 1996, made the most of his chance to establish a regular place in the first team. In those early days, despite being a young local lad, he was a victim of the boo-boys and was regularly barracked. He said: 'It affected me a lot. I'd been playing for no more than a year, not much else was really happening at the club and this seemed to catch the headlines. I really didn't need that at the time, but I just tried to do my best to shrug it off.' Like Trevor Putney at Norwich before him, Scowcroft worked his way through the jeers and eventually won the fans over. Some time later he would be voted into 31st place in the *EADT* readers poll for the top 100 Town players of all time.

Despite an unfortunate habit of missing penalties – eight were fluffed that season – Town cast aside their pre-Christmas form to progress up the table and into the play-offs in 1997-98. A key three points *en route* were won at home to Norwich in February, an occasion still referred to years later among Ipswich folk as 'the Demolition Derby'.

The pattern was set after just 64 seconds when Alex Mathie rifled in a Jamie Clapham throw. Before the half-hour, Gus Uhlenbeek and Mick

Stockwell combined to set up Scot Mathie with his second goal. Norwich looked in poor shape and their fragile defence crumbled again before half-time, Mathie swooping on a Stockwell pass to clinch his hat-trick. The hero of the hour failed to appear after the interval due to an injury, but Town continued to pile forward and Bobby Petta sprinted into the box to fire low past Andy Marshall. Hard-working Matt Holland then set up Petta again for the fifth and final goal. Norwich's night was typified by Robert Fleck's dreadful miss in front of an open goal. It was the third time Town had beaten City by 5-0 down the years, and Mathie had become the sixth Ipswich derby hat-trick scorer, albeit the first for eighteen years. It was an occasion to treasure for the home contingent, with Norwich being made to look exactly like a side drifting along in fourteenth place. Even today, a DVD of this game still sells well in Town's club shops.

One Town fan who recalls the day vividly is John Bowers: 'I was not paying attention for the first, and most brilliant goal, so to balance football karma I solemnly vowed to mark any other Town goals by celebrating with both feet off the ground. I duly did this, not having realised four more goals would follow. The next day I could hardly walk and my legs were black with bruises in a narrow but painful band between knee and hip – but I was supremely happy.'

Manager George Burley, who would ultimately have eight years at Portman Road as a manager, placed this game among his best memories in football. He recalled: 'Local derbies are normally very close, keenly contested affairs. So to win 5-0 was a great achievement. Alex Mathie became a hero for life with the fans after scoring a first-half hat-trick that day. On his day Bobby Petta was a real match winner and that day he was really on top of his game. His first goal was particularly spectacular. Norwich have turned us over at Portman Road a couple of times since I have been manager, so this was a real treat for the fans and a game that I am sure none of them or the players will ever forget.' The win set up Town's run to the play-offs, but once again they failed to win promotion, going down 0-2 on aggregate to Charlton at the semi-final stage.

Ipswich and Norwich's first meeting of the 1998-89 campaign, on a Tuesday evening in October, was the first taste of an East Anglian derby for Bruce Rioch, the former Scotland World Cup star who had taken over as City manager. His predecessor, Mike Walker, had departed after spending the entire 1997-98 season in the lower half of the table. Now, both clubs were in the top ten of the Nationwide Division One, and there was little to choose between them at Portman Road until the deadlock was broken on 53 minutes. Ipswich had not conceded in 410 minutes of football until Erik Fugelstad's cross was headed home by young Welshman Craig Bellamy. There was no further scoring, despite Scowcroft and Iwan Roberts both striking the woodwork, and Norwich celebrated a measure of revenge for the 0-5 drubbing eight months earlier. Some visiting fans evidently celebrated a little too much and the local press reported extensive damage to property and outbreaks of fighting in local streets. These reports were highly exaggerated according to a writer in the City fanzine 'Man Utd are on the Tele Again': 'I'm not going to pretend to be one of those fans who relishes the ugly side of football in local derbies, so unwelcome memories of some of the violence at this fixture in recent years flashed through my mind as we entered Suffolk. However, there is nothing I want more from a season than a glorious campaign and beating those bastards twice. This match was perfect, the atmosphere intense – despite their fans being a little quiet – and despite sensational local newspaper reports, very little trouble except some smashed toilets. For once the rival teams slugging it out on the pitch made the news, rather than the rival fans outside Ipswich station. Which made for, in my opinion, the most enjoyable City game seen since we were in Europe.'

Most fans love an intense atmosphere, but agree it is a shame when local derby passion spills over into violence of any sort. Norwich fan Graeme Davies touched on this point when recalling Norwich's 1-0 win in 1998: 'The East Anglian derby is normally played in an atmosphere of unbridled hatred, and it is usually the team that wants to win the most on the day that prevails, regardless of current form. Drawn derbies are rare. Also, the attitude of supporters at derbies often spreads to the players on the pitch. I've come to appreciate that for us to win the game we have to hate them more than they hate us. It's because I can sense the mood in the visiting fans' area that I can predict the probable outcome. If it's too relaxed I know I need to worry. If it's tense and downright nasty then I get a sudden surge of confidence. In more reflective moments I know that such behaviour is no real cause for pride. I've never been involved in hooliganism, nor do I wish to condone it, but when I'm at a derby I know the atmosphere has to be aggressive for us to win. This particular match was a case in point.'

Revenge might have been sweet in October 1998, but after beating Ipswich the season didn't shape up as Rioch and Norwich would have wished. By the spring of 1999 they had slipped to halfway and it was Ipswich who were again challenging strongly for promotion, enjoying a return of 31 points from a possible 36. The return derby at Carrow Road on a Sunday afternoon in April saw Town in second place and desperate to hurdle the dreaded play-offs and gain automatic elevation. Nineteen-year-old goalkeeper Robert Green made his debut for City, and he did well in the red-hot atmosphere, playing a big part in the resulting 0-0 draw. Town were marginally the better side and were angry when referee Taylor halted Mick Stockwell in his tracks when he was about to score, unwilling to apply the advantage rule. Green covered himself in glory in the final minute, leaping to save David Johnson's firm downward header and ensuring the first draw between the two rivals in a competitive game for sixteen years. The season would end in more Ipswich heartbreak, this time Bolton inflicting an 'away-goals' defeat in the play-offs, following a 4-3 extra-time thriller at Portman Road.

# 15

# To Hell and Back in an Extraordinary Week

## (1999-2003)

Ipswich and Norwich's last confrontation of the 20th century was a goal-less bore which will go down as possibly the dullest East Anglian derby of them all. However, the single point gained in this sleepy Sunday lunchtime affair at Carrow Road in November 1999 was very welcome as far as City boss Bruce Rioch was concerned, for his side were clawing their way up the table after a poor start, their squad decimated by injuries. George Burley, on the other hand, had steered his men into the top six again, and to keep them there had recently extracted a promise of more cash for players from his chairman David Sheepshanks.

Mike Bacon of the *Green 'Un* warned Town fans beforehand that this game might not be pretty: 'Whereas at Manchester City and Blackburn [recently], Town fans were ready to accept, albeit grudgingly, just the one point from the two games because of the way the side played – at Carrow Road it will be about the result only.' Some fans reckoned the midday kick-off – on police orders – had a tranquilising effect on fans and players. Designed to minimise trouble, and nothing to do with Sky TV, the lunchtime start was roundly condemned by fans who regarded it as inconvenient. In a further measure to deflate trouble, Norwich kitted their staff in the away fans' refreshment huts in blue Ipswich shirts! Town fan Steve Curtis was not impressed:

'The ladies did not look comfortable in them and Town fans could see through this stunt.' And even with Delia Smith now on the board, the Norwich pies received a poor review from Curtis: 'Mine was lukewarm and the filling consisted of gravy and nothing else, not even a piece of gristle could be found. The pie was like the game – lacking in substance.'

The dodgy pies and poor fare on the field meant the fans had to find inspiration and amusement from other sources. Top marks for invention went to the Norwich fans who conceived of waving their car keys at Town's Gary Croft, awaiting sentencing for motoring offences, including driving while disqualified.

During the 1999-2000 season Bruce Rioch must have cast envious eyes towards his opposite number at Portman Road, who had money to spend on strengthening his squad. With Norwich battling debts of around £7 million, even the sale of local hero Darren Eadie to Leicester, plus cash windfalls from sell-on clauses involving Chris Sutton and Danny Mills, failed to loosen the Norwich purse strings. Eventually the situation became impossible as far as Rioch was concerned and in March 2000, shortly after the club chose to invest in its Academy rather than the first-team squad, he decided enough was enough. Poor results were also a factor and he quit, with the club's Director of Football, the former Ipswich favourite Bryan Hamilton, being placed in temporary charge. By a quirk of the fixture list, the first game of Hamilton's tenure would be the local derby at Portman Road against his former club.

Although the previous two derbies had been goalless yawns, there was a feeling this one might be different. BBC Suffolk sports reporter Terry Baxter and his counterpart at BBC Norfolk, Roy Waller, exchanged the usual banter in the build-up. Baxter chirped: 'Whenever we start to feel that things aren't going our way at Portman Road we only have to look north of the border to feel heaps better.' He said he'd heard Norwich were hoping to expand the Barclay End of their ground – not to house more fans but to improve the catering facilities: 'Some corporate clients are more interested in Delia's delights than the football on show.'

Although Ipswich lay second at the time, and Norwich a depressed fifteenth, not all Town fans were entirely happy with life. When the Town crowd was criticised in the local press for being too quiet, one of their number, Harry Crowther, hit back by saying many supporters disliked the team's current style of play, which lacked excitement: 'Think about how much it can cost a rural fan to attend at Portman Road. Apart from £14 to gain admission, which may take some people five hours to earn, there's the cost of transport, programmes, etc. Don't attack fans for not yelling. Make a visit to Portman Road more exciting instead.'

Prior to the game, fans of the two clubs staged a game of their own at the Gainsborough Sports Centre in Ipswich. The 'Punch Drunk' team won 4-1 against their Norwich counterparts, gaining revenge for earlier results.

Amid all the jollity of the big-match build-up, however, there was sadness at news of the death of 79-year-old Ron Ellis, a man Ipswich chairman Sheepshanks once described as 'our greatest fan and a fantastic servant to the club'. Ron's first game had been in 1935 – prior to which Ipswich and Norwich had only ever met in a handful of friendlies or Norfolk and Suffolk League fixtures. In his subsequent 65 years of following Town, Ron probably witnessed more East Anglian derby games than anyone else. As well as a devoted fan on the terraces, he would help the club on a voluntary basis by ferrying players' boots to his friend the cobbler, deliver the club's mail to the post office and give players and officials lifts to and from the station or ground after away games. A bachelor who devoted himself to football and cricket, he became a local legend for his incredible feats of memory. As well as helping journalists with facts and figures about Town, he would amuse players by answering with amazing accuracy any questions they could throw at him about their own careers and statistics. Car registration numbers and dates of birth were his specialities.

Naturally the media spotlight focused on Bryan Hamilton before the big game, and the new Norwich boss admitted he 'must be mad' for accepting the challenge: 'My wife Collette, kids and pals all think I'm crackers. The only explanation is that I'd like to help a very decent board of directors. I've worked for some prats in my time but certainly not here. I understand the high standards Bruce sets himself in management; he was at Arsenal and wants more of that level. Maybe Norwich couldn't match his ambitions. To be honest, I wanted one more go before settling for golf and gardening.' Hamilton's popularity among Norwich fans was already on shaky ground because of his Ipswich connections, and he didn't help things much by admitting: 'I hope Ipswich will finally be promoted this season. I am a fan of Ipswich, for they are a good side and pass the ball well and have some excellent players.'

Even the optimistic Hamilton cannot have expected the dream start he got as City manager. The Canaries made the better opening and within twenty minutes had grabbed a deserved lead. Ipswich could only clear a corner to the edge of the box, where Iwan Roberts fired in a shot which struck a defender and fooled keeper Richard Wright, who went the wrong way. Roberts' toothy grin was even wider when Norwich broke from defence and he grabbed his second goal. Kenny Dalglish's son Paul crossed for Roberts, who chested the ball down, turned inside Fabian Wilnis, and curled a beauty into the corner. Shell-shocked Ipswich withdrew record signing Marcus Stewart at half-time but couldn't find a winning combination and by the end looked far from promotion material, despite still retaining second place in the table.

Town defender Mark Venus was frank in his message for fans after the game: 'We let you down. No messing, no excuses, no rubbish. We let ourselves, the whole club and, most importantly, we let the fans down. I don't think I've ever seen everyone at the club so low. It was a rank bad performance.' He said Norwich probably wouldn't play any better all season, but that was no consolation. He'd felt sick when he got home and couldn't stomach any dinner, watch football on TV or even sleep properly. 'We don't just drive home and forget all about it. It hurts us just as badly [as the fans], believe me.' Manager Burley made the team watch the entire video of the game, something he'd never done before. There was reportedly 'shouting and arguing' during this session as everyone had their say. A furious Burley called it the worst display of the season and within days he'd plunged into the transfer market for Dutch forward Martijn Reuser on loan from Vitesse Arnhem.'

Ipswich fans were devastated by the defeat. P Lillistone of Battisford reckoned it was the worst derby display in thirty years by Town and he accused the players of lacking passion and 'bottling it' on the big day. The *Green 'Un* called it 'one of the most extraordinary weeks in East Anglian football. The two managers have experienced every emotion possible as their sides have taken them to hell and back. Burley looked and sounded like a man at the end of his tether after the game; usually such a calm character, he was almost shaking with rage.' The editor reported that his postbag had been bursting that week with many fans writing for the first time to complain about the display. One, Steve Curtis, said upon returning to work he found his desk awaiting him covered in yellow and green bunting and Delia Smith cookbooks, the work of two City supporters in his office.

The inquests at Ipswich seemed to have a positive effect, for Town bounced back to win at Tranmere a few days later, finishing the season in third place and making the play-offs for a fourth successive season. This time, at last, it would end in smiles, with Barnsley being beaten in a 4-2 Wembley thriller. Top-flight football would be back at Portman Road in August 2000 after a five-year gap. Norwich followed the derby win with a miserable home defeat by bottom-of-the-table Swindon, and their season petered out to a mid-table finish. The mood of the fans at either end of the A140 couldn't have been more contrasting.

In the spring of 2000 one of Norwich's most popular figures from the past, winger Dale Gordon, 'did the unthinkable' and joined the payroll of Ipswich Town. He quit his position as manager of local side Gorleston to set up an ITFC Academy in nearby Lowestoft. Gordon, who had left Norwich for Glasgow Rangers in 1991, had been one of the many stars sold for big money during the Robert Chase era. Born on the Norfolk coast, he'd scored 43 goals in 248 appearances for the Canaries, but few of his admirers realised that as a boy he'd been an avid Ipswich fan, or that Paul Mariner had been his personal hero: 'I will always remember Mick Mills lifting the FA Cup in 1978 and being sat at home in full Ipswich kit, with the flag and everything. [After joining Norwich] I remember sitting on the bench outside the training ground at Trowse with my Ipswich kit on. John Bond came by and gave me an unbelievable amount of stick. It seems funny now. I was an Ipswich supporter, it didn't mean anything to me. It was different at that time, not as intense as it is now.'

Around this time, Ipswich Town gained two new nicknames, one which would become 'official' and the other strictly for derogatory use by Norwich fans only. Previously, the club had never had a distinctive nickname, usually being known as 'Town' or occasionally 'Superblues'. However, the story goes that an impromptu chant by Leeds fans put this matter right and a new nickname was born.

The occasion was the Premiership fixture at Leeds in September 2000 in which Ipswich fell behind early on to a Lee Bowyer goal. To the tune of the Pet Shop Boys' hit *Go West*, the Leeds fans started taunting their Ipswich counterparts by chanting 'No noise from the Tractor Boys'. Later in the game, goals by James Scowcroft and Jermaine Wright saw the visiting fans amend these lyrics for their own use – '2-1 to the Tractor Boys'. Initially some supporters were dubious about being known as Tractor Boys (which had been intended as an insult by the Leeds fans) but slowly it caught on, and before the long the club gave it an official seal of approval.

The 'other' nickname certainly didn't get any seal of approval. Ipswich fans' habit of speaking of 'Budgies' instead of 'Canaries', when referring to Norwich, was bound to one day lead to an equivalent. The term 'Binmen' eventually got the vote at Norwich and filled this gap. It was a reference to an episode of the TV drama *Lovejoy*, during which a council refuse collector rescued blue and white Ipswich favours from a dustbin and started wearing them.

Ipswich enjoyed a fine return to the top flight, finishing 2000-01 an impressive fifth and qualifying for Europe. Norwich, toiling in the lower half of the First Division, were desperate for promotion, but this was looking a distant dream. In early December the directors allowed Bryan Hamilton to invest in Manchester United striker Alex Notman, but when Notman's debut ended with City's fifth successive defeat, a weary Hamilton decided to resign. Coach Nigel Worthington took over, initially as caretaker, later landing the role full-time. Hamilton revealed that part of the problem was his unpopularity with the supporters:

'It was all down to a hard core of disaffected fans and a hostile press. I decided to walk away rather than sour three years with a smashing club. Fortunately, I'm at a stage in life where I can pick and choose what I do. I'm not sorry I had a go with Norwich, and I'm convinced we'd have become promotion candidates with patience. Some people weren't prepared to wait – they were probably sore about our neighbours Ipswich

doing so well. I'm not the sort to hang around when I feel unwanted –
even by a smallish group with undue influence.'

Iwan Roberts, the Norwich folk-hero whose goals had got Hamilton's
tenure off to such a great start, reflected later: 'He was a nice enough
man, but I never saw eye-to-eye with him. At the end of the day Bryan's
an Ipswich man. After he got the sack here he went to Ipswich and the
first thing he said was 'I'm back where I belong.' Frankly I couldn't agree
more.'

The Norwich fans had clearly turned on Hamilton, due to his Ipswich
background, and they soon had another figure upon whom to direct similar ire. Goalkeeper Andy Marshall moved to Ipswich in the summer of
2001 after more than 200 games for Norwich. The move went down like
a lead balloon in Norfolk. Supporter Ian Lindsay pointed out that
although Marshall had won the most recent Player of the Year award, his
'cocky attitude' had annoyed many City fans.

Bryan Gunn, Marshall's predecessor as Norwich goalkeeper, commented: 'I wouldn't have considered doing that [moving to Ipswich]. Not
in my time, because we were in a higher position than Ipswich. I can't
remember Ipswich being above us in the League during my time here.
Andy probably left under different circumstances, because he wanted to
play in the Premiership, and unfortunately Norwich couldn't have offered
him that opportunity. The only offer that he had was to go down to
Ipswich. He made a professional decision and it's just like anyone out
there looking to move jobs. He might have to go to the nearest competitor but he's probably going to get double the salary, an opportunity to set
up his family for life. You can't really give him too much stick for that.'

The *Evening Standard* columnist Mick Dennis, a Norwich fan, reckoned
Marshall's move was 'an act of betrayal' which defied reason. 'Does he
not realise that walking out on the club who nurtured him to join the
hated but (temporarily) more successful neighbours means that he will
not be able to go out socially without being abused by supporters who
feel that his move is a personal and particularly hurtful slight? Fans who
worshipped him now abhor him.'

During 2001-02 Ipswich tumbled from their previous season's lofty
fifth into the relegation mire. The writing was on the wall after a crucial
six-pointer was lost at Bolton, the home side scoring four in the first half.
Norwich were even partly to blame for this, according to one Town fan:
'The defence was a mess, Andy Marshall was at his flapping and mis-
kicking worst – never trust an ex-Norwich player – and up front and in
midfield players looked badly out of sorts.' Town finished eighteenth and
were relegated along with Derby and Leicester.

The blow to Ipswich of demotion in April 2002 was cushioned for their fans when Norwich missed out on promotion, the Canaries losing on penalties in the play-off final at Cardiff to Steve Bruce's Birmingham City. It had been Norwich's best season since the early 1990s, and hope was restored that manager Nigel Worthington was building a side capable of taking the club back to the top. The sixth-placed finish in Division One had been followed by a thrilling play-off semi-final victory over Wolves to set up the Cardiff showdown. In the Millennium Stadium, Welshman Iwan Roberts' extra-time goal was cancelled out by Geoff Horsfield, creating the penalty shoot-out, won by Birmingham after Daryl Sutch and Phil Mulryne missed their kicks. An estimated 32,000 Norwich fans had a wonderful day out – barring the result – enjoying the superb atmosphere created by a 70,000-plus crowd.

So, East Anglian derbies were back on the agenda for 2002-03, albeit in English football's second flight. The shenanigans commenced in the days before the first sell-out clash in September, at Portman Road, with Suffolk CID called in to investigate the theft of 245 match tickets. These were part of Norwich's 2,200 allocation sent by courier, but found to be missing when the sealed package was opened at Carrow Road. Police believed the tickets had found their way to the black market. Ipswich reprinted the missing tickets and barred entry to anybody holding the stolen ones.

Meanwhile Ipswich appeared to gag goalkeeper Marshall after being swamped with requests for press interviews with the former Norwich man, who would be making his first appearance against his old mates. The motive seemed to be to protect Marshall and minimise the antagonism being stirred up against him for being a 'turncoat'. It wasn't a blanket ban, for Marshall was quoted in one paper: 'I'm in quite a unique position because I've played in an East Anglian derby from the other side of the fence. The atmosphere will be electric. Portman Road is an amazing place now, although it has always had a great buzz about it. But now the fans are turning it into a cauldron, especially with the redeveloped stands. I haven't been to many derby games around the country but the East Anglian clash is right there at the top as far as I'm concerned. In any walk of life you keep in touch with old friends, but on the pitch I won't have any time for the likes of Mackay and Green. They are the enemy from kick-off and my only friends are those wearing the blue shirts.'

George Burley tried to defuse some of the tension: 'I think it would be nice if both teams went up [this season]. We have not had a derby for a while. They are so special and hopefully we can turn in the sort of display we are capable of.' Town striker Darren Bent was full of confidence, saying he couldn't remember losing to Norwich, and in around six games at youth level he'd hit about fifteen goals against them.

Live Sky coverage and a Sunday lunchtime start were once again part of the mix, but this time there was a noticeably more noisy atmosphere than at recent derbies. Although Ipswich saw more of the ball, particularly in a tense final ten minutes, Norwich carved out the better chances. Marshall, jeered mercilessly by visiting fans, was relieved when Paul McVeigh's ambitious forty-yarder drifted wide. Marshall also failed to get to a Iwan Roberts header, which crashed against the bar. Then he had to push away a Roberts right-foot effort.

Worthington's men took the lead in the second half, to silence most of the 29,122 crowd, Ipswich's biggest for a decade. Marshall was buffeted by Roberts, allowing McVeigh to cross and defender Malky Mackay to net. Town's pressure finally paid off in a dramatic finale when, three minutes into stoppage time, Adam Drury handled a Pablo Counago cross. City's Paul Heckingbottom was booked for holding up play for two minutes with supposed cramp before teenager Bent took the spot-kick and hit the post. Darren Ambrose volleyed the rebound back into the danger area and Counago swooped to score from close range. The roar of relief must have been heard miles away.

Joy was so unconfined that Ipswich fans invaded the pitch – a very rare event at Portman Road. Stewards ushered them off, but not before a handful had jostled and abused certain Norwich players. The incident was reported to the FA. Burley tried to play down the trouble: 'There was a lot of hype about the match. The stewards got the fans off the pitch very quickly and I don't think any harm was done. It is one of those things that can happen in derbies.'

Burley was right to suggest that people act in uncharacteristic fashion, due to the passions of a local derby. A Town fan known as 'Bracknell Blue' was apparently shocked by the reaction of his small son to Town's equaliser: 'When Pablo equalised in injury-time, my son aged nine rushed down the stand, cheering, screaming and then shouting abuse at the nearest Budgie player. I just sat there open-mouthed. I never trained him, it's just genetic I guess. He even went up to a Budgie in the street, of a similar age, and gave him a real verbal volley, and he's usually very quiet and shy.'

This 1-1 draw had a sad postscript for City forward Alex Notman, as he was later forced to retire aged only 23, on account of a freak injury suffered in this game. The Scot, who cost £250,000 from Manchester United, damaged an ankle in blocking a venomous free-kick from Mark Venus. To make matters worse, as he was stretchered off he was shown a yellow card for encroaching from the wall. The injury would require surgery but the damage could not be fully repaired and poor Notman's career was over. He recalled:

'To be honest I almost wish I'd let the shot go now – and I certainly wish I hadn't broken out of the wall so quickly. I wouldn't have got a yellow card, and more importantly probably wouldn't have got the injury either. That was the fourth time I'd done my ankle and as soon as the ball hit it I knew straight away that there was a problem. You don't think you should get injured when the ball hits you, but Venus has got a very hard shot. I just jumped up and the ball hit me on the ankle and it twisted round. It was very painful and to add insult to injury the referee gave me a yellow card because he reckoned I had broken out of the wall too soon. I was also getting a bit of stick from the Ipswich fans when they took me off on a stretcher. They obviously felt I was making a meal of it, but what has happened since has proved that I wasn't.'

The correspondent from the *Independent* found the match a fascinating example of how derby games generate almost illogical levels of passion. He reckoned: 'Something about local derby matches affects supporters as if they are kids on the last day of term. They behave as if normal rules don't fully apply, as if the whole occasion forms one extenuating circumstance. It is possible that the Birmingham fan who taunted Villa's keeper for his [recent] second-half blunder by making obscene gestures in front of him and then patting him on the cheek, believed he was being no more than playful. But such befuddled initiatives can often engender ugly consequences. Ipswich fans staged their own pitch invasion after the 93rd-minute penalty, and the visiting defender Darren Kenton was taunted in a similar fashion. Now Ipswich don't do pitch invasions. A long-standing season ticket holder who watched the match could not recall another occasion when the Portman Road faithful had overstepped the mark in such a fashion.

'Why are derby matches so important to supporters? The idea of territorial supremacy or local bragging rights may be at the heart of it for many. For those who support rival teams in the same town or city, losing to a neighbour prefigures a more enduring torment of the kind for which the Villa fan was preparing himself. But it is more than that. Like Ipswich, Watford are a club who traditionally provide one of the game's peaceable havens. Trouble flared there earlier this month, however, during a match against Luton Town. Watford is in Hertfordshire; Luton in Bedfordshire. This, though, is the closest thing either club has to a derby match. If the only football teams in Britain were Land's End Rovers and John O'Groats Athletic, they would be local rivals.

'I remember watching Luton play at Vicarage Road as a schoolboy in the days when Bruce Rioch was a promising young midfielder for them. It was one of the ugliest matches I can recall and the atmosphere around the ground was evil. The same flexible geographic principle operates in East Anglia with Ipswich and Norwich. After the latter team had been excruciatingly beaten by Birmingham City in last season's First Division play-off final at the Millennium Stadium, missing out on penalties after extra-time, their fans were left to queue in desolation at Cardiff station for specially chartered trains home. Conversation was, as you might expect, subdued. But then, one of the green and yellow horde found a comforting form of words as he looked ahead to a fixture list that would now include their relegated rivals. "We'll bloody smash Ipswich next season, anyway," he said. "Smash 'em." The mood brightened. The long, impending journey east was becoming something that could be borne with equanimity. Everybody needs somebody to hate. We're all happier that way.'

Less than a month later, Ipswich slumped into the bottom three after a lifeless 0-3 defeat at Grimsby, a result which prompted the shock sacking of George Burley after eight years in charge. Just seventeen months earlier he'd been the Premiership's Manager of the Year. Ipswich were now in disarray, saddled by huge debts following relegation from the top flight and losing vast sums by the week, thanks to the huge 'Premiership salaries' being paid to most of the staff – including, no doubt, Mr Burley. At that time Norwich were up in the division's top three, which intensified the grim mood south of the border.

Before long, the leading candidate for Burley's job emerged as the currently unemployed former Everton and Manchester City manager Joe Royle – whose CV also included the small matter of having played for Norwich. After a depressing home defeat by Gillingham, disgruntled Town fans, seizing on the fact that Royle was an ex-Canary, staged an after-match protest against his impending appointment. It wasn't as if Royle had spent a huge part of his life or career in Norfolk (just 42 League games in two seasons), but simply having worn the yellow and green was clearly enough to cause the antipathy.

Once Royle's name was confirmed, on 28 October, he announced he was ready to face down his critics and win over the doubters: 'If people who aren't happy with my appointment want to meet me, I'd have no problem with that. From what I've been told, there was just a feeling of frustration on Saturday [v Gillingham]. I think the Norwich thing is a factor, although I was also alleged to have once said Ipswich was a small town. My message to the fans is give us a little bit of time.'

Would Royle win over his critics, as defectors Trevor Putney and Keith Bertschin once had, or would he forever remain a 'Judas', as per Bryan Hamilton? Only time would tell.

# 16

# 'LET'S BE HAVING YOU!'

## (2003-05)

As the winter set in during the 2002-03 season, it was becoming clear that Norwich had survived the icy chills of their financial crisis and were building impressively for the future. For Ipswich, however, the battle to overcome mounting debts was only just beginning. In January 2003, Delia Smith announced via the *Evening Standard* that she was abandoning her TV career and recipe books to concentrate fully on being a Norwich City director and running her catering empire at Carrow Road. Meanwhile, on the field, both Ipswich and Norwich established themselves in the top ten of Division One soon after the Christmas holiday period, so that their meeting at Carrow Road in March 2003 was inevitably labelled a 'six pointer' in terms of the play-off chase.

Events would lead to this game being dubbed 'The Dean Bowditch Derby'. Supporters will forgive players almost anything, if at some time they can make a lasting impact in the furnace of a local derby. Some never manage it, but Bowditch did the trick at the age of just sixteen, with his very first involvement in senior football. After seventy hectic but goalless minutes, Joe Royle sent on sub Bowditch and within sixty seconds the deadlock had been broken. Bowditch's first touch put him clear, as defender Craig Fleming crumpled with a foot injury that would see him ferried to hospital. Bowditch laid the ball back and, in the bagatelle that followed, Fabian Wilnis rifled home. In injury-time, as Norwich piled men forward, Bowditch launched a breakaway raid which Bent completed with a fine low shot.

Bowditch was in dreamland. At sixteen, he'd not even been given a squad number until a few days previously, and certainly never expected such a baptism of fire: 'The boss told me to go out there and enjoy it, and I was standing there waiting to go on, and standing there, and standing there. I couldn't wait to get going but the ball wouldn't go out of play. I must have been waiting for five minutes or so and in the end I was almost pleading for someone, anyone to knock the ball off so I could get on. I got the ball straight away and their right-back fell over so I thought "that's not my problem" and raced on with it. When Fabian Wilnis put the ball in the net, at first I wasn't sure what to do. Then I could see the Ipswich fans going crazy so I thought "that's a good idea – I'll join them".'

It was certainly a day to cherish for the blue folk – their first win at Carrow Road for eleven long years – and a sweet occasion for Andy Marshall in particular, who kept a clean sheet despite a torrent of abuse from the home fans. One of the longest faces to be seen among Norwich people was that of veteran radio broadcaster Roy Waller. The result meant he had lost a public bet and would spend the week sporting an Ipswich shirt in public.

There was much discussion after the game about how, just as Darren Bent was composing himself to shoot Ipswich's second goal, the Carrow Road announcer decided to interrupt proceedings. The *Green 'Un*'s Elvin King said: ' A cynic would suggest Norwich were attempting something underhand. Surely this was not the case and Darren Bent admitted he heard nothing. But if the chance had been missed and Norwich had equalised it would have proved a very embarrassing situation for the Canaries.'

Bent admitted: 'So many people have asked me about it and wondered whether it put me off. But to be truthful I never heard a thing. I was focused on putting the ball into the net. City's media spokesman, Joe Ferrari, added: 'At any given time in any game, control room announcements dealing with crowd safety matters will be issued on the advice of police. Late in the game against Ipswich, two such announcements were made.'

The defeat left Norwich seventh with thirteen games to go, but they failed to recapture the consistency of earlier in the season and ended up eighth, five points adrift of the play-off zone. Meanwhile, the three points won at Carrow Road pushed Ipswich up to eighth, a remarkable rise, having been as low as twentieth in the autumn. Town were stronger in the run-in than City and overtook them, but also fell short of the play-offs by a handful of points. It left the two rivals among the hot favourites to do well in 2003-04 season, alongside the likes of relegated West Ham and West Brom.

Sure enough, 2003-04 proved a thrilling season in East Anglia, with Ipswich and Norwich both in Division One's top four as Christmas loomed. Both looked strong enough to maintain a challenge for promotion to the Premiership and the Portman Road derby on the Sunday prior to Christmas aroused enormous interest. In his autobiography *All I Want for Christmas*, popular Norwich striker Iwan Roberts recalled his thoughts that week: 'A very special week for everyone at the club. The gaffer will try and play everything down by saying it's just another game, because he wants the lads to relax. But everyone knows what a huge match it is – the biggest of the season. [While out Christmas shopping] people wish me all the best for Sunday and plead with me to make sure we beat Ipswich. It's at times like this you see just how much people care and you realise what a big effect you have on people's lives. The gaffer might play it cool by telling the press it's just another game, but believe me we all know it's anything but. I would take a point right now: anything rather than lose and ruin everyone's holiday. Joe Royle's been mouthing off on the radio, saying that Ipswich have too much pace for us to cope with and that will be enough for them to go on and win the game. The last thing the gaffer says to us is – to go out there and ram his words down his throat.'

It was another of those dreaded, unpopular Sunday lunchtime kick-offs, but there was no shortage of atmosphere as a crowd in excess of 30,000 assembled. Norwich fans were aware this could turn into a real party if City won, for the three points would put them top of the division for the first time that season – and right in front of the old enemy too.

Canaries boss Nigel Worthington boldly fielded a new strike-force for the game, his two new signings Leon McKenzie (Peterborough) and Matt Svensson (Charlton) making their debuts. Although it was Joe Royle's men who started the brighter, creating more chances and forcing several good saves from Robert Green, first blood went to the Canaries on 37 minutes. New-boy McKenzie was the hero of the hour. Following a half-cleared free-kick, Kelvin Davis scrambled desperately for the loose ball, but the unmarked McKenzie swivelled to clout home a half-volley from close range. The 2,200 away fans, already out-singing the home contingent, went into overdrive. After the break the tension mounted and there was an ugly flashpoint as Svensson and sub Richard Naylor clashed, provoking a brawl. Town's Darren Bent went agonisingly close to an equaliser, Green foiling him when clean through. Town's frustration turned to despondency with less than fifteen minutes left, when McKenzie clinched a marvellous win for Norwich. Gary Holt floated over a fine cross and McKenzie looped a header over Davis.

City fans could hardly take it all in. They'd avenged the 0-2 home defeat earlier in 2003, beaten the local enemy on their own turf, and taken over at the top of the table – all in one fell swoop. It didn't get much sweeter than this. One of their number that afternoon was Karen Buchanan, former editor of esteemed football magazine *FourFourTwo*. She recalled: 'It's my favourite ever Norwich City memory. In fact, it's one of my favourite ever memories. One of the absolute best days of my life. I would like to pay special tribute to the stewards that day, who kept us in for a full thirty minutes afterwards. Without their consideration we'd never have got to see [directors] Delia, Michael, Roger *et al* dancing on the pitch and genuflecting at us. I don't think I've ever been as ecstatic, before or since. The memories of our board of directors taking over the 'Portaloo Road' pitch and dancing for us will live with me for a lifetime.'

Veteran Iwan Roberts, who'd come on as sub, shared the fans' enthusiasm for the occasion. He recalled: 'We had a few chances to go top of the League before and had not taken them. How ironic that we should finally do it [at Ipswich]. Ask any Norwich supporter and they'd say we couldn't have done it better. We have played better, but we ground it out and defended superbly.'

The result meant a miserable Christmas for Town fans, and for one in a particular it was a painful experience, mentally and physically. Tom Kay was a disc jockey at the Yarmouth and Lowestoft radio station 'The Beach'. He explained: 'I've been a blue all my life but I serve an area where about 60 per cent of listeners are yellows. Whenever there's an opportunity I try to wind the Canaries fans up and gloated for many months after Ipswich beat them in the March 2003 derby. I'm also fond of "accidentally" switching off our sports presenter's microphone whenever there's some not so positive Ipswich news. With Canaries supporters taking this abuse for several years I thought maybe I wasn't being fair, so decided to put my neck on the line and make a pledge that if Norwich beat Ipswich in the December derby I'd have "NCFC" tattooed on my bottom live on air. As we all know, Norwich beat Ipswich 2-0 and the following day listeners jammed the switchboard asking when it would happen. We booked the local tattooist, who arrived at the studio with the sharpest of needles and I spent an agonising fifteen minutes being engraved, with whimpers and screams transmitted across the region. We received so many calls from listeners reckoning it was just a set-up that after the show I drove to all the major east coast towns parading my bottom and charging listeners a quid to touch it, donating the cash to the radio station's 'Help An East Coast Child' appeal. Ever since then, people still grab me in the street and ask to see the tattoo. I even got stopped by a Canary fan policeman who wanted a look.'

Norwich didn't look back after the win at Portman Road, remaining top of the division for the rest of the season, and lifting the championship by an eight-point margin from Gary Megson's West Brom. Fifteen of the 22 games after Portman Road were won, including the return with Ipswich in early March 2004. It was City's first League double over Town for seven years and even the most partisan Ipswich supporters couldn't dispute who owned local bragging rights now.

A capacity crowd of 23,942 created a stirring atmosphere at the return game and, in time-honoured local derby fashion, it started at breakneck speed, tackles flying in from all angles. Town skipper Jim Magilton needed treatment in the first minute after a heavy challenge, and his teammate Drissa Diallo was booked for a bad tackle as chances were created and spurned at both ends. Ian Westlake and Bent both hit the woodwork as Ipswich ended the first half ahead on points. Roberts, again a sub that day, recalls that the half-time break featured a dramatic intervention in the Norwich dressing room by manager Nigel Worthington: 'The gaffer doesn't lose his cool too often, but I've never seen him lose it in quite the spectacular way he does [here]. He gives you the full hair-dryer treatment, goes absolutely mad and has every right to.'

Red-faced Worthington got the response he demanded, and after the interval the game changed completely. The champions-elect took the lead on fifty minutes when defender Mackay was left unmarked to head in a free-kick. Nine minutes later it was Mackay again, netting from close-range after venturing up for another free-kick. With sixteen minutes left Diallo hauled down the dangerous Darren Huckerby and was shown a red card.

Ten-man Ipswich gave themselves hope on 86 minutes when Tommy Miller netted from the spot after a push on Richard Naylor. But Norwich's anxiety was quickly dispelled when a Huckerby shot flew past Kelvin Davis after striking a defender. The 3-1 win left City three points clear at the top with a game in hand, but sent Ipswich sliding out of the top six. It was a bitter pill to swallow in Suffolk and after Fabian Wilnis told reporters he felt Norwich would not survive if they got promoted, Roberts responded: 'It seems they all drink wine made from sour grapes over at Portman Road now.'

Town recovered their composure with a run of six wins from seven games shortly after the derby defeat to reach the play-offs once again. However, a 1-2 aggregate defeat by West Ham saw them fail to accompany jubilant Norwich into the Premiership for 2004-05. Town fans were once again left feeling they were stuck in a sort of 'no man's land' twixt Premiership and First Division. In the past eight years the club had suffered four play-off defeats, one promotion and one relegation.

With Norwich taking their place among the elite, the only local derby on offer during 2004-05 was in the nationwide Masters Tournament, in which a team of Town old boys met Norwich counterparts. The game ended 2-2 with Jason Dozzell and Steve McGavin on target for Town and Robert Fleck and Peter Mendham for City.

Earlier on, in the absence of a true local derby, a few Norwich fans made their way to Portman Road to see their former hero Iwan Roberts playing against Ipswich for his new club Gillingham. Roberts, making his

debut as the Gills player-coach, responded to the cheers of his own special fan club by getting stuck in early – and was booked after only thirty
seconds following a foul on Diallo. The Norwich fans defended their
decision to go into 'enemy territory' on the grounds that City had no
game that day.

Boosted by the goals of Darren Bent and Shefki Kuqi, Ipswich spent
virtually the entire 2004-05 season in the top three of the newly named
Championship, ultimately coming a cropper yet again in the play-offs.
West Ham again did the damage and sentenced them to another season
(at least) in the second tier. Ipswich had finished twelve points ahead of
the Hammers, but were unable to beat them on the two occasions it
counted most. Before the first leg, the *EADT* told the tale of an Ipswich
fan who suffers the perils of living deep inside Norwich territory. David
Street of Poringland apparently received his tickets for the West Ham
game through the mail, complete with a message scribbled on the back
of the envelope by person or persons unknown: 'Tickets to the Ipswich
Town "Not Going Up Again" party enclosed. Yellow Army'

Yet another play-off defeat was hugely depressing, but at least Town
fans had enjoyed a good laugh earlier, when Delia Smith made a much-
publicised intervention on the pitch at Carrow Road. With her beloved
Canaries two goals down to Manchester City and staring relegation in the
face, Delia decided the home crowd needed rousing. She strode on the
pitch at half-time and grabbed a microphone: 'A message for the best
football supporters in the world,' she boomed. 'We need a twelfth man
here. Where are you? Where are you? Come on! Let's be having you!'

The moment was captured by TV cameras and a disbelieving nation
later watched the news bulletins wide-eyed as this normally composed
and restrained 63-year-old showed a brand new side of her personality.
The faux Cockney persona she'd seemingly adopted (dropping her
'haitches' and 'gees' in the word 'having'), was particularly fascinating and
many observers wondered whether she'd indulged in too many of the
armagnac prunes in her stadium restaurant.

On the other hand, plenty of others applauded such a passionate
show of commitment to the City cause. Down in Ipswich, her profile as
a target for fun was raised sky-high. Her intervention ultimately backfired
because the crowd was no less subdued in the second half, especially
when Norwich were reduced to ten men and the visitors took all three
points with an injury-time goal. Relegation ensued, and Norwich found
themselves back alongside Ipswich after just one season away.

Earlier in the season Delia Smith had also unwittingly made news in
East Anglia, following an incident involving Ipswich fans at Cambridge

railway station. A spokesman reported that a number of supporters had complained and refused to board a train because it bore Delia's name. The fans were trying to get from Cambridge to Ipswich to see the home match with Brighton but refused to board Anglia's Delia Smith service. The train operator explained it had a number of trains named after local celebrities, including the former Ipswich manager Sir Alf Ramsey, but unfortunately that particular one had been busy elsewhere.

Norwich's relegation and Town's play-off failure at least meant both sets of fans could take comfort from the return of their favourite fixture. The build-up to the first of the 2005-06 derbies effectively began the moment it was clear they would be playing in the same division. Website message-boards and other communications paraphernalia were soon bursting with messages of mutual 'goodwill'. A Norfolk farmer received publicity for creating a 'Norwich City Maze' on his land, in which he no doubt planned to 'lose' any Ipswich visitors. And Anglia TV joined in the summer's fun by introducing a bizarre new quiz show called *Sportyfacts*. Set in what appeared to be a courtroom, presided over by a 'judge', teams representing Ipswich and Norwich battled it out. John Wark's side beat Bryan Gunn's by 19-18.

# 17

# ENTER 'THE CANARY CRUSHER'

## (2005-07)

After a local derby hiatus of 12 months, Ipswich and Norwich prepared for battle again at Championship level in mid-September 2005. It had been a lively summer, to say the least, with London awarded the 2012 Olympics, the outrage of the tube and bus bombings the following day, and the thrilling Ashes win over Australia all combining to take our minds off the forthcoming football season.

Nevertheless, Norwich sold a record 20,200 season tickets for 2005-06, meaning the prospect of many more sell-out games at Carrow Road was on the cards, despite relegation out of the Premiership. In fact, up to the end of 2004-05 season, City had managed capacity crowds at 65 of the last 70 home league games, a record many clubs looked upon with envy. Chairman Roger Munby urged fans to overcome their relegation blues, claiming the club had made genuine progress in recent times, and although a number of players left in the summer, crowd favourites like Darren Huckerby stayed put and there was genuine hope the Canaries could bounce back at the first attempt.

This optimism evaporated very early in proceedings, however. With Coventry's new Ricoh stadium not ready for action, there were amendments to the fixture list and Norwich started the new campaign with four of their first five league games at home. It was a great opportunity to get points on the board early, but City blew it in a big way. After half a dozen fixtures had passed, they were still waiting to chalk up a first win.

South of the border, Ipswich were faring only marginally better, and clearly had problems of their own. Town fans were appalled by the pre-season player sales at Portman Road, which were said to have ripped the heart out of the team. The lethal strike partnership of Darren Bent and Shefki Kuqi, goalkeeper Kelvin Davis, midfielder Tommy Miller and striker Pablo Couango – 502 appearances and 140 goals between them – all departed. To make matters worse, their replacements looked woefully inadequate. There was some sympathy over the restrictions being imposed on manager Joe Royle, but most fans would settle for nothing less than a promotion chase. To the neutral eye, mid-table mediocrity was on the cards at Portman Road for 2005-06 – and so it would prove.

The two troubled neighbours prepared for their first derby meeting of the season woefully short of confidence and optimism. In fact, both seemed to be dreading the occasion. Ipswich were badly hit by injuries and still reeling from a demoralising 0-4 home drubbing by mid-table Preston, while Norwich remained winless and looked ill-at-ease with life in their new Championship surroundings. Some local pundits called it the 'least heralded local derby of recent years', although the fans gave it the seal of approval with a bumper 29,184 turn-out, despite the midday Sunday kick-off. With Sky's live TV cameras opting to go elsewhere, here was proof that this unpopular kick-off time was purely designed to suit the police and not down to TV scheduling.

Many fans yearned for a return to the traditional 3pm-on-a-Saturday routine. A *Pink 'Un* columnist spoke for many when he complained: 'When it was a 3pm or night kick-off, you could spend the whole day soaking up the atmosphere and getting into it. Now we get dragged down there for some banal early kick-off on a Sunday. We are herded from the station to the ground, and back again. And while the noise levels at Portman Road have always been discreet at best, the last few times we have been down there the home fans have been obscenely quiet. You can't help but feel they miss the later kick-off times as well. It's all very well the police saying they do it for security reasons, but surely we have served our time now, and a sensible start time should be brought back onto the agenda. I don't know whether the Drum and Monkey [pub] still exists, but I fantasise about going in there for a pre-match pint once again.'

Town boss Royle played in the East Anglian derby three times in the early 1980s for Norwich, and before then had first-hand experience of the famous Merseyside and Manchester contests. He was therefore ideally placed to comment on how our local contest measured up: 'When I first came down here I was surprised at the intensity of these derby games. But I can safely say that it means every bit as much to the supporters of Ipswich and Norwich as the derby games do to fans in Liverpool, Manchester or Glasgow. While we as professionals have to treat it the same as any other game, there is certainly more at stake for the fans, who want the East Anglian bragging rights. You can rest assured our players will certainly be up for the game.'

Town chairman David Sheepshanks was also keen to talk the game up, calling it 'The Big One' and announcing that Sir Bobby Robson would be a special guest at the match, as would two members of the Royal Anglian Regiment currently serving in Iraq, Town fan Lance Corporal Lewis Shenton and City fan Private John Pearce. It was unclear whether the two soldiers were seated together for the game, and whether war broke out between them if they were!

Norwich were coming to Portman Road on the back of their worst run of away form for 26 years – but they did have history on their side as far as this fixture was concerned. City had managed a positive result in each of their previous four visits to Suffolk, even though Nigel Worthington's men had failed to record a single away win in their last 22 League games. Their paltry tally of just seven points from a possible 66 in recent away games told a depressing story.

More than 200 police were drafted in to keep the peace as Norwich set about proving that recent form is irrelevant in the Old Farm derby. The mercurial Huckerby was left on the bench by City, but Worthington's decision would be justified shortly after half-time in dramatic fashion. At 0-0, and with Ipswich down to ten men, tricky Huckerby was thrown into the fray at the interval and announced his arrival in brilliant style. Gary Doherty's long ball saw Town's inexperienced keeper Lewis Price advance too far and get caught in no-man's-land, and Huckerby was able to dance round him and net with a superb finish. It proved to be the winner.

The game had already been marred by the early red card shown to Town full-back Sito Castro for a challenge on Kevin Lisbie, a decision which horrified and disrupted Ipswich. Referee Lee Mason's hasty decision seemed ludicrously harsh at the time, and sure enough was duly rescinded the following week – but that was little compensation for the Spaniard's family who'd flown in to see the match. A man short, Ipswich forced the pace for most of the game, coming close to an equaliser when Blackburn loanee James McEveley tried his luck from 30 yards, only to be foiled by the diving Robert Green. Kevin Horlock blasted another good Town chance over the bar and Huckerby also bungled an open goal attempt. Young McEveley was sampling his first East Anglian derby, as was fellow new signing Sam Parkin. The latter was struggling for form in attack and being mercilessly barracked by impatient sections of the home support.

This defeat left Ipswich 13th in the table and Norwich 17th, far lower than both clubs expected to find themselves even at this early stage, but City emerged with renewed confidence for the future, having ended their eighteen-month winless away run. The 140th East Anglian derby had certainly been no classic, but the fact that close to 30,000 people turned out on a Sunday lunchtime to watch two out-of-form sides proved that local derby fever remained as virulent as ever.

Afterwards City remained unbeaten over the next five games and by mid-October had caught Ipswich in mid-table, while Sheffield United happily romped clear at the top. Ipswich made early exits from both cup competitions, meaning their unhappy fans only had 180 minutes of cup action to enjoy all season – the lowest in 46 years. Even worse, by the turn of the year Town had sunk to the lower reaches of the division and looked to be heading for their lowest league finish in 46 years, too. Norwich slipped back again and, as winter set in, it was clear both clubs were under-achieving.

The return game at Carrow Road was scheduled for February 2006. As matchday loomed City were fretting over a run of five games without a win while Town were in slightly better shape, although still short on goal-power: they'd amassed just 34 goals in 33 games in all competitions, one of the worst records in the division. With last year's goal aces Bent and Kuqi now long gone, and their replacements Parkin and Forster mis-firing and injury-prone, manager Royle persuaded his cash-strapped boss-es to loosen the purse strings for a striker. He paid £100,000 in mid-January to Cardiff for feisty six-footer Alan Lee, a 27-year-old Irishman. Lee bagged two goals at Southampton in his second match for the club and his arrival immediately made Town more dangerous. City had also been looking lightweight in attack, having accepted a bid of £7.25 million from West Ham for leading scorer Dean Ashton shortly before the derby. Worthington signed West Brom's Rob Earnshaw for a third of the amount received for Ashton, and borrowed Charlton's Jonathan Johansson to fill the gap. This pair made their full debuts against Ipswich, along with another loanee, Fulham defender Zesh Rehman. Norwich fans were pleased to see change, but seething over the departure of the popular Ashton.

Another Sunday showdown saw the best crowd of the season click through the Carrow Road turnstiles, curious to see how City's new-look side would cope with a derby. It was the men in blue who looked the more dangerous early on, but Norwich who drew first blood. In the 33rd minute Johansson sprang the offside trap to finish with a right-foot lob over Price from the edge of the area. The cheers had barely died down when Ipswich drew level. Jimmy Juan's 25-yard free-kick flew just inside Green's right-hand post after taking a wicked deflection off City's defen-sive wall. Matt Richards hit a Norwich post and Johansson did likewise at the other end as tempers began to fray towards the end with Ipswich well on top. It was a game they always deserved to win, the home defence decidedly uncomfortable against the physical presence of Lee and the pace of young sub Danny Haynes, who came on early. It was this duo who manufactured a dramatic winner two minutes from time. Richards' cross from the left was headed back across the goal by Lee, and Haynes bundled the ball into goal, with defender Doherty appearing to get the last touch. TV replays proved Haynes directed the ball with his arm rather than his head, a fact missed by many in the initial blur of action. Those in the Norwich camp who had spotted the offence were furious, but could hardly argue that Ipswich didn't deserve the points.

Prior to the handball controversy, the home fans spent vast amounts of energy giving Town defender Fabian Wilnis a hard time. This was payback time for the injudicious comments Wilnis made about Norwich on his previous visit, back in 2004. Back then he expressed the frank opinion that Norwich weren't good enough to top the Championship table, and were an ordinary side who wouldn't survive if they went into the Premier League. They would need to sign fifteen new players if they went up, or would be relegated by Christmas, he reckoned. Although Norwich did indeed subsequently fail the survive their one season at top level, his words infuriated Canaries followers and the episode had nasty repercussions. Wilnis admitted: 'I got letters saying I was a dead man and threatening to break my arms and legs if I ever set foot in Norwich. At the time, it was really frightening. I upset and offended some of their fans and for that I really am sorry.'

Although his comments were disrespectful to the title-winning side, and were surely little more than sour grapes, Wilnis seemed genuinely remorseful and shocked by the reaction to them. In the hope the whole thing would die down, he initially kept the death threats to himself and only told his wife and the Ipswich management later on. But Norwich fans have long memories and he was obliged to go on the record and apologise and endure major abuse on all subsequent visits to Carrow Road. As he observed himself, it had the reverse effect at home games and his popularity with Ipswich fans increased immensely! Songs referring to Wilnis 'hating Norwich' were composed by Town fans to be sung at subsequent derbies, and a huge banner appeared on the same theme. Wilnis was asked if he wanted to keep this banner as a memento, but wisely refrained from getting involved further.

So this first return to Norwich was an ordeal: 'People were screaming abuse at me from the minute we pulled up at the ground. I was public enemy number one and [Norwich] even put a bit in the programme reminding people what I'd said, which I thought was a bit irresponsible. Norwich went in front and all I could hear was their fans singing 'Wilnis, what's the score?' [After] our winner courtesy of Danny Haynes' famous "Hand of God" goal, how I celebrated. It was such a huge relief and I remember jumping and dancing in front of our ecstatic fans. I was happy and can remember them singing 'Fabian Wilnis is a blue – he hates Norwich'. To be honest I felt a little uncomfortable about that, too, because I didn't like being the centre of attention. All I can say is that I'm happy our coach was able to pick us up right outside the dressing rooms. I didn't fancy the prospect of walking through their fans much. This time I got straight on [the bus] without doing any interviews.'

Supporters of a statistical bent may have noted that this Ipswich triumph meant there was parity once more as regards the 141 meetings between the clubs at first-team level since hostilities began in 1902. Ipswich had now won 58 of the games, Norwich also 58, with 25 drawn. Remarkably, it was still neck and neck after 104 years. But although a win apiece in 2005-6 left Old Farm honours even, the big picture favoured Norwich. They finished the campaign in ninth place in the Championship, six points ahead of Town who were down in 15th, matching their worst finishing position on the League ladder since 1959. This led to much discontent in the stands, and the feeling grew that Ipswich were going nowhere fast and radical change was called for. The problem was this: if Royle, with his vast experience and impressive CV, couldn't inspire progress, then who could? Similarly, up the A140, there was no shortage of City fans feeling Worthington had also done all he could and should be replaced, too. Modern football imposes huge pressures on managers to produce results and the days when a rookie manager like Bobby Robson could pitch up at Portman Road and be given years to create a winning formula were long gone.

When a groundswell of opinion surfaces from within such large fanbases, directors generally sit up and take notice sooner rather than later. Sure enough, just eleven days after the final game of the 2005-6 season, Royle parted company with Ipswich, ostensibly by mutual consent. He'd spent four years at the helm, during which the club entered voluntary administration, sold a clutch of its best players to Premiership clubs, but twice reached the play-offs, losing to West Ham both times. It was a reasonable record in the circumstances, but not good enough to meet the high expectations of the Ipswich faithful.

Once Royle had gone, a month of speculation went by before a replacement was announced. The directors' choice was a big surprise – 37-year-old Town midfielder Jim Magilton, who had just quit playing and was on the look-out for a coaching role somewhere. After 52 Northern Ireland caps and 580 career appearances, Magilton had kicked a ball for the last time in the defeat at Plymouth which left Town in their worst position in 46 seasons. Six weeks later he was the youngest manager in the Championship.

There were changes at Norwich, too, but to the dismay of his harshest critics, Nigel Worthington was spared the axe, and instead coach Steve Foley was made scapegoat for City's below-par season. Just a month later, the amiable Foley would join the enemy ranks at Ipswich where he was appointed technical coach. The 53-year-old thus became only the second man to coach both City and Town at first team level, and also one of a rare breed to have represented all three major East Anglian clubs, Ipswich, Norwich and Colchester.

Barring a superb start to the new season, Worthington must have known he would soon be a dead man walking. The fans wanted change and nothing less than a serious promotion challenge would satisfy them. Hope flickered briefly with three wins and a draw from the first five games, leaving Norwich second in the table, but four games without a win in September then plunged Carrow Road into gloom. After a lacklustre 1-3 defeat at Plymouth, the club's majority shareholders, Delia Smith and husband Michael Wynn-Jones, formally apologised to the 776 fans who had trekked to Devon, and publicly demanded an improvement from Worthington and his players.

It didn't work. Eight days later the team crashed 1-4 at home to Burnley in a Sunday afternoon televised game, and the abuse that came Worthington's way from the stands reached new levels of intensity. He put on a brave face at the post-match press conference, but a parting of the ways was inevitable and duly took place within the hour. Worthington reportedly trousered a £600,000 pay-off, and before long was being linked with vacancies at Sheffield Wednesday, Barnsley, Hull, Swansea and Luton. He chose to take an extended break before a short stint in charge at Leicester was followed by his appointment as manager of Northern Ireland.

Naturally, Ipswich fans took the opportunity to revel in their neighbours' distress, which at least took their minds off their own demoralising defeat at Colchester's tiny Layer Road ground. Although Colchester is geographically far nearer to Ipswich than is Norwich, the so-called 'A12 derby' has never been anything like as potent or intense as the Old Farm equivalent. This is no doubt due to the Essex club operating for nearly 50 years at a lower league level than Ipswich. There has long been a theory in these parts that large numbers of people from the Colchester catchment area jumped on the Ipswich bandwagon back in the 1970s and early 80s during Town's glory days, when the U's were down in the old Fourth Division. Colchester and Ipswich battled it out for regional supremacy in the 1950s until the Suffolk club were promoted in 1957, which led to rivalry with the U's fizzling out almost completely. Now, half-a-century on, the Essex outfit had finally caught their neighbours up, and their 1-0 win spelt a very bad night for Magilton and his troops. It was embarrassing for Ipswich, but nothing like as bad as losing to Norwich.

For a few days Norwich languished managerless in the relegation zone, before the board's new man was unveiled in the shape of Peter Grant, a former Canary and long-time Celtic midfielder, who had recently been assistant to West Ham boss Alan Pardew. The Canaries now had to take stock and effectively start their season all over again. Over subsequent weeks, with the first Ipswich derby of the campaign looming on the horizon, the two clubs' respective positions in the table would be reversed. Town slipped down to 17th while City enjoyed a mini-revival under their new manager.

For their first managerial East Anglian derby, both Grant and Magilton were naturally far more interested in winning valuable league points than in local bragging rights. However, both knew plenty about the importance of Old Farm meetings, and understood what they meant to the fans. Both had appeared as players in the fixture in the past. Magilton played in eight derbies, dating back to 1999, while his opposite number appeared in the two contests of the 1997-8 season, including the so-called 'destruction derby' when Town ran out 5-0 winners. After many years at Celtic Park, Grant had also sampled the white-hot intensity of Glasgow derbies.

They lined up at Portman Road on the sunny late morning of Sunday 19 November for another game covered live by Sky TV. In the usual lively atmosphere, nervy defending by Ipswich allowed Norwich debutant Luke Chadwick to fire the Canaries ahead, but a quality finish by Sylvain Legwinski levelled matters before the interval. Chadwick, a former starlet at Manchester United, was carried off after colliding with advertising boards. There were close shaves in both goalmouths, but the match's turning point didn't arrive until less than fifteen minutes from time. Magilton sent on sub Haynes, scorer of the controversial winner in the previous derby, and the teenager instantly swooped to head Town ahead, minutes later grabbing a second with a curling drive that went in off a post. The lad from Peckham's emphatic entrance in successive derby games gained him cult hero status and before long he was being referred to as 'Canary Crusher'.

It was Town's first win over the old enemy at Portman Road for nearly nine years, but the feelgood factor didn't last. Only one of their next six games was won and Magilton's first Christmas as a manager saw his charges languishing miserably in the lower half of the table. Peter Grant must have secretly sympathised, for he too was having a tough introduction to management at Carrow Road. He'd even upset some of the club's own fans, suggesting that for long periods in matches they often didn't make enough noise. After an uninspiring 0-0 draw against Southend on

Boxing Day, City found themselves one place behind Ipswich, with few genuine signs at this point that the new regime would fare much better than Worthington's.

Grant welcomed in the new year of 2007 by opting for drastic action. Team changes galore were accompanied by rumours of discontent within the camp. Moroccan midfielder Yussef Safri, who reportedly brawled with teammate Dickson Ethuhu after one defeat, said he would demand a transfer if asked to repeat his experience on the sub's bench for the Southend debacle. It was clearly a period of transition and City fans would need to scale down their hopes and be patient. The team scraped together enough points to stay above the relegation zone, but only just.

Doing sterling service in a number of roles was veteran Dion Dublin. This popular giant, who actually started his career at Carrow Road as a junior nineteen years earlier, had returned to his old stomping ground in the dying days of Worthington's tenure. Now 37 and approaching 600 first-team appearances at nine clubs, Dublin held things together in difficult circumstances, showing unexpected enthusiasm and determination. If he had been hoping to see out his playing days with a relaxed and comfortable ride in sleepy Norfolk, he was mistaken. He weighed in with a few goals on the way to winning the player of the year award, and was as enthusiastic as anybody when the return derby with Ipswich came along towards the end of this difficult season.

Both clubs were by now out of trouble, drifting together just below halfway in the table. The only issue to be decided was who would finish with their noses ahead. Promotion and relegation excitement was rife all around the country by mid-April 2007, but not in East Anglia. Ipswich fans pinned their hopes on Canary Crusher Haynes, who at that point was second leading scorer behind Lee with seven goals, despite 25 of his 29 appearances being as a substitute. Magilton liked to use him as an impact sub late on. Peter Grant, meanwhile, had high hopes resting on another slippery striker, Rob Earnshaw, whose first full season at Norwich had been rudely interrupted by a groin injury picked up in training. He recovered to make his first start in seventeen league games against Ipswich, at the expense of youngster Chris Martin. The expensively purchased Earnshaw had led the divisional scoring charts at the time of his injury and had been badly missed.

Norwich made a flying start in front of the raucous full house, midfield destroyer Etuhu burying a firm header at the near post from Huckerby's cross after just five minutes. City frequently went close to a second, and the interval arrived with Ipswich relieved to be still in the contest. Sure enough, they emerged with renewed energy and before long

David Wright had crashed home an angled drive to equalise after his first attempt at a cross had been blocked. The visiting fans then got highly exited as Haynes was brought on with twelve minutes left, but he couldn't find a way through and it was Dublin, celebrating his 38th birthday, who went closest to grabbing a winner. The contest finished all-square for only the 26th time in its 143 stagings. Dublin wasn't the only veteran to impress, for Town's Wilnis had a fine game at the grand old age of 36. The Dutch-Surinamese defender had been out of the first-team picture for long spells lately, but rolled back the years with a polished performance. Wilnis was praised for his efforts in front of Canary fans baying for his blood once again. Particularly fulsome in his tributes was Town coach Foley, who was delighted to avoid defeat on a first return to the club that had disposed of his services.

The draw left both teams with two games apiece remaining in 2006-07, Ipswich a point ahead with the pair marooned in mid-table. Ipswich were twelve points adrift of the play-off places, while Norwich were twelve clear of the drop zone. *Comme ci, comme ça*. It all added up to an unremarkable season whichever way you looked at it, with even the two derby games failing to produce much genuine drama or controversy.

# 18

# SLEEPING WITH THE ENEMY

## (2007-10)

The summer of 2007 saw Ipswich quietly planning for the new season, while north of the border life appeared altogether more stressful. Spanish-born striker Pablo Counago rejoined Town after an unhappy two years with Malaga, and Magilton also used his Irish charm to entice a quality goalkeeper – Edinburgh-born Neil Alexander – to sign from Cardiff. Both looked like excellent captures.

There were fewer happy faces at Norwich's Colney training ground, however, for a buy-out clause in Rob Earnshaw's contract enabled Derby to swoop and pay a club record £3.5 million for him, against Peter Grant's wishes. The manager was also angry to lose Dickson Etuhu, who headed to Sunderland for £1.5 million. He reacted by restructuring the squad, appointing young defender Jason Shackell as captain and signing former Norwich favourite Jamie Cureton from Colchester for £825,000 to fill the gap left by Earnshaw.

Both clubs enjoyed a good start to the campaign, Ipswich winning a penalty at home to Sheffield Wednesday just 35 seconds into the first game. Two wins and a draw in the opening three league games saw Town soar to second in the table, while Norwich also notched two wins and a draw in the season's opening week, lifting hopes that the two clubs might spend the season battling it out at the top of the Championship.

But after stumbling at Hull, things soon went steadily downhill for the Canaries and the club found itself facing another autumn of discontent, just like twelve months earlier. A shortage of goals was the problem and after a nightmare sequence of five games without a win and without a goal, Grant fell on his sword. He departed Carrow Road the day after a grim single-goal defeat at fellow-strugglers QPR, one of only two clubs lower in the table. Grant's assistant Jim Duffy took caretaker charge, as the board wearily repeated the process of recruiting a new manager.

Virtually a full month was needed to find the right man, by which time City were four points adrift at the bottom. They needed an experienced trouble-shooter and opted for a man with experience at high level, the former West Ham and Newcastle boss Glenn Roeder. He became the club's 22nd manager since the war, inheriting a team bereft of confidence that had collected a meagre eight points by the beginning of November and were looking relegation fodder. Although he was taking over one of the recognised bigger Championship clubs, it was clear Roeder's main priority must be to prevent the humiliation of dropping into the lower divisions for the first time since 1960. Some fans were struggling to believe their side could be so entrenched near the bottom of the second tier, less than three years after trouncing Manchester United in the Premiership.

Roeder, a well-travelled figure, whose low points included relegation and a brain tumour while at West Ham, was eager to take on the rescue job. He admitted he had not been head-hunted by Delia and her colleagues, but had contacted City himself immediately on hearing about the vacancy on TV.

Will Buckley, Norwich fan and Sunday newspaper columnist, reckoned this was further confirmation that out-of-work managers spent their days watching Sky Sports News with mobile phone in hand. Once Roeder had got himself on the short-list, it was a foregone conclusion he would be appointed: he prided himself on giving quality job interviews, having now totalled five, with a 100 per cent success rate. He clearly talked a good game if nothing else.

When Roeder consulted the fixture list he must have smiled wryly to himself when finding his first game in charge would be a true baptism of fire – Ipswich at Carrow Road. Even though new managers often enjoy a honeymoon period after taking over a new team, Ipswich fans regarded this as an ideal time to face the old enemy, for by now Town were flying high in fourth place and unbeaten in five games. Some of those who had doubted the wisdom of appointing an untried manager in Magilton were even beginning to soften a little.

Having cracked three goals past both Colchester and Wolves in their previous games, Town maintained their form in the first half of the derby on Sunday, 4 November 2007. The home faithful were silenced as Lee fired the Blues ahead and Counago netted a disputed second from close range before the interval. City looked to be down and out, but Roeder's debut half-time team talk did the trick and they completed a brilliant second-half comeback, boosted by debutant Martin Taylor's header going in off Owen Garvan not long after the turnaround. A point was salvaged by Cureton's first goal since mid-August, a neat finish with twenty minutes left. All the recent uncertainty and misery was blown away in an instant and Carrow Road was rocking again. Even going down to ten men shortly afterwards – Huckerby banished for a dangerous tackle on Jon Walters – failed to dampen the party spirit. Given the nature of the revival and the clubs' respective positions in the table, this felt more like a win than a draw once referee Rob Styles had sounded the final whistle. The glum Ipswich faces underlined that view.

Roeder and Magilton both seemed relieved to get their first manage-rial Old Farm derby out of the way. Breathless and exhausted as any of the players, they no doubt necked a quick stiffener before calming down in time to face the media. Roeder said: 'I've missed football and it's great to be back. It was very satisfying the team put in so much effort. At half-time, even though we were two down, I didn't go in screaming because the players knew they had played well.' Magilton was magnanimous: 'You have to give credit to the opposition. They threw all caution to the wind and had a real go. It's amazing what a new manager does to a team.'

The joy at pegging back their local rivals and silencing the premature Ipswich victory chants seemed to invigorate City for the fight ahead. Once the Roeder regime had settled into place, the team went on a thir-teen-match unbeaten run that effectively saw off the relegation threat. The Roeder revolution during this time involved shipping out seven of the first-team squad, including promising young goalkeeper Joe Lewis for £400,000 to Peterborough. And at the season's end the number of play-ers departed in barely six months reached a remarkable sixteen. The retir-ing Dion Dublin, plus Roeder himself, hinted that over the years Norwich had been 'too nice' a football club, and they needed to get real, harden up and undergo a revolution such as this.

Down the road, Magilton's manoueverings were less drastic in com-parison, although the form of both clubs since Roeder's arrival proved similar: From the weekend of the 2-2 derby draw, through to the end of that season, Town and City notched up near identical points tallies, 47 and 46 respectively. But Ipswich's better start to the season meant they were contesting play-off places, and not fighting relegation like City, when the clubs came together for the return match at Portman Road on Sunday, 13 April, 2008. The top five had pulled away by now but one final play-off spot was within Town's reach if they could finish the campaign strongly. It meant the derby was vital for the blue half of the region, not so for Norwich, who were clear of the bottom four and not looking seri-ous relegation candidates. A whole clutch of clubs could still go down, but several looked in far worse shape than Norwich, and a mid-table fin-ish was on the cards whatever the outcome at Portman Road. This was just as well, because the Canaries put on a mediocre show that disap-pointed their followers intensely.

A bumper crowd of almost 30,000 was the biggest to watch an Old Farm derby since the December 2003 clash at Portman Road. The visi-tors engineered a great start, scoring a spectacular shock opener though Ched Evans, a lively young Welshman recruited before Christmas on loan from Manchester City. He seized on a loose ball and his low 25-yarder flashed beyond keeper Stephen Bywater, Ipswich's recent loan recruit from Derby. Town fans were temporarily in despair, but were soon galvanised by their team's efforts to strike back quickly. Shefki Kuqi, borrowed from Crystal Palace and making his first full appearance since rejoining the club, looked lively in attack, with Canary Crusher Haynes and Counago also causing City problems. Just nine minutes after Evans' devastating strike, Ipswich were back on terms. The outstanding Counago played in Haynes, whose low drive ended up in the net after deflecting off the shins of City's Alex Pearce. For the remainder of the game there only looked one winner, Ipswich the far hungrier of the two sides. Shortly before the interval, City keeper David Marshall dashed out to beat Jon Walters to a dangerous through ball, but lost possession to Counago, who was able to set up Haynes to slot home what would prove the winning goal.

Haynes had done it again, maintaining his hoodoo over Norwich, having now scored four key goals against their first team, not to mention netting against them at all other levels. It was proving stern punishment for the Canaries, who had failed to sign Haynes when they had the chance several years earlier. Despite the narrow victory margin, this was one of the most one-sided derbies in recent memory and there was much harrumphing in Norfolk that the Canaries had under-performed and let their fans down on their big day. It was an isolated episode though, and most seemed to feel the new Roeder regime was generally taking their club in the right direction. He and his much-changed backroom team were providing what he called 'a complete redecoration, not just a lick of paint' at the club. Proof of the fans' faith came when a remarkable total of 18,500 season tickets for the following season were renewed, even before City were 100 per cent sure of avoiding relegation. That figure soon exceeded 20,000 once safety was assured by thumping QPR 3-0. Meanwhile, Ipswich fans celebrated long and hard after their 2-1 derby win, their enthusiasm only waning after subsequent draws with Wolves and Preston meant they fell agonisingly short of reaching the play-offs. It meant Town now had a seventh successive season in football's second tier to anticipate. And Norwich's survival meant it would be the Canaries thirteenth season at this level out of the last fourteen. At least it meant more derbies to come.

There was much determined talk in Norwich about getting off to a better start to 2008-09 following the previous season's early calamities. They were widely expected to be among the promotion chasers, alongside relegated Reading and Birmingham, not to mention Wolves and Ipswich. Once again, however, it failed to work out that way and Canaries feathers were soon drooping after a dismal start. Wolves and Birmingham were forging ahead at the top, and although Ipswich were well above Norwich, their fans also felt less than satisfied. The clubs were due to meet for the first of the 2008-09 Old Farm derbies at the halfway point of the season in December. By then City had already suffered ten league defeats and another battle to avoid the drop was looking on the cards. The natives were, unsurprisingly, distinctly restless. Roeder had by now been charge for just over a year, 56 competitive first team games in all (18 wins, 14 draws and 24 defeats), and throughout that period the club had been mired in the lower half of the table.

Consequently, rarely has a Norwich manager gone into a derby match needing a win as badly as Roeder did at Carrow Road on Sunday, 7 December 2008. Jim Magilton was also feeling the pressure at Ipswich, although not to the same extent. His second season in charge had seen yet more of the inconsistency that has frustrated and infuriated Town fans in recent years. They had crept as high as eighth in the table in November, but generally again looked little better than a moderate mid-table outfit.

By now, striker Kevin Lisbie had joined the exclusive list of players who had played for both Ipswich and Norwich, having arrived at Portman Road from Colchester for £600,000. Lisbie had played half-a-dozen games for Norwich during a loan spell three years earlier, a period that included the derby game at Portman Road in which he was involved in the challenge that saw Ipswich's Sito Castro harshly sent off. Lisbie reckoned he had happy memories of his stay at Norwich and, perhaps mindful of the treatment dished out to Fabian Wilnis, promised he wouldn't celebrate if he scored against them for Town: 'I'm not one for going over the top, or rubbing it in their faces,' said the laconic Londoner. 'I never really knew the depth of feeling [in Old Farm derbies] until I played in one and it took me a bit by surprise. As soon as the whistle blew you could understand what all the talk was about, with the crowd so intense.'

Sampling the derby for the first time was Ipswich skipper Gareth McAuley, a seasoned Northern Ireland international who had joined the club six months earlier from Leicester. His previous local derby experience came with Lincoln (versus Grimsby) and Leicester (versus Forest, Derby and Coventry) but he knew those clashes simply didn't compare with the intensity of the Old Farm version: 'Lincoln v Grimsby was pretty good, but it won't be on the same scale as this. The players tell me the atmosphere is really intense, so this will be special. One of the reasons to be in the game is to play in these sort of games.'

Ipswich boss Magilton was also feeling bullish as the big game approached. He described it as Eastern England's very own version of El Clasico (Real Madrid v Barcelona) and he called for referee Lee Probert to take into account the intense rivalry and make appropriate allowances for the extra adrenalin and commitment both sets of players would be showing: 'Derbies are usually the most frenetic of games and the team that wins is usually the side that can string a few passes together and stay composed,' he warned.

As per usual, recent form counted for little once the 146th derby got underway on a cool, crisp lunchtime Carrow Road. It was the home side which dominated proceedings, banishing their unhappy memories of the previous clash and working hard for a well-deserved 2-0 victory. Ipswich's new central defensive partnership of McAuley and Alex Bruce (son of former Norwich skipper Steve), put on a brave and determined display which saved their side from a bigger hammering. Town were battered during the opening half but somehow kept the scoresheet blank, and after the break looked a little brighter following a roasting from the manager.

After Walters missed a good opportunity when clear on goal, City once again gained the ascendancy and took a deserved lead as winger Lee Croft swerved a blistering drive from 25 yards past Richard Wright, to get the home fans singing again. In his fourth derby appearance, Croft had conjured up what he called the best goal of his career, and at a crucial time, too. Town reacted by instantly introducing the talismanic Haynes, but this time the Canary Crusher failed to work his magic, although going close with one header.

The points were finally clinched by Norwich eight minutes from time in controversial circumstances, with Town's key defender McAuley forced off the pitch at the time of the goal. Blood had been seeping from a head wound, which the referee had not noticed, but McAuley was in no mood to leave the field at such a vital time. It was only after City striker Leroy Lita sprinted 30 yards to tell the referee about the blood that he was forced to go off for treatment. Without his commanding presence, David Bell's swinging free-kick found Matty Pattison at the back post, and the ball was scrambled home for 2-0. The Ipswich camp were furious at Lita for telling tales, feeling he should have minded his own business, but once he had calmed down Magilton admitted it had been 'a clever move' by the Norwich man to get McAuley removed.

'On the Ball City' was by now ringing out at volume, but the Ipswich management will no doubt still have heard the chants of 'What a load of rubbish' and 'We want our money back' from their own disillusioned fans, many of whom were calling for Magilton to be removed sooner rather than later. For his part, the manager rued the fact that his team seemed to save their worst performances for these big occasions, games where live TV cameras were in attendance.

Nothing upsets Ipswich fans more than a defeat by Norwich and, combined with inconsistency in other games, the pressure quickly grew on Magilton, who after 30 months as boss had failed to convince many of them. A season of consolidation, followed by one of just missing the play-offs, plus the current mid-table position, was seen as simply not good enough. Claiming to be speaking for the majority of fans, the *East Anglian Daily Times* mounted a campaign designed to bring about a change of manager. All this undoubtedly contributed to the angry scenes at Portman Road shortly after the derby, when Magilton stormed out of a press conference after being questioned about reports that he had held secret crisis talks with certain players.

Whatever the nature of those secret meetings, some improvement in results came about and Town slowly climbed the table during the remainder of 2008-09, albeit not quite rapidly enough to secure a play-off place. It was not enough to silence the moaners, but did mean Magilton was still in a job by Easter.

Glenn Roeder, on the other hand, must have hoped his 2-0 derby victory would signal a change of fortunes. The three points took City out of the bottom four and brightened the general atmosphere at Carrow Road considerably. However, it was to prove a false dawn, and by the end of 2008 City had been stuck in 20th place in the table for several weeks. As was the case at Ipswich, many Norwich followers were singularly unimpressed by their manager's efforts. His drastic changes both on and off the field had failed to yield any tangible progress in terms of results and many still refused to forgive Roeder for not renewing the contract of Darren Huckerby in the summer, meaning they were unable to give their hero a proper send off. The internet messageboards and the local paper letters columns remained full of criticism for the two managers, on both sides of the Waveney Valley.

First to fall off the tightrope was Roeder, who was gone by mid-January, the announcement coming the day after Norwich lost to bottom-of-the-table Charlton at Carrow Road in an FA Cup replay. Charlton had not previously won in eighteen games, and the crescendo of criticism meant Roeder duly became the 27th manager to part company with a League club since the season started five months earlier. Roeder had won exactly a third of the 60 matches under his command at Norwich, which was inferior to his predecessors Peter Grant and Nigel Worthington, although better than the three men before that – Bryan Hamilton, Bruce Rioch and Gary Megson.

The popular former City goalkeeper Bryan Gunn was surprisingly made caretaker-manager. Twice Norwich's player of the year in his twelve years as a first-teamer, Gunn had worked in a number of roles at Carrow Road, including sponsorship sales, community ambassador, goalkeeping coach and head of player recruitment. Taking charge of the home game with Barnsley, he was initially seen as little more than a stop-gap, but after City roared to a 4-0 victory he was given the job until the end of the season, with former colleagues Ian Crook and John Deehan brought in to assist him. Ultimately, however, putting three playing legends in charge of a club in big trouble proved a romantic notion doomed to failure. Only four wins from the next fifteen games meant the Canaries remained at the heart of the relegation battle. The return derby at Ipswich on Sunday, 19 April, 2009 – the third-to-last fixture of the season – saw them desperate for points to avoid dropping into the lower divisions for the first time in 49 years. Charlton were already doomed at the bottom, and would be joined by two from Norwich, Forest, Barnsley or Southampton, this foursome separated by just two points.

Ipswich were by now marooned in mid-table again, so the three points from the derby meant little *per se*, apart from local pride, plus the potential delight in plunging Norwich into further difficulties. A further interesting aspect to the game was the presence of former Town favourite Alan Lee in the Norwich No 10 shirt. The big striker had left Ipswich around nine months earlier for Crystal Palace, but had now been recruited by City on loan. He thus became the fourteenth player to wear the colours of both clubs in a competitive game since Ipswich turned professional in the 1930s.

The two teams served up a rousing derby which featured five goals for the first time in sixteen meetings. But it would once again be overshadowed by controversy resulting from a refereeing decision. In the Portman Road sunshine, loanee David Mooney headed City ahead in front of the snarling North Stand end, only for Alan Quinn to drive home a sweet equaliser a few minutes later. After the turnaround came the game's pivotal moment, a penalty decision that would have had Bryan Gunn tearing his hair out had he possessed any. An innocuous challenge involving City keeper David Marshall and former Canary Lisbie was deemed worthy of a spot-kick, a decision even Lisbie and Town boss Magilton felt was harsh. In-form loanee Giovanni dos Santos stepped up to put Ipswich ahead and they increased their lead near the finish when Jon Stead raced clear to score from an angle. There was just time for City to pull one back, via Sammy Clingan from another disputed penalty, but it was too little too late and the trapdoor beckoned Norwich more ominously. Results elsewhere meant they dropped into the bottom three with just two matches remaining. They would contrive to lose both – conceding four at bottom-placed Charlton – and were duly relegated.

In the warm afterglow of a derby victory, Jim Magilton could have been forgiven for enjoying a respite from the criticism and the pressure. What he surely couldn't have expected was the sack three days later. It transpired that the club's secretive owner Marcus Evans and his senior henchmen had been tracking the availability of former Sunderland boss Roy Keane for some time, and Magilton's number was already up, whatever the derby outcome. The comings and goings that week also included appointment of a new chief executive in former British Olympic Association boss Simon Clegg, plus the exit of assistant manager John Gorman. Barely 24 hours after the anti-Magilton brigade began digesting news of his departure, the club unveiled Keane as their new man. Here was a huge name, an appointment that excited the fans, and put Ipswich Town back in the national spotlight. And a further 48 hours on, the first match of the Keane era saw an impressive 3-0 win at Cardiff. The season was now virtually over, and there had been more excitement in this one week than the rest of it put together.

With Norwich taking the plunge into League One, the 2009-10 season would see Ipswich alone in the second tier and a division higher than their local rivals, for the first time in 49 years. Norfolk and Suffolk police may have welcomed this situation, but not so the supporters. The annual joust with the old enemy is always badly missed, even though one set of fans can extract much pleasure from the other's relegation. But by romping to the League One title in 2010 under the no-nonsense command of Paul Lambert, Norwich duly returned to the Championship in some style. City fans were suddenly more optimistic about the future than for many years, although their Town counterparts much less jolly following a disappointing first season under Keane, in which they finished below mid-table yet again. The *East Anglian Daily Times* called it 'the dullest of seasons' at Portman Road, and the absence of a local derby was partly responsible for this. The modern football fan demands instant gratification, and while Ipswich and Norwich remain outside of the Premiership, more than ever their Old Farm derby is a major highlight of their season. Both camps were therefore relishing the return to battle in 2010-11.

Despite the contrasting nature of their fortunes, the two clubs have continued to attract much-envied levels of support in recent years. Early season ticket sales for 2010-11 indicated both are likely to exceed 20,000 crowds for all, or nearly all, home games in the near future. City's joint-majority shareholder Delia Smith proudly described Canaries fans as 'the best in the world' after statistics showed that, of the 22 Football League clubs with ex-Premier League experience, only Norwich could boast higher average attendances in 2010 than during their stint in the top flight. During their League One title-winning romp the club averaged a close-to-capacity 24,600 – compared to 24,354 during their last spell in the Premiership. South of the border, Ipswich were recently being watched by an average of around 3,400 fans per game fewer than in their last season in the top tier (2001-02). However, Town could still pull in a healthy average of nearly 21,000 in what was a hugely disappointing and relatively uneventful campaign. These stats can only improve now that the derby is back on the calendar again.

Those addicts who badly missed their annual derby 'fix' during 2009-10 were able to gain a little relief thanks to a special match arranged in Great Yarmouth by Dale Gordon, a boyhood Ipswich fan and later a star winger for seven years at Norwich. Gordon, who nowadays runs the Legends Lounge at Yarmouth's Wellesley Road stadium, invited Town and City stars of the past to take part in the fund-raising game. Managed by Kevin Beattie and Ken Brown, the sides donned appropriate colours and did battle in time-honoured fashion, Ipswich Legends prevailing 2-1, goals from Alex Mathie and David Johnson cancelling out one by Darren Huckerby. It was less hectic than the real thing (one local paper called it the 'Older Farm Derby') but it certainly whetted a few appetites, and when the fixture lists for 2010-11 were published there was no doubt over which two games the fans of Ipswich Town and Norwich City were looking for first.

Why a game of football between Ipswich and Norwich should be so important is hard to define. The answer must lie in some sort of deep-rooted tribalism instinct, for fans (who rarely, if ever, change 'tribes') treat a derby with much more intensity than players (who switch allegiances frequently and with impunity). Very few footballers are deeply motivated by a local derby, over and above other big games. Terry Butcher of Ipswich was one notable exception.

Yes, local derbies really are different. They defy logic. They provide the opportunity, gleefully accepted, for otherwise intelligent and articulate people to behave in strange, illogical ways. Why else would a profession-al woman like Karen Buchanan of Norwich mutter 'scum, scum, scum' under her breath every time her train passes through Ipswich? And why else would former local government officer Mark Jarman of Ipswich refuse to mend plugs because they contain a yellow and green wire?

It would, I think, be fitting for the last word in this story to go to these two representatives of the people to whom a local derby matters most. Buchanan admitted: 'I did go through a phase of not wearing jeans, but then I realised they're not Ipswich blue and had to admit to myself I was taking things a bit far. All the plates and mugs in my house are yellow and green, as are my cushions, and all the lighters I buy. I cannot buy a blue lighter: if it's the last one in the shop I would get matches instead. When I pass through Ipswich on the train, I have to sit there quietly muttering 'scum, scum, scum' under my breath until we've pulled out of the station. And I once bought two useless baby chairs from IKEA purely because one was green and yellow and the other was yellow and green. Norwich manager John Bond once said too much was made of the Ipswich game, for it was just three points like any other. Rationally speaking, he was right. But since when did rationality have a part to play in football?'

And the normally laconic Jarman confessed: 'When we beat Norwich 5-0 in the 1990s I went into the East Stand bar after the game. When we staggered out some time after 6, we were walking along a near-deserted Portman Road when the Scum team-coach emerged. I was rather more agile in those days, so was able to join in the charge after them, screaming and jeering at Darren Eadie as he cowered in his corner on the bus. We kept pace to the traffic lights at the station, which were red, and forced the hapless Scum players to get more and more embarrassed while we danced our little dance. On another occasion, I was eating in an Indian restaurant just down the road from where Delia Smith was holding court in another, posher restaurant. I glued my eyes to the window and scowled at her, and stared her out.'

In early 2010, Danny Baker's popular Saturday morning BBC radio show instigated a campaign called 'The Shirt of Hurt' to aid Sport Relief coffers. It involved football fans pledging sums for someone else to wear the shirt of their most hated rivals. The respondees included a Norwich fan who revealed that on her recent hen-night she was forced to pay a forfeit involving parading in public in an Ipswich shirt and hat. She subsequently walked up the aisle still not recovered from the trauma. In response, an Ipswich fan contacted the show to confess he never ate sweetcorn and peas in the same meal because they represented Norwich's colours.

Another fan forced to publicly wear the shirt of 'the other lot' was Greg Wosahlo, the son of Roger, a Town forward in the late 1960s. Greg's ordeal attracted considerable publicity after TV cameras caught

sight of him in a yellow-and-green Norwich shirt in among the blue
hordes of the away end at Newcastle in April 2010. BBC's Late Kick-Off
programme showed the footage and appealed for information on the
mystery. Greg was named as the man in question, and he explained he
was forced to undergo the ordeal by his mates during a stag weekend. He
only escaped a lynching by repeatedly explaining to fellow Ipswich fans
that the shirt was being worn as a punishment and not out of choice! To
prove his point he had to celebrate even more wildly than usual when
Town scored.

Entering the hell-hole of the opponents' territory while incognito is
not unheard of in Old Farm history. In April 2008 the *Eastern Evening
News* sports desk in Norwich conducted an experiment, sending reporter
Peter Walsh undercover to find out what it would be like for a City fan to
watch a local derby 'from where no Norwich fan had gone before' –
behind enemy lines at Portman Road. Wearing neutral colours and keeping his comments and emotions well under wraps, the uncomfortable
Walsh's every move in Ipswich's North Stand was captured by a photog-
rapher. Like Wosahlo, he emerged relatively unscathed, and his eventful
day provided amusing copy for his editors. Ipswich won the game 3-1 and
he concluded: 'It was a miserable game and a miserable experience.'

He will no doubt have been cheered up soon afterwards when his
newspaper rifled through its picture files, located shots of some of the
best goals from Norwich City history and set about recreating them in
the manner of the Fantasy Football TV show feature 'Phoenix from the
Flames'. Former players and various stand-in actors gathered at a chilly
and otherwise deserted sports-field to try and re-create Canaries history
in front of a video camera. A highlight was the sight of Darren Eadie
staging a re-run of his fine goal in the 2-1 win over Ipswich in September
1997. Looking as nimble as ever, despite the eleven-year interlude, Eadie
had to repeatedly jink around somebody impersonating Ipswich keeper
Richard Wright before slamming home a shot from a tight angle. There
was nostalgia and mirth aplenty when the resulting stills and video
footage subsequently appeared in print and on the internet.

Naturally, Ipswich and Norwich fans rarely see eye to eye and generally shun the company of their opposite numbers. So there was widespread horror and amazement at news in early 2010 that Town fan James
Croome and City follower Oliver Back, both 26, had subjected themselves to an unprecedented torment: They would spend two months con-
fined in a small space together, with no means of escape. The pair joined
forces in a trans-Atlantic rowing race, completing 2,934 miles from the
Canary Islands to Antigua in 59 days, 16 hours and 17 minutes, winning

the pairs class and raising thousands for a hospice charity. Football was apparently not a major topic of conversation during the ordeal.

Croome and Back's friendship successfully crossed the Old Farm divide and, on a similar theme, a wedding took place soon afterwards involving devoted supporters of the rival clubs. Ipswich fan Lucy French tied the knot with Norwich devotee Ashley Holland. Instead of brushing their footballing differences under the carpet, they plumped for a football-themed wedding. The bride arrived on a tractor decorated with blue and white ribbons, discreetly sporting a garter belt with an Ipswich Town badge on it. Guests sat on tables named after Town and City players and enjoyed slices of a wedding cake decorated with an Old Farm theme. Proceedings reportedly remained civilised and obscene chanting was kept to a minimum.

Less restrained were the postings on social networking websites in the spring of 2009 when Norwich were heading for relegation out of the Championship. Nearly 2,000 Ipswich fans gleefully joined a Facebook group inviting all and sundry to attend a 'Relegation Party' in Norwich and a further 800-plus Tractor Boys signed up to a gathering at Portman Road to celebrate the Canaries' downfall.

Even the General Election of May 2010 failed to pass without being infected by Old Farm fever. When it was announced that the constituency of Waveney had 'turned blue again' after the election of Peter Aldous, most outsiders assumed this was merely a reference to the Tory man toppling the sitting Labour member. But, as many voters knew, Mr Aldous was a born-and-bred Ipswich fan and his blue credentials extended further than merely political affiliation.

Should anyone still be in doubt over the intensity of the Old Farm rivalry, an academic study of local rivalry provides fairly conclusive evidence. *The Football Rivalries Report* of 2008 was commissioned by The New Football Pools Company, owners of Littlewoods, and involved research among thousands of fans. The strength of various rivalries across England and Wales was analysed and a league table of intensity compiled. To the surprise of non-East Anglian folk, Ipswich v Norwich came second, ahead of the well-documented rivalries on Merseyside, Manchester and other major cities – and was only pipped for top spot by the Black Country rivalry of West Brom and Wolves.

Even more remarkably, the Old Farm rivalry is – the survey concluded – the most reciprocated in the entire English game, with 99 per cent of fans from both clubs naming their opposite numbers as most hated opponents. And this despite the fact that the gap of 44 miles between the two clubs is the biggest between any in the survey's top ten.

The report marvelled at the strength of the Old Farm evidence, and included an account of how during a UEFA Cup-tie at Portman Road, even fans from Helsingborg in Sweden chanted 'stand up if you hate Norwich' – much to the delight of the home crowd. The report concluded the rivalry went much deeper than just football and was related to the fact that Norwich has city status and Ipswich doesn't, plus the fact that many Ipswich folk are said to dislike the quiet, rural traditions of East Anglia and would prefer to be more closely associated with the metropolitan feel of London – unlike their Norfolk rivals.

The FRR survey's top 30 rivalries:

1. West Brom and Wolves; 2. IPSWICH AND NORWICH; 3. Liverpool and Manchester United; 4. Portsmouth and Southampton; 5. Cardiff and Swansea; 6. Aston Villa and Birmingham; 7. Sheffield United and Sheffield Wednesday; 8. Bristol City and Bristol Rovers; 9. Newcastle and Sunderland; 10. Brighton and Crystal Palace; 11. Derby and Nottingham Forest; 12. Blackpool and Preston; 13. Darlington and Hartlepool; 14. Luton and Watford; 15. Blackburn and Burnley; 16. Port Vale and Stoke; 17. Arsenal and Tottenham; 18. Grimsby and Scunthorpe; 19. Everton and Liverpool; 20. Leeds and Manchester United; 21. Chester City and Wrexham; 22. Chesterfield and Mansfield; 23. Northampton and Peterborough; 24. Bury and Rochdale; 25. Manchester City and Manchester United; 26. Coventry and Leicester; 27. Millwall and West Ham; 28. Accrington Stanley and Morecambe; 29. Colchester and Southend; 30. Macclesfield and Stockport.

# STATISTICALLY SPEAKING ...

By the end of the 2009-10 season, Ipswich Town and Norwich City had met on 147 occasions in all competitions at first-team level. This figure includes non-competitive games such as friendlies and testimonials. It also includes the eight meetings between 4 November 1905 and 26 December 1936, during which time Norwich were a professional club but Ipswich were still amateur, which meant these games were effectively Ipswich's first team versus Norwich reserves.

Both clubs have had many ups and downs during the 108 years since their first meeting, but the stats show there is little to choose between them. Norwich have won 59 encounters and Ipswich 61, with 27 drawn. Norwich have netted 201 goals and Ipswich 216.

The highest crowd for an East Anglian derby game was the 39,980 who squeezed into Carrow Road for the thrilling FA Cup third round tie which ended 1-1 on Saturday, 27 January 1962. The biggest crowd for a derby at Ipswich was the 35,077 who witnessed the First Division game won 2-0 by the home side on Tuesday, 23 September 1975.

### BREAKDOWN OF THE 147 MEETINGS

FOOTBALL LEAGUE/PREMIER LEAGUE:
Played 83, Ipswich won 38, Norwich won 29, drawn 16 (Ipswich scored 128, Norwich scored 91).

FA CUP:
Played 3, Ipswich 0, Norwich 2, drawn 1 (2-4).

LEAGUE CUP:
Played 8, Ipswich 2, Norwich 4, drawn 2 (9-12).

TEXACO CUP:
Played 2, Ipswich 2, Norwich 0, drawn 0 (4-2).

FULL-MEMBERS CUP:
Played 2, Ipswich 1, Norwich 1, drawn 0 (1-2).

SOUTHERN LEAGUE:
Played 4, Ipswich 1, Norwich 3, drawn 0 (6-8).

SOUTHERN LEAGUE CUP:
Played 1, Ipswich 0, Norwich 1, drawn 0 (0-1).

DIVISION THREE SOUTH (NORTH) CUP:
Played 2, Ipswich 1, Norwich 1, drawn 0 (4-1).

NORFOLK & SUFFOLK LEAGUE:
  Played 6, Ipswich 1, Norwich 4, drawn 1 (4-12).
FRIENDLY/TESTIMONIAL/CHARITY GAME:
  Played 36, Ipswich won 15, Norwich 14, drawn 7 (58-69).


PLAYERS WHO PLAYED FOR BOTH IPSWICH AND NORWICH:
John Roy (Norwich 1934-36, Ipswich 1946-47), Allenby Driver (Norwich 1947-50, Ipswich 1950-52), Peter Morris (Ipswich 1968-74, Norwich 1971-72), Bobby Bell (Ipswich 1968-72, Norwich 1972), John Miller (Ipswich 1968-73, Norwich 1974-76), Clive Woods (Ipswich 1969-80, Norwich 1980-82), Keith Bertschin (Ipswich 1975-77, Norwich 1981-85), Clive Baker (Norwich 1977-81, Ipswich 1992-95), John Deehan (Norwich 1981-86, Ipswich 1986-88), Trevor Putney (Ipswich 1982-86, Norwich 1986-89), Louie Donowa (Norwich 1982-83, Ipswich 1989-90), Andy Marshall (Norwich 1994-2001, Ipswich 2001-03), Kevin Lisbie (Norwich 2005, Ipswich 2008-10), Alan Lee (Ipswich 2006-08, Norwich 2009). In addition, John Friar, Harold Joy and Jon Sheffield signed for Ipswich from Norwich but never made the Town first team. A number of other Ipswich players guested for Norwich in wartime football.


MOST APPEARANCES AND GOALS (NOT INCLUDING FRIENDLIES):
John Wark played in 25 derbies for Ipswich and Kevin Keelan 23 for Norwich. Wark hit nine goals for Town in derby games and Hugh Curran five for City.


OTHER CONNECTIONS:
Bryan Hamilton played for and coached Ipswich and later coached and managed Norwich; Steve Foley has coached at both clubs; Joe Royle and Mick O'Brien both played for Norwich and later managed Ipswich; Sammy Chung, Colin Suggett, Willie Donachie and Roy McCrohan all played for Norwich and later coached Ipswich; Stephen Wright played for Norwich and was later trainer at Ipswich; Dale Gordon played for Norwich and later worked for Ipswich's youth academy; Malcolm Webster coached goalkeepers at both Ipswich and Norwich; Trevor Whymark played for Ipswich and later coached at both Ipswich and Norwich at schoolboy level; Kevin Beattie played for Ipswich and later scouted for Norwich.

Printed in Great Britain
by Amazon